Adobe LiveMotion™ Shortcuts

Keep this handy rundown of shortcuts close to your keyboard for quick reference.

Toolbox Shortcuts

You can use the toolbox shortcuts in two ways:

- Tap a toolbox shortcut key to switch to a tool.

- Hold down a toolbox shortcut key to use the tool temporarily—this will allow you to use the tool until the key is released.

The following toolbox shortcuts are identical on the Macintosh and PC platforms.

Tool	Shortcut
Crop tool	C
Edit Mode/Preview	Q
Ellipse tool	L
Eyedropper tool	I

Tip: Hold down I+Shift to transfer an object's style.

Tool	Shortcut
Hand tool	H
HTML Text tool	Y
Layer Offset tool	O
Paint Bucket tool	K
Pen tool	P
Pen Selection tool	S
Polygon tool	N
Rectangle tool	M
Rounded Rectangle tool	R
Selection tool	V
Subgroup Selection tool	A
Drag Selection tool	U
Transform tool	E
Type tool	T
Zoom tool	Z

Palette Shortcuts

Palette	Mac	PC
Opacity palette	F5	F5
Color palette	F6	F6
Layer palette	F7	F7
Properties palette	F8	F8
Transform palette		F9
Styles palette	F10	F10
Rollovers palette	F11	F11

File Menu Shortcuts

Action	Mac	PC
New	Cmd+N	Ctrl+N
Open	Cmd+O	Ctrl+O
Close	Cmd+W	Ctrl+W
Save	Cmd+S	Ctrl+S
Save As	Shift+Cmd+S	Shift+Ctrl+S
Revert	F12	F12
Place	Cmd+I	Ctrl+I
Place Sequence	Opt+Shift+Cmd+I	Alt+Shift+Ctrl+I
Replace	Shift+Cmd+I	Shift+Ctrl+I
Export Settings	Opt+Shift+Cmd+E	Alt+Shift+Ctrl+E
Export	Cmd+E	Ctrl+E
Export As	Shift+Cmd+E	Shift+Ctrl+E
Preview In Browser	Cmd+0 (zero)	Ctrl+0 (zero)
Page/Print Setup	Shift+Cmd+P	Shift+Ctrl+P
Print	Cmd+P	Ctrl+P
Quit/Exit	Cmd+Q	Ctrl+Q

Edit Menu Shortcuts

Action	Mac	PC
Undo	Cmd+Z	Ctrl+Z
Redo	Shift+Cmd+Z	Shift+Ctrl+Z
Cut	Cmd+X	Ctrl+X
Copy	Cmd+C	Ctrl+C
Paste	Cmd+V	Ctrl+V
Paste Style	Cmd+B	Ctrl+B
Select All	Cmd+A	Ctrl+A
Deselect All	Shift+Cmd+A	Shift+Ctrl+A
Duplicate	Cmd+D	Ctrl+D
Make Alias	Cmd+M	Ctrl+M
Break Alias	Opt+Cmd+M	Alt+Ctrl+M
Edit Original	Shift+Cmd+M	Shift+Ctrl+M
Preferences	Cmd+K	Ctrl+K
Composition Settings	Shift+Cmd+N	Shift+Ctrl+N

Object Menu Shortcuts

Action	Mac	PC
Bring to Front	Shift+Cmd+]	Shift+Ctrl+]
Bring Forward	Cmd+]	Ctrl+]
Send Backward	Cmd+[	Ctrl+[
Send to Back	Shift+Cmd+[	Shift+Ctrl+[
Group	Cmd+G	Ctrl+G
Ungroup	Cmd+U	Ctrl+U
Make Actual Size	Opt+S	Alt+S
Apply Last Filter	Cmd+F	Ctrl+F

Layer Menu Shortcuts

Action	Mac	PC
New Layer	Cmd+L	Ctrl+L
Select Layer 1	Cmd+1	Ctrl+1
Select Layer 2	Cmd+2	Ctrl+2
Select Layer 3	Cmd+3	Ctrl+3
Select Layer 4	Cmd+4	Ctrl+4
Select Layer 5	Cmd+5	Ctrl+5

Timeline Menu Shortcuts

Action	Mac	PC
Show Timeline Menu	Cmd+T	Ctrl+T

Tip: Once the Timeline window is present, this command toggles between the Composition and Timeline windows.

Action	Mac	PC
Make Time Independent Group	Shift+Cmd+G	Shift+Ctrl+G
Next Keyframe	Opt+K	Alt+K
Previous Keyframe	Opt+J	Alt+J
New Position Keyframe	Opt+Shift+P	Alt+Shift+P
New Rotation Keyframe	Opt+Shift+R	Alt+Shift+R
New Scale Keyframe	Opt+Shift+S	Alt+Shift+S
New Opacity Keyframe	Opt+Shift+T	Alt+Shift+T
New Anchor Point Keyframe	Opt+Shift+A	Alt+Shift+A

View Menu Shortcuts

Action	Mac	PC
Active Export Preview	Cmd+9	Ctrl+9
Preview Mac/ Windows Gamma	Cmd+8	Ctrl+8
Preview AutoSlice Area	Cmd+7	Ctrl+7
Hide Object Edges	Cmd+H	Ctrl+H
Preview Motion Path	Shift+Cmd+H	Shift+Ctrl+H
Zoom In	Cmd++	Ctrl++
Zoom Out	Cmd+-	Ctrl+-
Actual Size	Opt+Cmd+0 (zero)	Alt+Ctrl+0 (zero)
Show Grid	Cmd+'	Ctrl+'
Snap To Grid	Shift+Cmd+'	Shift+Ctrl+'
Show Rulers	Cmd+R	Ctrl+R
Show Guides	Cmd+;	Ctrl+;
Snap To Guides	Shift+Cmd+;	Shift+Ctrl+;
Lock Guides	Opt+Cmd+;	Alt+Ctrl+;
Show/Hide Toolbox And Palettes	Tab	Tab
Show/Hide Palettes	Shift+Tab	Shift+Tab

Timeline Shortcuts

The following Timeline shortcuts are available when the Timeline window is the active window.

Action	Shortcut
Move backward one frame	Page Up
Move forward one frame	Page Down
Move backward 10 frames	Shift+Page Up
Move forward 10 frames	Shift+Page Down
Move to start of Timeline	Home
Move to end of Timeline	End
Start or Stop an animation	Spacebar

Tip: To move an object or group with its animation intact, hold down Opt+Cmd (Mac) or Ctrl+Alt (PC) while dragging.

Adobe LiveMotion™

f/x & Design

Daniel Gray

President, CEO
Keith Weiskamp

Publisher
Steve Sayre

Acquisitions Editor
Beth Kohler

Marketing Specialist
Patti Davenport

Project Editor
Melissa D. Olson

Technical Reviewer
Jon Shanley

Production Coordinator
Meg E. Turecek

Cover Designer
Jody Winkler

Layout Designer
April Nielsen

CD-ROM Developer
Michelle McConnell

The Coriolis Group, LLC
14455 N. Hayden Road
Suite 220
Scottsdale, Arizona 85260

(480)483-0192
FAX (480)483-0193
www.coriolis.com

Library of Congress Cataloging-In-Publication Data
Gray, Daniel, 1961-
    Adobe LiveMotion f/x and design / by Dan Gray.
        p.   cm
    ISBN 1-57610-676-4
    1. Computer graphics. 2. Computer animation. 3. Adobe LiveMotion. I. Title.
T385.G737453   2000
006.6'96--DC21   00-055511
                                                                          CIP

Printed in the United States of America
10 9 8 7 6 5 4 3 2 1

Other Titles for the Creative Professional

Looking Good on the Web
By Daniel Gray

Flash™ 4 Web Animation f/x and Design
By Ken Milburn and John Croteau

Paint Shop Pro™ 6 Visual Insight
By Ramona Pruitt and Joshua Pruitt

QuarkXPress™ 4 In Depth
By William Harrel and Elaine Betts

Adobe PageMill® 3 f/x and Design
By Daniel Gray

Illustrator® 9 f/x and Design
By Sherry London

Painter™ 6 f/x and Design
By Sherry London and Rhoda Grossman

Photoshop® 5 In Depth
By David Xenakis and Sherry London

Adobe InDesign™ f/x and Design
By Elaine Betts

For every Web monkey who has worked through the night,
this one's for you.

About the Author

Daniel Gray has been writing about graphics and online topics since 1990. Most recently, he worked with the Adobe LiveMotion development team to produce content (tutorials and goodies) for the LiveMotion product CD-ROM. Dan's recent books include *Adobe ImageStyler In Depth, Looking Good on the Web*, and *The Complete Guide to Associate and Affiliate Programs on the Net*. His Web site can be found at **www.geekbooks.com**.

Acknowledgments

Adobe LiveMotion f/x and Design could not have come to fruition without the kind help and hard work of many people.

First and foremost, I would like to thank the Adobe LiveMotion engineering and quality assurance crew—the folks that make the magic and burn the midnight oil: Chris Prosser, Steve Troppoli, Ken Rice, Norm Stratton, Colin Day, Andrew Geibel, Craig D'Andrea, Larry Sullivan, and Joe Bowden. To Ralf Berger, the great kahuna, thanks for steering an amazing ship. And to Debbie D'Andrea thanks for keeping everything (including me) on course. It's been a privilege to work alongside you guys. Let's do it again.

To the fine folks in marketing who keep the faith and spread the word on a global scale: Daniel Brown, Michael Ninness, John Nack, and Lynly Schambers. And to the folks who get the word to the street: Pati Stoop, Kiyo Toma, and especially Tim Plumer for his help and insight. Thank you all kindly.

Many thanks to a great crew at The Coriolis Group: Keith Weiskamp, Steve Sayre, and Beth Kohler for rolling the dice with yours truly once again; Ellen Strader for her kind copyedits; Meg Turecek, April Nielsen, and Jody Winkler for a fabulous job with the layout and cover; and project editor par excellence, Melissa Olson. And many thanks to John Shanley, for another fine technical edit.

To Charlie Haywood for his awesome ImageStyler and LiveMotion artwork, I'm honored to have his work appear in this book.

My deepest gratitude goes to my readers and my wife and kids. I need you all to be able to do what I do. Thanks for putting up with me.

If you should ever have a LiveMotion question that is not answered in this book, please do not hesitate to drop me a line via email at **dan@geekbooks.com**.

—*Daniel Gray*
Somewhere in the swamps of Jersey
www.geekbooks.com
July 2000

Contents at a Glance

Table of Contents

Introduction

Thank you kindly for picking up *Adobe LiveMotion f/x and Design*.

Adobe LiveMotion is a very different beast for me. I've been involved with the program's developers since the summer of 1998—well before the release of LiveMotion's predecessor, Adobe ImageStyler. When I saw what ImageStyler could do, I saw the future (and quit my day gig). While I wasn't the only one to see the promise in that program, I was the only author to write a book about it (*Adobe ImageStyler In Depth*).

The LiveMotion development team dug my ImageStyler book. So much so that they invited me to create content—tutorials, styles, textures, and even some shapes—for the LiveMotion CD-ROM. It was an evolutionary process. As the program changed in development, I edited the tutorials to reflect those changes. The experience was enlightening. My respect was heightened for the folks who build the software we use every day, as I was humbled by the magic they were called on to produce. Software development can be a long, grueling road filled with potholes. And sometimes, when you *finally* get to the beach, you find out that there's a red tide or a jellyfish.

After writing *Adobe ImageStyler In Depth* and working on the tutorials for the LiveMotion product CD-ROM, I almost feel that this is my *third* book on LiveMotion. If you were one of the folks who purchased my ImageStyler book, I offer my heartfelt thanks. You'll find that a good bit of this book is based on that first book. While Adobe may have changed the name, there are many folks who consider LiveMotion to be the second version of ImageStyler. It's all marketing, folks!

f/x and Design Philosophy

This f/x and Design book will help you gain a better understanding of Adobe LiveMotion's intermediate and advanced features. Learn about key features, such as behaviors, and push ordinary features into extraordinary effects. This book goes beyond the product documentation to demonstrate cutting-edge techniques, using extensive illustrations and real-world projects for you to try yourself. The book's easy-to-read, hands-on approach explains what works and what doesn't. *Adobe LiveMotion f/x and Design* was written to inspire you to explore and experiment with LiveMotion's feature set.

Who Needs This Book

Whether you're a professional designer, student, or hobbyist, this book can help you get the most out of Adobe LiveMotion. If you're expanding your skill set or moving up from Adobe ImageStyler, this f/x and Design book's easy step-by-step format will help you master the coolest design, animation, and interactive aspects of LiveMotion.

It's likely that you're using Adobe LiveMotion because of the program's ease of use in creating animated SWF Flash files. But LiveMotion is about more than just Flash. This book will show you exactly where the program's capabilities lie.

How This Book Is Structured

Adobe LiveMotion f/x and Design sets out to quickly take you from the basics of LiveMotion into its most exciting features. Each chapter provides professional-level projects and creative tips. The color LiveMotion Studio displays a host of cool techniques and design treatments. The companion CD-ROM is packed with LiveMotion example files and a host of goodies, including LiveMotion styles, textures, and shapes—many of which are displayed in the appendixes.

The chapters start with the basics of LiveMotion and its object-oriented editing methods. As the book moves along, you'll gain mastery of each of LiveMotion's tools and commands—from standard and remote rollovers through animation and advanced behavior techniques. You'll quickly get up to speed, building layouts with sliced graphics and JavaScript, animated GIF banners, and full-blown SWF Flash files with interactivity.

Without further adieu, it's time to strap in and blast off. Let's put LiveMotion into orbit!

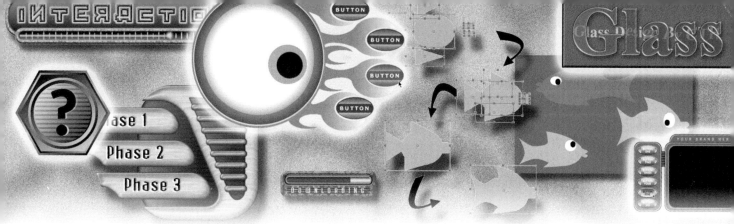

Chapter 1

LiveMotion's Mojo Methodology

In this chapter, you'll learn the magic behind Adobe LiveMotion's object-oriented approach, with an introduction to shapes, text, color, gradients, layers, and paths.

What's the Deal with Objects?

LiveMotion is a no-nonsense tool. It has no fluff in its feature set, no bloat in its code, no sacrifices to legacy. And although Adobe's engineers adhered largely to Adobe's hallmark user interface—making the program highly accessible to loyalists long familiar with their category leading tools—LiveMotion grew out of the technology initially developed for Adobe ImageStyler. Hence, if you're familiar with Photoshop, Illustrator, or ImageStyler, you already know a good portion of the drawing tools and methodology in LiveMotion.

Whereas LiveMotion provides an object-oriented drawing environment—along the lines of Adobe Illustrator, Macromedia FreeHand, and CorelDRAW—the program's magic goes far past those print-focused tools. This chapter dives right into the basics of LiveMotion's mojo methodology. It will help you quickly grasp the essence of the program and its drawing tools. As you proceed through the projects, you'll create a button bar—a common Web graphics chore, made easy.

Before I get into the specifics of each type of object, you need to absorb two basic concepts that apply to every object in a LiveMotion composition.

Everything's an Object

In LiveMotion, everything—including shapes, paths, text, and imported bitmaps—is an *object*. As such, the program is an equal opportunity graphics editor. You can instantly alter objects in a host of ways. You can colorize, resize, crop, texturize, and style them, and more. You can non-destructively alter and distort bitmapped images through the use of built-in palettes, as well as with Photoshop plug-ins. Non-destructive editing is at the core of LiveMotion's approach. If you change your mind about an effect, you can always go back to the original, or you can cruise back to any stop along the way. Figure 1.1 shows a progression of effects, created with just a handful of clicks.

Figure 1.1
Multiple object layers allow for an amazing array of effects.

The Toolbox

The LiveMotion toolbox echoes the toolboxes of Photoshop and Illustrator, with twists of its own. Here's a rundown on the LiveMotion toolbox, along with keyboard shortcuts for each tool:

Tool	Description	Shortcut
Selection tool	Selects and manipulates (moves, scales, and rotates) objects.	V
Subgroup Selection tool	Selects and manipulates objects within a group.	A
Drag Selection tool	Selects objects via a marquee. (It's great for digging a single object out from underneath a clump of objects.)	U
Layer Offset tool	Manipulates individual layers.	O
Rectangle tool	Creates rectangles and squares.	M
Rounded Rectangle tool	Creates rounded rectangles.	R
Ellipse tool	Creates ellipses and circles.	L
Polygon tool	Creates geometric objects, with three to ten sides.	N
Pen tool	Draws objects with a traditional Bézier pen tool.	P
Pen Selection tool	Manipulates control points.	S
Type tool	Creates graphic text.	T
HTML Text tool	Creates HTML text areas.	Y
Crop tool	Trims any object.	C
Transform tool	Skews and rotates objects using the center handles and corner handles, respectively.	E
Paint Bucket tool	Fills objects with the current fill color.	K
Eyedropper tool	Selects color from existing objects.	I
Hand tool	Drag-navigates the composition.	H
Zoom tool	Zooms into the composition. (Hold down Option/Alt to zoom out.)	Z
Current Fill Color	Shows the color of the currently (or most recently) selected object.	
Document Background Color	Shows the composition background color.	
Color Scheme	Show the currently selected complementary color scheme.	
Edit Mode/Preview Mode	Toggles between modes.	Q

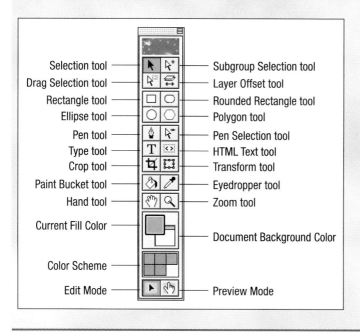

Objects with Layers, Not Layers with Objects

What makes LiveMotion different? Instead of placing objects *on* layers, the objects themselves *have* layers. This concept may seem alien to you—unless you're a veteran of ImageStyler, which pioneered the idea. Multiple layers allow you to build up an effect, creating basic illusions, such as drop shadows, and more complex illusions, such as multiple surfaced effects. Any LiveMotion object can consist of up to 99 layers. (ImageStyler was limited to five layers.)

Go ahead and fire up LiveMotion, if you haven't already. You're ready to blast off.

Working with Shapes

LiveMotion gives you the ability to easily create rudimentary objects—rectangles, rounded-corner rectangles, ellipses, polygons—and text. You can create more complex objects (and tweak them) with the Pen tool or construct them with the Combine feature. You can also place (import) artwork from external sources as a shape. Let's start out with the most basic shapes.

Creating Basic Shapes and Lines

Drawing basic shapes is a straightforward affair. Simply select the appropriate drawing tool—Rectangle, Rounded Rectangle, Ellipse, or Polygon—and then click and drag in the composition window. When you release the mouse button, the object's bounding box appears, as shown in Figure 1.2.

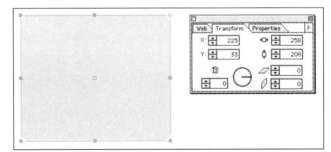

Figure 1.2
It's a click and drag thing. The Transform palette displays the object's size, as it's drawn.

Two keyboard modifiers apply to all of the object tools:

- *Draw a symmetrical object*—Click and drag while holding down the Shift key to draw a perfect square, rounded-corner square, circle, or polygon.

- *Draw from center*—Click and drag while holding down the Option (Mac) or Alt (PC) key to draw from the center of the object.

Let's take a look at some of the cool things you can do with shapes:

- *Switch shapes*—Instantly change the shape of an object using the drop-down menu on LiveMotion's Properties palette. You can swap a rectangle for a rounded-corner rectangle in the blink of an eye.

- *Convert to path*—Turn a rectangle, rounded-corner rectangle, ellipse, or polygon into a path by choosing Path from the Properties palette's drop-down menu.

- *Set a rounded-corner radius*—Set this radius from 0 to 50 pixels (in $1/4$ pixel increments).

- *Create polygons*—Define these to have three to ten sides.

"Hey, how can I just draw a simple line?" you ask. LiveMotion lets you draw lines in one of two ways. You can draw a really skinny rectangle with the Rectangle tool, or you can use the Pen tool. Figure 1.3 shows a skinny rectangle, along with the Transform palette. (The Pen tool is covered later in this chapter.)

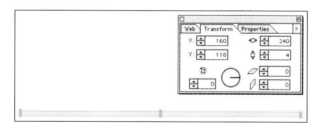

Figure 1.3
It's a rectangle *and* a line.

Combine Shapes

LiveMotion's *Combine* features—Unite, Unite With Color, Minus Front, Intersect, and Exclude—give you five powerful mechanisms to create complex shapes from the program's basic rectangles, ellipses, polygons, and rounded rectangles, as well as from objects drawn with the Pen tool or imported from other programs. The Combine functions are accessed via the Object|Combine menu. Let's take a rundown of each function.

Unite

Selecting this function, after selecting multiple objects, fuses objects. The new object maintains the outline or fill characteristics of the bottom object, as shown in Figure 1.4.

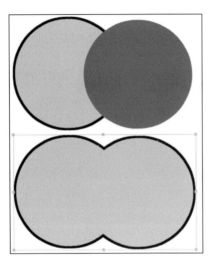

Figure 1.4
Unite performs the Vulcan mind meld.

Unite With Color

Selecting this function also fuses objects, as shown in Figure 1.5. The individual elements of the new object maintain their original characteristics such as color, texture, 3D effects, and opacity of both objects.

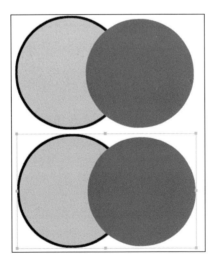

Figure 1.5
Unite With Color goes one up by preserving surface attributes.

Bitmap or Vector?

When used with two pure vector objects, Unite with Color is the only Combine function that will automatically convert the combined object into a bitmap upon SWF export. In Figures 1.4 through 1.8, the bottom circle is a two-layer object. When a two-layer object is combined with a one-layer object in this manner, the resulting object will convert into a bitmap upon SWF export.

Minus Front

Selecting this function deletes the top object entirely and subtracts the overlapping area from the bottom object. The new object maintains the outline or fill characteristics of the bottom object, as shown in Figure 1.6.

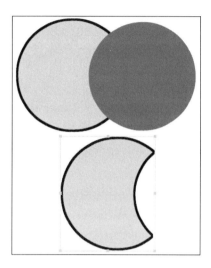

Figure 1.6
Minus Front cuts away the area behind the top object—just like a cookie cutter.

Intersect

Selecting this function subtracts all but the overlapping area from the bottom object. The new object maintains the outline or fill characteristics of the bottom object, as shown in Figure 1.7.

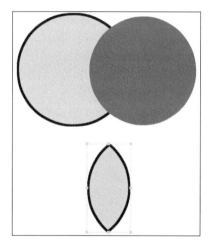

Figure 1.7
Intersect leaves only the area common between the objects.

Exclude

Selecting this function fuses the objects (like Unite), but subtracts the overlapping area (like Intersect) from the combined object. The new object maintains the outline or fill characteristics of the bottom object, as shown in Figure 1.8.

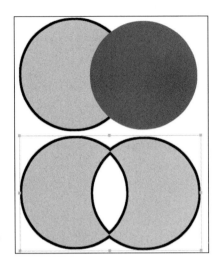

Figure 1.8
An example of the Exclude function. Mom never had this much fun in the kitchen.

Building Shapes with Combine

Now that you've seen the basics of LiveMotion's Combine feature, let's apply that knowledge and create some cool shapes. The following section demonstrates a handful of techniques you can use to create donut, half moon, crescent moon, rounded-corner tab, and other shapes that are commonly used in interface design.

Donuts

It's easy to make Homer Simpson's favorite see-through shape. Begin by drawing a large circle; then, draw a smaller circle on top of it. Select both circles and choose the Object|Align|Centers menu item. Finish by punching the hole through the donut with Object|Combine|Minus Front, as shown in Figure 1.9. Donut objects are often used to create fancy bezels and frames.

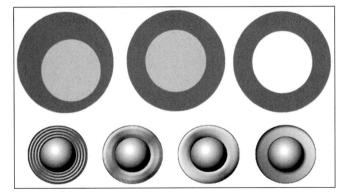

Figure 1.9
By placing a donut on top of an ellipse with a radial gradient, you can create the illusion of an offset radial fill.

Half Moons

Splitting a circle in half is a quick trick. Start by drawing the circle; then, draw a rectangle a bit taller and a tad larger than half the width of the circle. Drag the circle so that its center handles intersect the side of the rectangle, as shown in Figure 1.10. Select both the circle and the rectangle and choose the Object|Combine|Minus Front menu item to cut the half moon.

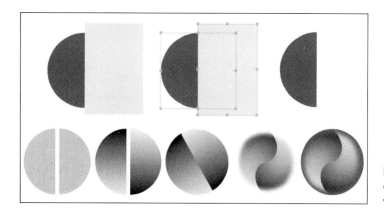

Figure 1.10
Careful alignment is essential
when chopping elements.

PROJECT Building a Yin-Yang Orb

What good is a half moon? The following exercise demonstrates how to build a yin-yang orb—a design element that might find its way into a rollover interface or other composition. Figure 1.10 shows the creative progression of a yin-yang orb. Here's the blow-by-blow on the additional steps:

1. Choose the Edit|Duplicate menu item to copy the half moon.

2. Select Object|Transform|Flip Horizontal to change the orientation of the duplicated half moon.

3. Give each half moon a linear (light gray to dark gray) gradient; run the gradients in opposite directions.

4. Push the two half moons together. Zoom in, if necessary, to be sure the sides meet exactly.

5. Select both half moons and choose Object|Combine|Unite With Color to combine the objects.

6. Click and drag the combined object's top right handle to rotate it counterclockwise 30 degrees. (Hold down the Shift key to constrain the rotation to 15 degree increments.)

7. On the Distort palette, select Twirl from the drop-down menu. Set the number of Turns to 31 and the Band Size to 1.

8. On the Layers palette, set the Width to -9 and the Softness to 10.

9. Create a new layer with the Cmd/Ctrl+L keyboard shortcut, then select a dark gray from the Color palette.

Crescent Moons

To make a single crescent moon, begin with two identically sized ellipses. Place one over the other, align them carefully, select both ellipses, and choose the Object|Combine|Minus Front menu item.

Crescent moons can also make interesting bezels by adding a cat's-eye appearance to a button, as shown in Figure 1.11. This technique uses Object| Combine|Exclude with two sets of ellipses to create the upper and lower eyelids (mirrored crescents). Then, choose Object|Combine|Intersect to create the eyeball. (The cat's eye at the bottom right uses two separate crescents.)

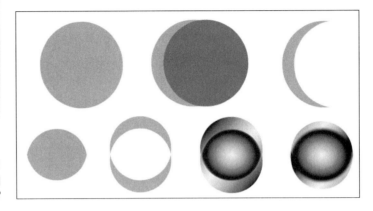

Figure 1.11

How about an eye, à la Hal from 2001?

PROJECT Creating Rounded Tabs

Here's another clichéd design metaphor. Rounded tabs are an all too common design element in interface design—be it for Web sites (think Amazon.com) or software (take a look at the tabs in Adobe's floating palettes). Here's a quick step-by-step:

1. Start with a rounded-corner rectangle. Duplicate it, and then apply horizontal skew (in opposite directions) to each rectangle via the Transform palette.

2. Slide one rectangle over the other. (I've changed the color of the top object to make it easier to see.)

3. Select both objects, choose the Object|Align Vertical Centers menu item, and choose Object|Combine|Unite.

4. Draw a rectangle to cover the bottom of the new object.

5. Shift-click on the new object, and choose Object|Combine|Minus Front to trim the bottom of the tab.

Figure 1.12 shows three variations on the theme. You can further modify the combined tab objects by editing them with the Pen Selection tool.

Combining Text and Objects

You can combine text with other objects to create interesting shapes, letterforms, and symbols. Figure 1.13 illustrates a range of cool effects created by combining the letter *A* with an ellipse. The top row shows the original *A* and ellipse,

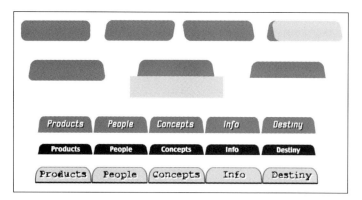

Figure 1.12
How do you like your tabs—
businesslike or grungy?

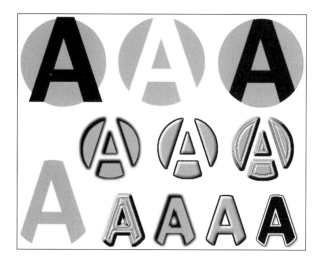

Figure 1.13
Try punching a text character out
of an object to create a cool
button, distinctive bullet, or
snazzy logotype. Text remains in
an editable state when it's combined with other objects.

along with the result of Object|Combine|Minus Front. (I placed a black ellipse
behind the rightmost combined object in the row.) The center row demonstrates some layer and 3D effects, and the bottom row shows the results of
Object|Combine|Intersect, along with some other nifty effects.

Importing Shapes

LiveMotion takes a simple approach to importing images. Without having to
fiddle around choosing an import filter, you can use the Place command to
import Adobe Illustrator, Amiga IFF, BMP, Encapsulated PostScript (EPS),
FilmStrip, CompuServe GIF, JPEG, PCX, Photoshop, PICT, Pixar, PNG, Targa,
and TIFF files, in addition to other LiveMotion (and ImageStyler IST) documents. Although this list consists mainly of bitmap options, the ability to import
Adobe Illustrator and EPS ensures that you'll be able to import vector artwork,
as well.

Why Use Vector Artwork?

Vector-based artwork is the lingua franca of the graphic design and print world;
it's used chiefly for logos and line art. Vector art is created with mathematical

equations, rather than bit-by-bit representations. The advantage of vector art is that you can scale it infinitely, without any loss in image quality. Scale a vector logo to three times its size, and it will scale smoothly; scale a bitmap logo to three times its size, and it will turn into a jaggy mess, as demonstrated in Figure 1.14.

Figure 1.14
Bitmaps suffer when scaled upward, whereas vectors scale smoothly.

Every major drawing application has the ability to export Adobe Illustrator or EPS files (although some are more adept than others). LiveMotion can't import native CorelDRAW, Macromedia FreeHand, or Micrografx Designer files, but it's a no-brainer to export artwork from these programs in Illustrator or EPS format. Chapter 11 goes into depth on working with other applications.

How LiveMotion Treats Placed Vector Artwork

All vector artwork isn't created equally. LiveMotion can be particular about placing certain vector formats. Here are some details:

- *Encapsulated PostScript (EPS)*—This format carries the most information; it's the best format for complex artwork.

- *Illustrator (AI)*—This format works for most artwork, although LiveMotion may have a difficult time interpreting files from some applications.

- *Windows Metafile (WMF)*—While LiveMotion can import WMF files on the Windows platform, it doesn't recognize WMF files on the Mac.

Coloring Placed Vector Artwork

LiveMotion allows you to color simple vector artwork. If you've assigned an outline or fill other than black (in the drawing application), LiveMotion will place the object with the color(s) specified. If you need to color the new object (that was a color other than black), here's an easy workaround:

1. Place the vector artwork.

2. Use Cmd/Ctrl+L to add a new layer to the object. Select Color from the Layer palette's Fill With menu, and then, specify the new color.

This technique colors the entire object. Although you can use any of Live-Motion's cool fill techniques, you can't color individual elements within a placed Illustrator or EPS file—unless it's a properly constructed layered file. Layered Adobe Illustrator files can be converted into objects (Object|Convert Layers Into|Objects).

Alignment

In complicated Web graphic designs, it all comes down to the pixel. It's imperative to place each object precisely. Fortunately, LiveMotion provides all the alignment apparatus you need to create pixel-perfect images—it's up to you to use them. In addition to the Grid and Guideline features, you'll use the Alignment options—Left, Right, Top, Bottom, Horizontal Centers, Vertical Centers, and Centers—along with the Transform palette. The Alignment options allow you to quickly arrange objects in relation to each other, and the Transform palette lets you place objects precisely on the page.

PROJECT Building a Simple Button Bar

Ready to put LiveMotion to work? Let's take a look at how to use the Distribute features in concert with the Distribute option. Follow these steps to draw a handful of simple rectangles for use as a button bar:

1. Select the Rectangle tool. Draw a rectangle 100 pixels wide by 25 pixels high to create a button. (Use the Transform palette to set the width and height exactly.)

2. With the rectangle selected, create four duplicate rectangles (for a total of five buttons) by pressing Cmd/Ctrl+D four times. Each duplicate rectangle will be placed exactly on top of the rectangle from which it was duplicated.

3. Use the Rectangle tool to draw a rectangle 520 pixels wide by 35 pixels high. (You'll use this rectangle to help align the buttons.) Once again, use the Transform palette to set the width and height exactly.

4. To start the alignment procedure, select the first 100-by-25 rectangle (at the top of the stack), hold down Shift, and select the 520-by-35 rectangle. Then, choose Object|Align|Left to left align the two objects. Then, select the next 100-by-25 rectangle, hold down Shift, and select the 520-by-35 rectangle. Choose Object|Align|Right to right-align the two objects.

5. To distribute the five 100-by-25 rectangles, drag a marquee around them and choose Object|Distribute|Horizontal.

6. With the five 100-by-25 rectangles still selected, use Object|Align|Vertical Centers to line them up in a perfect row (if necessary), as shown in Figure 1.15. Use the Color palette to set the fill to R-102, G-102, and B-102 (for a dark gray) or a similar tone.

7. Save this file as button bar.liv—you'll come back to it shortly.

Figure 1.15

Pixel perfect: Create, align left, align right, distribute, and align vertically.

After completing that little exercise, you should begin to understand how the Align and Distribute features operate. After a while, they will become second nature to you. In the next section, you'll see how LiveMotion works with text.

Working with Text

LiveMotion's Type tool lets you work with a certain degree of interactivity. When you click on the page with the Type tool selected, the Type Tool dialog box will open and display specifications gleaned from the last chunk of text (or from the current settings in the Properties palette). This is convenient when you're creating a series of text objects with the same specs. As you change the specifications or the text itself, LiveMotion interactively displays the result of those changes on the page. If the Type Tool dialog box covers the position where you clicked on the page, simply click and drag the dialog box's title bar to uncover the text.

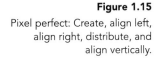 ## Adding Text to the Button Bar

Next, you'll add some text to the buttons created in the last exercise. You'll use Arial, a sans-serif font that's common to both the Macintosh and PC platforms. (If Arial isn't loaded on your system, feel free to use Helvetica or any other font that suits your fancy.) Follow these steps:

1. Set the Current Fill Color to white. (Select the Current Fill Color swatch on the toolbox, then select white from the Color palette.)

2. Select the Type tool.

3. Click on the centerpoint of the first button to open the Type Tool dialog box.

4. Set the Font to Arial Regular (or whatever font works for you). Set the Size to 14 and the Tracking to 7. Set the Alignment to Horizontal Center. Outline shouldn't be selected. (Leading doesn't matter in this case, because you're setting only one line of text.)

5. In the text entry box, type "products" and click on OK.

6. Use the Type tool to individually set the words "company", "support", "contacts", and "partners". Roughly position each word in the center of a button, as shown in Figure 1.16.

Figure 1.16
Don't worry about the exact placement of each chunk of text—you'll take care of that in a moment.

When you place text on the page, it remains fully editable. You can use the Properties palette to adjust the typographical specifications. To edit the text string, double-click on the text to open the Type Tool dialog box.

Aligning Text: A Caveat

At times, it can be a real trick to align multiple text blocks. It all has to do with the dimensions of the text blocks and their corresponding bounding boxes. Text set in all caps usually isn't a problem, but text set in uppercase and lowercase letters can be problematic. Some text blocks will have letters with descenders (as well as ascenders) and others won't, as demonstrated in Figure 1.17.

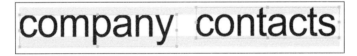

Figure 1.17
Consider the height of the bounding boxes. LiveMotion doesn't offer a baseline alignment option.

Let's review a handful of relevant typographic terms:

*   *x-height*—The height of a typeface's lowercase letters.

*   *baseline*—The "floor" that a typeface sits on.

*   *ascender*—The part of the character that rises above the character's x-height.

*   *descender*—The part of the character that extends below the character's baseline.

PROJECT Aligning the Button Bar Text

Things would be a piece of cake if all blocks of text had ascenders or descenders—you'd just select all the text blocks and use Object|Align|Top or Object|Align|Bottom, respectively. This not being the case, you'll have to work at alignment. Because four of the five text blocks in this project have descenders, you'll bottom-align them, and then top-align the word *contacts* to one of the other words.

> **Text Bounding Box Oddities**
>
> LiveMotion build 78 (the initial release version) does some odd things with text bounding boxes. Often, the bounding boxes appear to be oversized. This button bar text alignment project may or may not function as designed. (Some bounding boxes may interpret ascender and descender height correctly.)

Let's begin by horizontally centering each word within its respective button:

1. Drag a marquee around *products* and its button.
2. Choose the Object|Align|Horizontal Centers menu item.
3. Repeat Steps 1 and 2 for each button.
4. Select the words *products, company, support,* and *partners.*
5. Choose Object|Align|Bottom to bottom-align the words.
6. Select *contacts.* Press the down arrow until the baseline of *contacts* is visible below the rest of the words. (Don't worry, this madness has a method.)
7. Hold down the Shift key and select *partners.*
8. Choose Object|Align|Top to top-align the words.

> **Guideline Guidelines**
>
> You'll need to display LiveMotion's rulers in order to drag out a guideline. Select View|Show Rulers—or use the keyboard shortcut: Cmd/Ctrl+R to display the rulers. Next, select View|Show Guides (Cmd/Ctrl+;), then click and drag from the respective ruler.

Keep in mind that LiveMotion always aligns all the objects in a selection to the object furthest in the direction you're aligning. That's why you nudged *contacts* down. Here are a few more alignment pointers:

- Use the Transform palette's X and Y coordinates as a handy way to align to the pixel.
- Nudge with the cursor keys to get alignment just right.
- Drag out a guideline for exact alignment, as shown in Figure 1.18.

In the next section, you'll gain a basic understanding of layers.

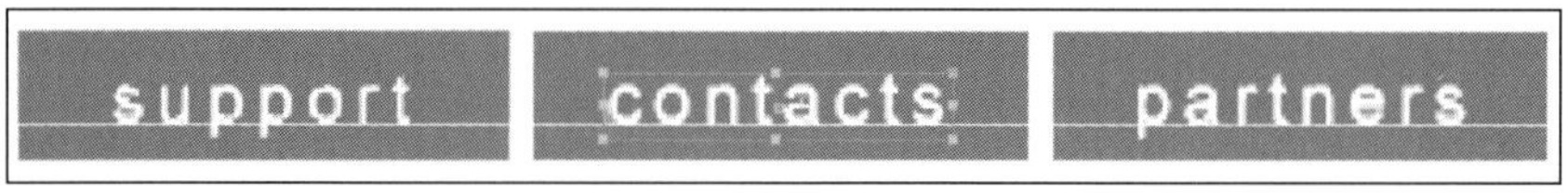

Figure 1.18
Guidelines, although absent from ImageStyler, have been well-implemented in LiveMotion.

Working with Layers

Object layers are at the heart of LiveMotion's mojo methodology. With as many as 99 layers per object, you have a powerful means to achieve a magical end. (ImageStyler was limited to just five layers.) You can create simple effects by adding only one more layer to an object, whereas complex effects may require two or more additional layers.

You'll use object layers to create, among others:

• Drop shadows

• Glow effects

• Outline effects

In the following sections, you'll learn how to create these essential effects.

Creating Drop Shadows with Layers

If you're accustomed to creating drop shadows with an older version of Photoshop (or another image-editing application that doesn't support automated drop shadows), you'll find that drop shadows are frighteningly easy to create with LiveMotion. The effects are infinitely variable, as well—LiveMotion affords complete control over the softness of the drop shadow, in addition to its color, width, offset, and opacity.

 ### Adding a Drop Shadow to the Button Bar

Let's take a look at how easy it is to create and modify a drop shadow. Using the button bar that you've been building, follow these steps:

1. Open the Object Layers, Layer, and Opacity palettes.

2. Select the word *products*.

3. Press Cmd/Ctrl+L to create a new layer. (New layers are filled with black by default, and they are automatically selected upon creation in the Object Layers palette.)

4. Adjust the new layer's X (horizontal) and Y (vertical) Offset with the Layer palette. Use an X Offset of -2 and a Y Offset of 2 to push the shadow layer to the left of and below the original layer. The further you push the shadow away from the object, the more the object will appear to float (up to a certain point), as shown in Figure 1.19.

> **Beware of Layers with SWF Export**
>
> Adding a layer to an object (or modifying a layer) will cause the object to be exported as a bitmap in the SWF file. Chapter 9 contains a list of conditions that may cause bitmapping.

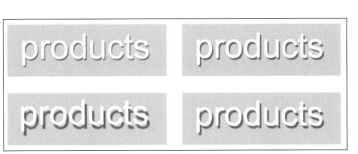

Figure 1.19
Watch the type float off the page.

5. Name the layer (optional) by double-clicking on the layer name (in this case, Layer 2) in the Object Layers palette. Doing so opens the Name dialog box. Assign the layer the name "Shadow" and click on OK.

6. Try adjusting the drop shadow's width and softness with the Layer palette.

Saving Styles

LiveMotion allows you to save complex layer effects via the Styles palette. Once you've saved a style, you can quickly assign it to another object at any time. To save a style, select the object that has the look you want. Then, click on the New Style button on the Styles palette (or simply drag the styled object to the Styles palette). When the Name dialog box opens, decide whether you want the style to ignore the color of the first layer. Then, enter the name of the new style and click on OK.

If Ignore Color Of First Layer *is* selected, LiveMotion assumes that you don't want to transfer the color of the first layer. In this case, the object that receives the new style maintains the color of its original first layer. If Ignore Color Of First Layer is *not* selected, LiveMotion assumes that you want to transfer the color of the first layer with the style.

Chapter 3 dives into the subject of styles in depth.

Keep these considerations in mind when you're creating drop shadows:

- *Keep small things simple*—When you're working with really small type and objects, a simple drop shadow works best, because you have only so many pixels to work with. Larger type and objects allow you to experiment more readily with the width and softness settings.

- *Watch file sizes*—Generally, the softer the shadow, the more individual pixel values and the larger the resulting file.

- *Get more pop*—Increase the contrast between the base and drop shadow colors to increase lift.

- *Use the Object Layer Opacity settings*—When you're creating drop shadows over textured objects or backgrounds, the Object Layer Opacity settings come in handy. Throttle the Object Layer Opacity setting back to allow the background to show through the shadow.

Creating Glow Effects with Layers

Glow effects are similar to drop shadows, with a couple of key differences. Glow effects always use softness and tend to be placed at the same X and Y coordinates as the base layer. The Layer palette's Width and Softness settings allow you to vary the effect, as demonstrated in Figure 1.20.

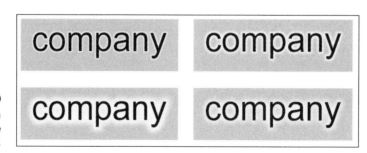

Figure 1.20
Glow effects are often used (in their many permutations) as the **over** or **down** state of a rollover.

Here's a quick way to create a glow. You'll practice on one of the buttons you created earlier:

1. Begin with the Object Layers, Layer, and Color palettes open.

2. Select the word *company*.

3. Press Cmd/Ctrl+L to create a new layer (Layer 2).

4. Assign a white fill to Layer 2 with the Color palette.

5. On the Layer palette, set the Width to 1 and the Softness to 2 to create the glow.

6. Name the layer (optional) by double-clicking on the layer name. Assign the layer the name Glow and click on OK.

7. Select Layer 1 on the Object Layers palette.

8. Assign a black fill to Layer 1 with the Color palette.

Glows tend to work best when sufficient definition exists between the base layer and the glow layer. Text can become indiscernible if the base layer and the glow layer consist of the same color—but, of course, if this is the effect you want, go for it.

Creating Outline Effects with Layers

Although you can assign LiveMotion objects either a fill or an outline, you can also create an outline effect by adding a slightly thicker layer behind the original layer. This technique allows you to create up to four separate outline bands by varying the width of each layer. Figure 1.21 demonstrates a number of outline effects.

Figure 1.21
Plenty of stops along the way—from a simple one- or two-layer outline to an intricate neon-like effect that uses five or more layers.

Let's assign a simple outline to one of your buttons:

1. Begin with the Object Layers, Layer, and Color palettes open.

2. Select the word *support*.

3. Press Cmd/Ctrl+L to create a new layer (Layer 2).

4. On the Layer palette, set the Width to 2 to create the outline.

5. Name the layer (optional) by double-clicking on the layer name. Enter the layer name "Outline" and click on OK.

Now, you might be thinking, "I thought that I could assign object outlines directly. Why should I use this technique?" Here's one of the primary reasons: Outlines assigned through the Properties palette (or via the Type Tool dialog box) fall within the character or object, not outside, as shown by Figure 1.22.

Figure 1.22
The words on the left have properties outlines, whereas the words on the right have layer outlines. On their own, properties outlines can create nice, incised effects.

For fast layer access, use the easy-to-remember keyboard shortcuts in Table 1.1.

In Chapter 5, you'll see how easy it is to turn this little navigational graphic into a functioning button bar, complete with URL hotspot links.

Without further adieu, let's jump into the world of color and gradients.

Table 1.1 Power layer editing.

Layer	Macintosh	PC
Layer 1	Cmd+1	Ctrl+1
Layer 2	Cmd+2	Ctrl+2
Layer 3	Cmd+3	Ctrl+3
Layer 4	Cmd+4	Ctrl+4
Layer 5	Cmd+5	Ctrl+5

Copying Layer Styles

You don't have to save a style in order to copy it from one object to another. LiveMotion includes a nifty Paste Style feature, complete with keyboard shortcut: Cmd/Ctrl+B. Let's try copying the drop shadow from the word *products* onto the other button text:

1. Select the word *products*.

2. Copy the word *products* to the clipboard with Cmd/Ctrl+C.

3. Select the word *partners*.

4. Paste the style to the word *products* with Cmd/Ctrl+B, or via Edit|Paste Style.

5. Select each of the remaining words in the button bar and paste the style. Notice how the pasted style wipes out the previous layer effects.

Now that you've assigned drop shadows to the button text, you may notice that the horizontal alignment of the text is a bit off-center. Select each button, together with its text, and choose Object|Align|Horizontal Centers to remedy the problem.

Working with Color and Gradients

Adobe LiveMotion takes a unique approach to specifying color. Together, the Color palette, the Eyedropper tool, the Gradient palette, and the Color Scheme palette form a powerful equation. Although the interface may seem a bit daunting at first, you'll soon see that the program delivers what you need most—and, where it falls short, you can easily find a solution.

Color

The first thing that many folks exclaim when they examine LiveMotion's Color palette is, "Hey, where are the color swatches?" The next question is, "Wait a minute, where's the Web-safe color palette?" I'll answer both of those questions right off the bat.

Swatches, Swatches, Wherefore Art Thou?

Yes, LiveMotion's engineers left out the familiar swatch method of color selection. But, one of the six color views—Saturation, Value, Hue, Hue-Saturation-Brightness (HSB), CIE L, or RGB—should offer a color-selection method that suits your working style. (Web color purists may be bummed—hex color specification is noticeably absent.) If you choose the right options, the Color palette can even take on a sort of pseudo-swatchy appearance. That brings me to the next point.

Web-Safe, Not Sorry

Lynda Weinman (**www.lynda.com**), author of *Designing Web Graphics* (and a score of other Web books), rode to fame and glory on the Web-safe palette. She was the first author to focus on the fact that 216 colors are common to the palettes of both Netscape Navigator and Microsoft Internet Explorer. These 216 magical colors won't dither when displayed in different browsers and on different platforms (although other colors might).

LiveMotion provides the means to specify Web-safe color, although it's easy to overlook the button that turns on the Web-safe color option. Selecting the Color palette's color-cube checkbox transforms the palette into Web-safe color mode. Visually, this change is most apparent in Saturation, Value, Hue, and CIE L modes. When the color-cube checkbox is unselected, the color sweeps are smooth; when the checkbox is selected, however, the sweeps become blocky, as shown in Figure 1.23. Each block consists of a Web-safe color—almost like a swatchbook, of sorts.

And that's not all. In RGB and HSB modes, the individual sliders automatically click to Web-safe color combinations. So, you can easily specify Web-safe color—you just need to become accustomed to LiveMotion's presentation method.

> **Hue or HSB—What's the Difference?**
>
> LiveMotion's Color palette has Hue and HSB modes. The Hue mode allows you to choose colors from a strictly visual palette, while the HSB mode allows you to specify colors via slider input or a numerical entry.

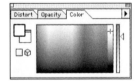

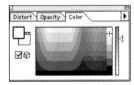

Figure 1.23
The Color palette—Saturation mode—in standard (top) and Web-safe incarnations.

Gradients

If you're accustomed to flat color, the smooth sweep of gradient color will open up a new world of design possibilities. Images feel more lively when they gain the illusion of dimensionality and sheen.

Gradient Types

LiveMotion allows for four different kinds of gradients, as shown in Figure 1.24:

- Linear
- Radial
- Burst
- Double burst

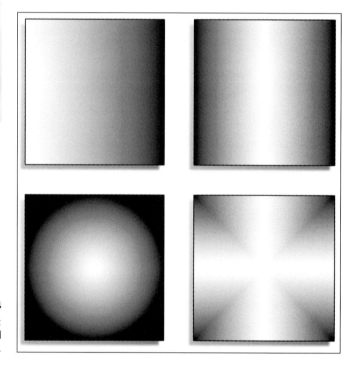

Figure 1.24
Clockwise from top left: linear, burst, double burst, and radial gradients.

When you begin using gradients, you can easily become addicted. High-traffic Web site designers know better: Take a trip to the major Web portals—the search engines—where fast image downloads are key, and you'll see that gradients are used sparingly, if at all. Most of the major players stick with flat-color graphics to ensure the smallest file sizes.

How Gradients Affect File Size

With that last comment thrown to the wind, let's take a look at some gradients and get a feel for how they affect file size. You should remember some salient points about gradient color and file size. In general:

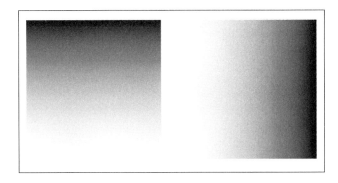

Figure 1.25
Vertical linear gradients yield smaller file sizes than horizontal linear gradients.

- Due to the manner in which images are compressed, vertical linear gradients (as shown in Figure 1.25), produce smaller files than horizontal linear gradients. Later in this chapter, the "Export File Size Comparisons" section provides some examples.

- The more color in the gradient, the larger the file.

- The smoother the gradient, the larger the file.

- Dithering adds smoothness to GIF gradients, but results in larger files.

- Short sweeps of color are less problematic than long sweeps.

PROJECT Experimenting with Gradients and File Size

In order to understand how gradients can affect file size, you'll next draw a 144-by-144-pixel square and fill it with a black-to-white linear gradient. (This isn't a scientific approach, but it should give you an idea of how gradients work.) You'll assign various orientations and file options to see how they affect the file size.

This experiment uses four palettes: Transform, Color, Gradient, and Export. Start with a blank canvas:

1. Select the Rectangle tool. Draw a 144-by-144-pixel square. (Use the Transform palette to set the square's width and height exactly.)

2. With the new 144-by-144 square selected, set the Color palette to RGB mode and open the Gradient palette.

3. Select Linear from the Gradient palette's drop-down menu.

4. Select the slider at the bottom left of the Gradient palette, and then click on the black swatch at the bottom right of the Color palette. This assigns black as the starting gradient color.

5. Select the slider at the bottom right of the Gradient palette, and then click on the white swatch at the bottom right of the Color palette. This assigns white as the ending gradient color.

6. Select the Relative option so that the gradient will rotate with the 144-by-144 square.

7. Try assigning different export options with the Export palette. Select View|Active Export Preview to display the exported file (and object) size at the bottom of the LiveMotion window, as shown in Figure 1.26. Try rotating the gradient object 90 degrees to witness the exported file-size difference in horizontal and vertical linear gradients.

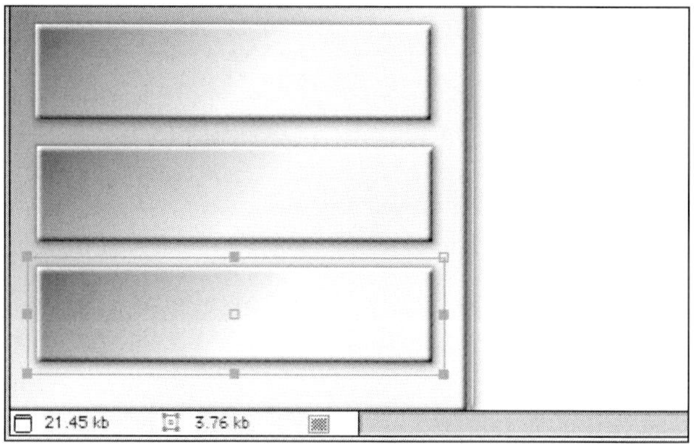

Figure 1.26
The Active Export Preview option (at the lower-left corner of the window) provides a live report of the exported file size and selected object size (center). The icon on the right reports whether the selected object will export as a vector or bitmap. (The pen icon indicates a vector, whereas the landscape icon indicates a bitmap.)

Do You *Really* Need All That Color?

Although LiveMotion's Gradient palette is relatively simple, it falls many steps short of what can be found in other imaging applications. But, you know what? In the world of high-volume Web graphics production, you don't need to bury yourself in gradient choices. Great Web graphics are tight little files: They don't include flawlessly smooth gradients with a gazillion colors. Web site visitors value speed over total color fidelity. If a design screams for a more impressive gradient and you can honestly make the point, go ahead and fire up one of those other programs (or try the complex gradient work-around in the next section).

You might draw a few additional conclusions from this experiment:

- JPEG compression tends to produce smaller files and better-looking blends.
- If you think you need dithering to create a decent-looking GIF image, try JPEG instead.
- Larger GIF palettes reach a threshold of return.

Export File Size Comparisons

Export settings have a significant effect on exported file size. Dithering is a double-edged sword. Sure, it can make your GIF blends look smoother, but check out the file-size bloat. If a blend covers a short distance, you can get by with no dithering—and the shorter the blend, the fewer colors you'll need.

Tables 1.2 and 1.3 demonstrate a range of options for this 144-by-144-pixel black-to-white linear gradient, along with the file sizes that they produce. The JPEG file format gets the nod for gradient images. (Your mileage may vary.)

The topic of file exports will be covered in depth in Chapters 5 and 8.

Building Complex Linear Gradients with the Combine Tools

Here's a workaround for those times when you have your heart set on creating a complex gradient, but you don't want to use another program to do so. Take the object in question and carefully chop it into little bits with LiveMotion's

Table 1.2   Effects of JPEG quality on file size for a 144-by-144 black to white gradient.

JPEG Quality	Horizontal Gradient		Vertical Gradient	
	Progressive Chroma	Reduced	Progressive Chroma	Reduced
10	887	818	784	793
30	953	885	822	837
50	994	927	852	885
70	1050	1007	878	931
90	1400	1330	1130	1220

Table 1.3   Effects of GIF quality on file size for a 144-by-144 black to white gradient.

Number of Gif Colors	Horizontal Gradient		Vertical Gradient	
	Non-Dithered	Dithered	Non-Dithered	Dithered
8	1500	3430	655	2540
16	2410	4460	986	3300
32	2890	4540	1400	3300
64	3770	5410	1400	4270

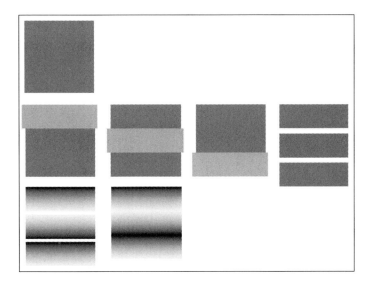

Figure 1.27
The complex gradient technique, used on a simple square.

Combine feature. Then, fill each of the little bits with a hyper-tuned gradient fill. When all the gradients are assigned, align the separate bits carefully and group them, as shown in Figure 1.27. Follow these steps:

1. Begin with the shape you want to fill with the complex gradient. Decide how many sweeps of color you'll need.

2. Draw a rectangle to dissect the shape. Duplicate the original shape and the dissecting rectangle. (This example uses two duplicates.)

3. Choose the Object|Combine|Intersect menu item to chop out the individual pieces.

4. Assign the gradient to each piece.

5. Reassemble the pieces so that each piece abuts exactly. Get ready to do some simple math; careful use of the Transform palette is essential.

6. Use Object|Group to wrap the pieces into a tidy package.

Honestly, this technique can be a lot of work. If you have a program capable of generating complex gradients (say, Photoshop or Illustrator), you may be happier using it to generate the gradient. Once you've created a nifty custom gradient, you can quickly bring it into the LiveMotion composition and use it as a texture. You might also want to experiment with LiveMotion's Mask feature. (Check out the step-by-step Desert Chrome example in the color section.)

Color Schemes

Do you have a difficult time selecting color combinations? Can't match colors to save your life? LiveMotion's Color Scheme palette provides a convenient means to create sets of complementary colors. Color schemes can consist of between two and six colors. To create a color scheme, follow these simple steps:

1. Deselect the Lock button on the Color Scheme palette.

2. Select the color scheme's base color from the Color palette (or with the Eyedropper tool).

3. Select the number of colors in the scheme on the Color Scheme palette, and then select the scheme type from one of the three buttons at the bottom right of the palette.

4. If you have colored the background of your composition, you can view the color scheme on the background color. Just click the button to the right of the Lock button, as shown in Figure 1.28.

5. Once you've created a color scheme you dig, select the Lock button.

Figure 1.28
The Color Scheme palette blends impressive color theory into a point and click interface.

Pop That Text

The individual colors within a color scheme work well with each other, but they don't always provide enough pop to break colored text off a colored object or background. Here are a couple of hints to maximize contrast between text and its underlying color:

- *Black and white*—It's tough to go wrong with black or white text, assuming you use black text on a light- to medium-colored background, or white text on a medium- to dark-colored background.

- *Invert*—Don't overlook this checkbox in the Adjust palette. Specify the same color for the text as the underlying color, and then select the Invert checkbox for maximum contrast.

The Pen Tool

LiveMotion sets itself apart from the competition (and its predecessor) with an authentic Bézier Pen tool. This familiar appliance is noticeably missing from both Macromedia Flash 4 and Adobe ImageStyler. If Adobe Illustrator is old hat for you, LiveMotion's Pen tool will make you feel right at home.

Pen Tool Basics

The Pen tool allows you to quickly create objects that consist of any combination of straight and curved lines, as shown in Figure 1.29. Line segments enter and exit through *nodes*. The line's attack and departure are regulated through the positioning of the node's *control points*. (The node sits on the line, whereas the control points are found at the ends of the antennas.) The following section provides a rundown on some Pen tool basics:

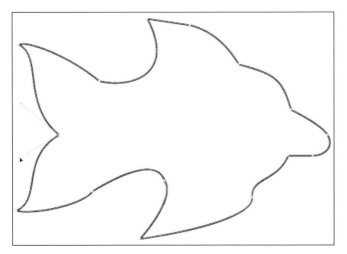

Figure 1.29
Knitting needles, alien antennas, nodes, and control points, call them what you will—they're the key to taking complete charge of your paths.

- *Drawing Straight Lines*—To draw a straight line segment, select the Pen tool, click the starting point of the line, and then click to set the ending point of the line segment. (Hint: Hold down the Shift key to constrain the lines in 45 degree increments.)

- *Drawing Curved Lines*—To draw a curved line segment, select the Pen tool, click the starting point of the line, and then click and drag to set the ending point of the line segment. As you drag the control point, it will affect the curve.

- *Altering Curves*—Once you draw curves, you can alter them with the Pen Selection tool. A number of methods exist to alter curves:

  - Click and drag on a line segment.

  - Click and drag a node.

  - Click and drag a control point.

  - Add or remove a node.

  - Change the node type.

- *Adding and Removing Nodes*—To add a node, hold down the Cmd/Ctrl key while positioning the cursor at the point where you want to add the new node, then, click to add the node. To remove a node, hold down the Cmd/Ctrl key while positioning the cursor over the node you want to remove, then click to remove the node.

- *Changing a Node Type*—To change a node type, Option/Alt click on the node you want to alter, then drag on the node to pull out the control points. To change a node from symmetrical to asymmetrical, Option/Alt click and drag on the control point.

Pen Tool Tips

Here are a handful of Pen tool tips:

- *Convert shapes*—You don't have to draw everything from scratch with the Pen tool. Instead, you can combine shapes, and then tweak the resulting path with the Pen Selection tool. (Note: Objects combined using the Unite With Color option cannot be path edited.)

- *Start with an outline*—Use the Properties dialog box to set the object type to outline before you start drawing with the Pen tool. This makes it easier to see the object shape. If you draw with a filled object, it can be difficult to discern the finished shape.

- *Close your paths*—Don't leave your paths wide open. If you're drawing a closed path, you'll want to be sure to click all of the way back to the starting node. (Hint: The starting node is red.)

- *Keep it simple*—Use the smallest number of nodes to create your objects. The fewer the nodes, the smaller the object, and the smaller the vector export.

Moving On

Getting started with LiveMotion is as easy as sitting down and launching the program. This chapter covered the basics of operation, with information on shapes, layers, objects, alignment, text, color, gradients, and the Pen tool. This discussion should provide a solid map to follow as you seek to discover the magic in LiveMotion. The next chapter gets all touchy-feely with the subject of 3D effects, textures, and backgrounds.

Chapter 2

3D Effects, Textures, and Backgrounds

Want to design Web pages that your audience can reach out and touch? This chapter covers 3D effects, textures, and backgrounds.

Making It Pop

LiveMotion's 3D effects and texture features can turn a flat-looking design into a sculpted interface that pops from the Web browser. These features allow you to create a wide range of graphics, buttons, and navigational elements—anything from subtle blind-embossed effects through chiseled heavy-metal looks. If your Web design schemes include images that appear to be wrought from the elements, whether hand-hewn or forged from steel, this chapter will help you achieve your alternate reality.

Creating 3D Effects with LiveMotion

LiveMotion makes 3D graphic creation easy and interactive. Although the program doesn't render full-blown 3D graphics, it makes quick work of cutouts, embosses, bevels, and ripples—all the goodies you'll need to knock out the elements of a nifty 3D interface. The 3D effects are all governed by the 3D palette, which provides the means to alter the depth, softness, and lighting (intensity, angle, and type) of each effect.

Let's dive right into the 3D effects to get a feel for how they work.

Cutout and Look Through

The *Cutout effect* emulates a stencil (or die cut) as if punching a hole through the current selection. The Depth control governs the (illusion of) distance between the stencil and what lies behind it by drawing a shadow within the selection. The higher the Depth setting, the deeper the shadow. Figure 2.1 demonstrates the progressive effect of depth on a gray piece of 96-point type set on a white background.

3D Effects and Flash

LiveMotion's 3D effects are way cool and way fast—to create. Be aware of the following, however, before you go off and start creating intricate 3D Flash interfaces: When LiveMotion creates a 3D effect, the resulting object is exported (in the SWF file) as a bitmap. Because bitmap objects are inherently larger than vector objects, this can lead to large SWF files and long downloads. Chapter 7 delivers the skinny on how to take the weight (and the wait) out of those downloads.

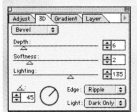

The 3D palette adds cool effects to objects, but you may want to use it sparingly with compositions that will be exported as SWF Flash files.

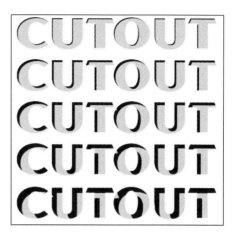

Figure 2.1

With Softness set to 0, it's easy to see how various Depth settings (3, 6, 9, 12, and 15) push the shadow around.

Want to lose that hard edge? The Softness setting lets you add a realistic blur to your cutout shadows. Figure 2.2 demonstrates those same Depth settings, each with a Softness setting of 6. A soft shadow helps to create the illusion of a 3D image.

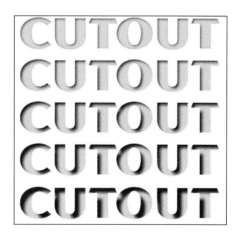

Figure 2.2

Softness adds realism to cutouts.

Filling a piece of cutout type with a texture can make the type pop between the dimensions. With some textures, the type appears (as you'd expect) as a cutout, whereas with other textures, the type appears to float on the surface of the page, as shown in Figure 2.3.

Here are some hints for using cutouts:

- Mild cutouts (those with a low Depth setting) are more likely to appear as if they're floating over the surface of the page. Higher Depth settings punch through the page.

- Encasing a cutout in a bezeled frame can create a porthole-like appearance.

- Cutouts make cool rollover **over** states, as you'll see in Chapter 4.

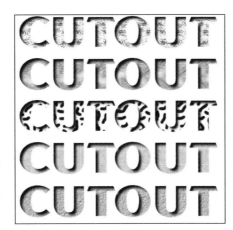

Figure 2.3
Careful use of textures,
lighting, soft shadows, and
a low Depth setting cause a
cutout to pop off the page.

Pressing Embosses

The *Emboss effect* can deliver a range of appearances—including the look of embossed paper or leather, or a stamped wax seal—depending on the options specified and the color or texture to which you apply the effect. You can choose from four types of embossed edges: straight, button, plateau, and ripple. Figure 2.4 demonstrates the differences between the Emboss effect's edges. The embossed characters in the top row are set with no softness, whereas the embossed characters in the bottom row are set with various degrees of softness.

Figure 2.4
A variety of embossed effects,
show edge variations, from left to
right: straight, button, plateau,
and ripple.

Here are some embossing tips, as shown in Figure 2.5 (from the top):

- To create a rounded pill-like effect, use a straight edge and push up the Softness setting.

- For a subtle blind-embossed effect, use a button edge and fill with the background (Layer|Fill With: Background).

- For a harder pill-like effect, use a plateau edge.

- Try a ripple edge to carve an interesting ridge.

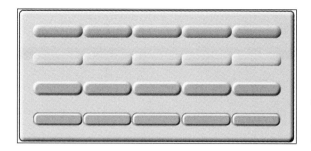

Figure 2.5
Embossed buttons tend to be softer than their beveled kin. From the top: straight-, button-, plateau-, and ripple-edged embossed buttons.

Carving Bevels

The *Bevel effect* is similar to the Emboss effect, albeit with a harder edge. Bevels have a more chiseled look that makes them more appropriate when portraying carved or forged designs. As with the Emboss effect, you can choose from four types of beveled edges: straight, button, plateau, and ripple. Figure 2.6 demonstrates the differences among the Bevel effect's edges. The beveled characters in the top row are set with no softness, whereas the beveled characters in the bottom row are set with various degrees of softness.

Figure 2.6
A variety of beveled effects, from left to right: straight, button, plateau, and ripple.

You may find yourself using smaller Depth settings with beveled buttons, as compared to embossed buttons, because a beveled edge looks a bit harder than an embossed edge. Compare the beveled buttons in Figure 2.7 with the embossed buttons in Figure 2.5. The beveled buttons have good definition with smaller depth settings.

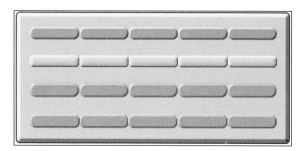

Figure 2.7
One more time, from the top: straight-, button-, plateau-, and ripple-edged beveled buttons.

Figure 2.8
Beveled text can carry
some weight.

Here are a handful of bevel tips, as demonstrated by Figure 2.8:

- Diagonal and curved bevels are prone to extrusion marks, especially on deeper cuts. Try pumping up the Softness setting to fade the marks.

- Adding a second, wider beveled layer can make text look beefier. Open the character tracking to keep the characters from touching each other.

- Adding an extra layer with a soft drop shadow really makes your beveled type pop off the page.

Ripples in the Pond

The *Ripple effect* is the most vivid of LiveMotion's 3D effects. At extreme settings, it can produce a hypnotic outcome, whereas at milder settings, you'll swear you've just thrown a coin into the fountain. Due to their circular nature, ripples may not be particularly useful for text effects, but you can use them to build wicked buttons and bullets. Figure 2.9 demonstrates the results of a variety of Depth and Softness settings.

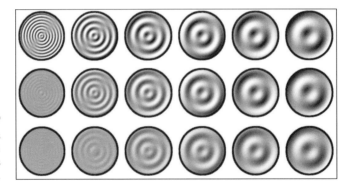

Figure 2.9
Flying saucers—the columns
show Depth settings of 1 through
6, and the rows show Softness
settings of 0, 4, and 8.

Here are some ripple tips:

- Push the Depth and Softness settings way up to create an airbrushed, cloud-like texture. It isn't 3D, but it isn't half bad, either. Crank the Lighting slider down to eliminate hot spots.

- Want to put your visitors into a trance? Amplify the hypnotic Ripple effect with variations in rollover states. Try switching from Light Only to Dark Only lighting.

Get an Edge

Sorting out the edge effects can be confusing. The figure provides some clues, by showing a simulated crosscut of each type of edge. The higher the Depth setting, the more extreme (larger) the edge.

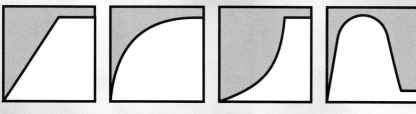

Pick an edge: straight, button, plateau, or ripple.

- A double-ripple 3D fill (ripple edge) is extra groovy, with twice the line density.

- Stay away from cheap wine with screw-off caps.

Lighting 3D Effects

Until this point, I've focused on depth, softness, and edges—perhaps the most obvious aspects of working with LiveMotion's 3D effects. Now, it's time to turn your attention to the subtle (or not so subtle) subject of lighting. The proper lighting can make or break a 3D effect. Too little light, and the image will become flat and lifeless; too much light, and the image will become harsh and glaring.

LiveMotion provides three primary lighting controls on the 3D palette:

- *Intensity*—Think of the Lighting slider as your dimmer control. Settings below 100 will become progressively muted; settings above 100 will become increasingly glary.

- *Angle of attack*—Take a gander at the Lighting widget: The radius line governs the light's angle of attack. Spin the widget (or dial in the degrees directly) to aim the light.

- *Type*—The pop-up menu allows you to choose from Normal, Light Only, and Dark Only settings. Try flipping through these choices for some radically different effects.

Figure 2.10 demonstrates the differences between the Normal, Light Only, and Dark Only settings, along with the effects of various light intensities. Notice how the buttons on the left are muted, whereas the figures on the right are highly contrasted.

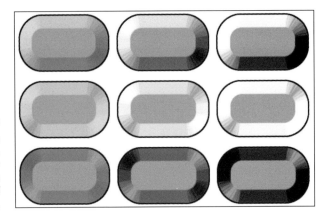

Figure 2.10

Candlelight or arc lamps? The rows show (from top) Normal, Light Only, and Dark Only settings, and the columns illustrate intensity settings of (from left) 50, 100, and 150.

Figure 2.11

My NiteLife style (included on this book's companion CD-ROM) creates an illuminated glass-like effect with two beveled layers and a drop shadow layer.

3D Effects and Web-Safe Color in GIF Exports

Let the beveler beware! When you apply a 3D effect to an object that's been filled with Web-safe color, the base color of the object remains Web-safe. However, the beveled, embossed, rippled, or cutout shadow probably will *not* be Web-safe. Select Web Adaptive in the Export palette's drop-down menu to avoid the possibility of color shifts and dithering in the browser. Select View|Active Export Preview (or select the Preview option in the Export palette) to see the changes before exporting the file.

Fiddling with lighting effects helps pop the image off the page while enhancing the illusion of a third dimension. Things start to get interesting when an object has two or more layers. I created the logo plate in Figure 2.11 with two objects—the text (set in the Metolurgy2 font) and a rounded-corner rectangle—and assigned both objects the NiteLife style. Although these letterforms are admittedly complex, take a look at how wild the bevels become in the text; the more complex the object shape, the more intricate the extrusion. The beveled layers both use the Light Only setting to highlight the bevels.

OBJECT Combining 3D Effects

Some of the most powerful results happen when you combine LiveMotion's 3D effects. By using a number of layers, you can sculpt ornate castles in the sand (without the fear of a rising tide), whether they're startlingly realistic or positively otherworldly. The NiteLife style illustrated in Figure 2.11 is an (admittedly over the top) example of what can happen when you combine two bevels. The Layer palette's Width slider affords up to 20 pixels of play between the widest and skinniest layers. This lets you choke the top layer down 10 pixels and spread the bottom layer up 10 pixels when working from the base layer—and that's more than enough room to create 3D effects for Web site interface design.

You'll find lots of reasons to combine 3D effects. Figure 2.12 shows a pair of examples (set in the Vag Rounded font) that use beveled frames behind cutouts. The first example uses three layers.

Figure 2.12
Two variations on a porthole theme.

Try re-creating this effect:

1. *The cutout*—Choke the Width -4 from the original layer. Use a 3D Cutout effect with a Depth setting of 11 and a Softness setting of 3.

2. *The bezel*—Spread the Width 5 from the original layer. Use a 3D Bevel effect with a ripple edge, a Depth setting of 3, and a Softness setting of 1. (Also apply a brushed metal texture.)

3. *The outline*—Spread the Width 8 from the original layer. You don't need to add any other effects to this basic black layer.

The second example achieves a very different look by adding one simple layer to the first example. I added a basic black layer (with no changes to the Width setting) directly behind the cutout layer. This layer reduces the visible width of the bezel without encroaching on the cutout.

The beauty of LiveMotion is that once you get a happening look, you can alter it to create something new and exciting without having to reinvent the wheel. Like that bezel? Hate that cutout? No sweat—just try altering the top layer. Figure 2.13 reuses the second porthole style, replacing the cutout with a ripple layer. This combination achieves a neat taillight effect when you use it on circles, ellipses, and rounded-corner rectangles.

Although the 3D effects can add an illusion of texture to an object, you'll often combine them with bitmap (or vector) textures. In the following section, I'll tackle that subject.

Figure 2.13
Hang a left. This ripple effect uses a Depth setting of 12, a Softness setting of 6, a Lighting setting of 96, a ripple edge, and the Light Only option.

Working with Textures

LiveMotion allows you to quickly apply textures to objects and backgrounds. Although the program ships with a small collection of textures, you can easily bring in textures from other sources—whether you've found them on the Internet, on a CD-ROM, or created them yourself. You can bring textures into LiveMotion on the fly for use in a specific instance by one of the following means:

- From a file with File|Place As Texture or from the Clipboard with Edit|Paste Special|Paste Texture.

- Bring them into LiveMotion's Texture palette for repeated use (either via the Texture palette's New Texture button, by dragging the object containing the texture to the palette, or even by dragging the texture file directly to the Texture palette from the Desktop).

I've got to admit it: I'm a texture freak. Over the years, I've created thousands upon thousands of original seamless textures—it's an addictive, even hypnotic craft. When I sit down to create a texture, I can't create just one. More often, I'll create 100 or more at a clip. I've included thousands of my textures on my books' companion CD-ROMs (and this book is no exception). In fact, the LiveMotion team tapped me to create some textures for LiveMotion—many of the textures you'll find on the original Adobe LiveMotion CD-ROM are my creations.

Achieving Seamlessness

Textures become *seamless* when you make their ends meet. Look at a properly prepared seamless texture: Its left edge should wrap around to its right edge; its bottom edge should wrap around to its top edge. You achieve seamlessness when the sides of the tile flow together both horizontally and vertically in a harmonious manner, as demonstrated by Figure 2.14.

Figure 2.14
It isn't nuclear, it's seamless.

Creating seamless textures can be a trivial or non-trivial matter, depending on your approach. Really great seamless textures always take a bit of work, however. The major image-editing applications all include some way to create seamless images.

Where Do the Textures Go?

Once you've imported a texture through the Texture palette, it's stored in LiveMotion's Texture folder. You can add textures directly to that folder (via the Mac's Finder or Windows Explorer), if you're so inclined.

Getting Seamless in Adobe Photoshop

Adobe Photoshop's Offset filter moves the edges of an image into the middle of the image, where you can easily discern and manually eliminate the seams. Once the seams are in the middle of the image, you use the Clone tool to obscure them. Let's cover this with a quick Photoshop step-by-step:

1. Choose Filter|Other|Offset to open the Offset Filter dialog box.

2. Set Horizontal to half the image's pixel width.

3. Set Vertical to half the image's pixel height.

4. Select Undefined Areas To Wrap Around. This setting pushes the seams into the middle of the image.

5. Click on OK.

Now that the seams are in the middle of the image, it's time to go to work with the Clone tool. You'll want to selectively clone pixels over the visible seams. This isn't a trivial process—you may have to move the Offset percentages a couple of times to get things just right.

Getting Seamless in Corel PHOTO-PAINT

The Offset filter found in Corel PHOTO-PAINT is similar to Photoshop's Offset filter—it enables you to slide (offset) the horizontal and vertical edges of an image. Once the edges have been offset to the middle of the image, you can use the Clone tool to terminate the visible seams, with extreme prejudice. Here's a PHOTO-PAINT 9 step-by-step:

1. Select Effects|Distort|Offset.

2. Select Shift Value As % Of Dimensions.

3. Set the Horizontal and Vertical Shift values to 50. These settings move the seams to the exact middle of the image.

4. Select Undefine Areas|Wrap Around.

5. Click on Preview to check things out (you may want to try different Shift percentages, depending on the texture).

6. Click on OK.

Use the Clone tool to obscure the visible edges, as in the previous section.

Getting Seamless in Fractal Painter

Fractal Painter's Wrap-Around Seams feature performs a similar function to Photoshop's Offset filter. The Wrap-Around Colors feature goes one better by carrying your brush strokes off one edge of the image and around to the opposite side. To create a pattern in Fractal Painter, you must either define the entire image as a pattern or capture a portion of an image as a pattern.

A Word about the Adjust and Distort Palettes (and Plug-ins, Too)

Once you've placed a texture in LiveMotion, the fun has just begun. The program's Adjust and Distort palettes allow you to take your textures into a whole new realm. The interactive nature of LiveMotion lets you create some startling results. I'll cover the Adjust and Distort palettes in Chapters 3 and 4, where you'll create styles that snap off the page and rollovers that sit up and bark.

Although LiveMotion provides the ability to use Photoshop plug-ins, it's only possible to apply plug-ins to images, not to textures or to vector objects.

Once an image has been converted into a pattern, you gain access to the Wrap-Around functions. To move the seams inward, simply hold down the Shift key while you drag with the grabber hand. This technique provides more feedback than Photoshop's method of specifying an offset in pixels.

In the next section, you'll see that although LiveMotion really isn't a texture-creation program, you can use it to create basic seamless images. The program is at its best when used in conjunction with a seamless tilemaker, such as Xaos Tools Terrazzo.

PROJECT Creating Simple Seamless Tiles

Let's take a look at how you can create a basic seamless tile in LiveMotion. Perhaps you want to create a simple watermark or a rudimentary pattern. In either case, you need to begin by creating a rectangular area to contain the repeating pattern. Then, you'll place the artwork onto the rectangle, taking care not to lay any objects over the edge. (If any objects are over the edge, LiveMotion will export the image with gaps.) Figure 2.15 shows two variations on a watermarked theme using this technique.

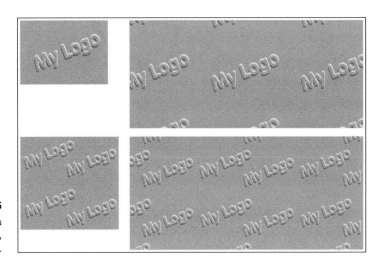

Figure 2.15
It isn't fancy, but it's fast. If all you want to do is tile your logo, LiveMotion can do the trick.

Here's a quick step-by-step:

1. Create and color the rectangle.

2. Place the motif (objects, logo, or what have you) in the rectangular area.

3. Specify the export format options on the Export palette.

4. Select the rectangle and all the objects within it.

5. Choose File|Export Selection, name the file, and click on Save.

Of course, you aren't limited to simple watermarks. I'll expand on this technique in the next section, which covers the topic of seamless background creation for HTML page design.

Background Basics

The days of drab gray Web-page backgrounds are long behind us. Today, every great Web page starts with an appropriate background. Thankfully, LiveMotion is proficient at both applying and generating seamless backgrounds. The previous section explained how to work with textures and create a simple patterned effect. This section goes into far greater depth as it builds upon those topics.

As you read this chapter, you'll find the *Adobe LiveMotion f/x and Design* companion CD-ROM to be an invaluable resource. The CD-ROM contains LiveMotion (LIV) files for all the background textures detailed here. Black-and-white figures can only show so much. You'll want to dig into the files to fully understand how all the aspects of our discussion fit together.

You should consider three key points when designing a tiled background image:

• Ensure readability.

• Less is more.

• Never let them see your seams.

It's imperative to ensure readability. The information contained in your Web site is more important than the electronic paper (the background) on which it's printed. So, you should avoid overly complex designs—they may confuse your visitors. Wild patterns can be fun, but use them only where they don't obscure the text. Strive for a clean, effective, seamless presentation.

Simple Background Colors

Sometimes, solid colors are best. If you value fast download speeds above all, you'll probably be content to set the HTML background color and leave it at that. Simple one-color backgrounds display instantly. With no background

LiveMotion and SWF Backgrounds

When you set up a composition with a background texture or pattern—as opposed to a solid color background—for SWF export, the background will be exported as part of the SWF file, not as part of the HTML container document. The SWF format allows for cool animated backgrounds. This allows background stripes (and the like) to slide into position.

file to download, the color will appear as quickly as the browser can parse the HTML code. You can set a background color a number of ways with LiveMotion:

- *Directly*—Select the Background Color square at the bottom of the toolbox and then select a color from the Color palette.

- *With the Paint Bucket*—Select the Paint Bucket tool, select a color from the Color palette, and click on the page background.

- *From an object*—Select the Background Color square at the bottom of the toolbox, select the Eyedropper tool, and select a color for the object. (Of course, you can also select a color from the Color palette with this method.)

Building Backgrounds

Earlier in this chapter, I touched on background building (in the "Creating Simple Seamless Tiles" project). Now, let's take a closer look at how to create background images with LiveMotion. Creating background images is straightforward. Basically, you have to create a GIF or JPEG file that tiles seamlessly in the browser. With simple backgrounds, this task is relatively easy to accomplish. But, as your designs grow more complex, you need to be a bit more vigilant in your composition.

Maximum Background Width and Height

Keep in mind that background images always tile out to fill the browser window. LiveMotion has a maximum page size of 1,024-by-1,024 pixels. This means that the backgrounds you design can't be larger than 1,024 pixels either horizontally or vertically. And that's okay—there's little reason to design a background wider or taller than that.

You should accommodate the widest audience by designing for the lowest common (practical) denominator—that is, the 640x480 display. As you do, think of all those folks browsing on 800x600, 832x624, 1,024x768, and higher resolutions. Strive to keep a consistent presentation for the whole crowd.

Backgrounds with a vertical pattern should be roughly 1,024 pixels wide by the smallest height that works (try not to go smaller than 2 pixels high—1 pixel high backgrounds can cause problems with some browsers). Although the live image area might only be 600 pixels, the remaining horizontal area prevents the image from tiling in the browser. Horizontally striped backgrounds can be trickier—you might aim for a maximum height of 768 or 1,024 by the smallest width that works (try not to go smaller than 2 pixels wide). I'll demonstrate these concepts in a moment.

Assemble, Export, and Place

Ready to get started? Fear not—this isn't rocket science. The steps to seamless background creation are as follows:

1. *Assembly*—This is where you craft the background tile. For a successful tile, you'll need to position the individually colored (or textured) chunks with precision.

2. *Export selection*—Select all the objects within your background tile; then, choose your export options and export the selection.

3. *Place Texture*—Choose File|Place As Texture to specify your background image within the new LiveMotion composition.

In the following sections, you'll learn how to create a wide assortment of seamless background patterns. Let's begin with vertical stripes.

Vertically Striped Backgrounds

Variations on the vertically striped background theme are among the most popular on the Web. You'll see scores of Web sites that use a dark stripe running down the left side of the page, with a lighter (usually white) body area. In the following section, I'll show you how to create solid-color stripes, 3D stripes, fading stripes, textured stripes, and curved stripes.

Solid Colors

The most basic vertically striped backgrounds use just two colors. Their slightly more complex brethren add a third area, beyond 600 pixels or so, to infer a dead zone. Figures 2.16 and 2.17 show the difference in appearance between these two common background schemes.

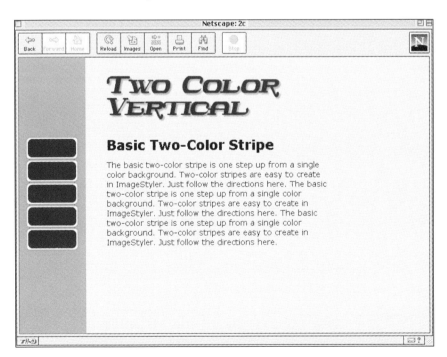

Figure 2.16
Two-piece vertical striped backgrounds are basic, yet effective.

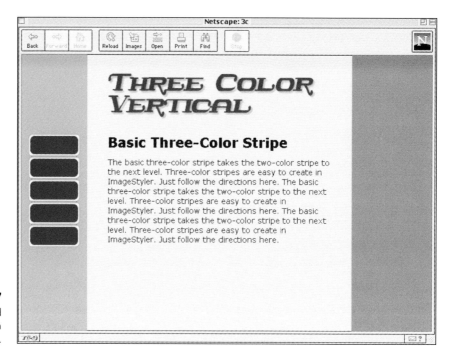

Figure 2.17
Three-piece vertical striped backgrounds define an out-of-bounds area.

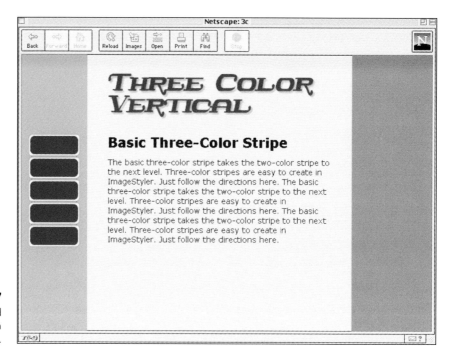 Keep It Simple: Two-Color Backgrounds

If you value display speed, but still want a striped background, you should stick with solid colors for your vertical stripes. Flat's where it's at—flat color, that is. The more complex your background designs become (and the more colors they involve), the larger the file size will be. And, the more intricate the background design, the more likely that it may overwhelm the page design.

Let's take a look at how easily you can build vertical stripes:

1. *Set the composition size.* Choose Edit|Composition Settings to access the Composition Settings dialog box. Enter "1024" in the Width field and "20" in the Height field. Select Entire Composition from the Export menu, then click on OK.

2. *Draw the colored stripe.* Select the Rectangle tool and draw a rectangle 120 pixels wide by 20 pixels high; it will represent the colored stripe. Use the Transform palette to set the width and height. (It's actually okay if the rectangle is larger than 20 pixels high.) With the new rectangle selected, choose a dark color from the Color palette.

3. *Position the colored stripe.* With the new (stripe) rectangle selected, enter "0" in both the X and Y fields on the Transform palette to place the rectangle at the upper-left corner of the composition.

Follow the Sequence

Object width and height affect positioning. Consequently, you should always set an object's X and Y coordinates *after* you've set its width and height.

4. *Set the background color.* Select the Document Background Color swatch on the Toolbox, then select a light color from the Color palette.

5. *Get ready to export.* Open the Export Settings palette by choosing File|Export Settings. Set the format to GIF and the number of colors to 4. Make sure that the Include Transparency Information button is *not* selected (otherwise, the file will be exported with transparency—and that's not something you'll want to do with background files.) Select the Preview checkbox to see how the file will appear when exported.

6. *Generate the background file.* Choose File|Export. Name the file and click on Save. (The first time you export a file, LiveMotion will ask you what the file should be named. Subsequent exports of the same file will be named identically. To use a different name, use File|Export As.)

7. *Place the background.* Open the file that will use the new background. Choose File|Place As Texture. Select the background file and click on Open to place the background.

Although these directions are explicit, creating vertical stripes really is a simple procedure. Using the Entire Composition export option is the easiest way to go. You can also build your background objects in a larger composition window and use File|Export Selection (with the pertinent objects selected). If you go that route, however, you should ensure that all of the objects are exactly the same height and are positioned with the same exact Y coordinate. If you fail to do so, you may end up with a not-so-seamless pattern—offensive horizontal lines will call attention to any misalignment.

If you like the idea of a clearly defined page, but you want more control over the whole screen, read on. The next section explains how to create a three-color background scheme.

A Step Up: Three-Color Backgrounds

Three-color backgrounds are only slightly more difficult to produce and only incrementally larger in file size then their two-color brethren. For just a handful of bytes, the "out-of-bounds" area provides a clear definition of what's on the page and what's off. Here's a detailed three-color how-to:

1. *Set the canvas size; draw and position the colored stripe.* Follow Steps 1, 2, 3, and 4 of the previous two-color background project.

2. *Draw the out-of-bounds area.* Select the Rectangle tool. Draw a rectangle; it will represent the out-of-bounds color. Use the Transform palette to set the width and height to 424 and 20 pixels, respectively. With the new rectangle selected, choose a dark color from the Color palette.

3. *Position the out-of-bounds area.* With the new (out-of-bounds) rectangle selected, enter "600" in the X field and "0" in the Y field on the Transform palette. Doing so butts the left side of the out-of-bounds rectangle to the right side of the body rectangle.

4. *Get ready to export.* Open the Export Settings palette by choosing File|Export Settings. Set the format to GIF and the number of colors to 5. Make sure that the Transparency option is not chosen. Select the Preview checkbox to see how the file will appear when exported.

5. *Generate the background file.* Choose File|Export As. Name the file and click on Save.

6. *Place the background.* Open the file that will use the new background. Choose File|Place As Texture. Select the background file and click on Open to place the background.

Now, let's see how to make those simple stripes pop.

3D Stripes

LiveMotion makes it easy to build backgrounds with 3D stripes that seem to pop from the browser. The following section demonstrates two techniques that you can use to create cool (and totally seamless) vertical 3D-striped backgrounds.

 Building 3D Stripes: The Automatic Way

Let's begin with a copy of the three-color stripe you created in the previous project. The trick is to use the same Entire Composition export, coupled with oversized objects that bleed off the top and bottom edges of the composition, as shown in Figure 2.18.

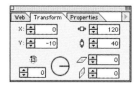

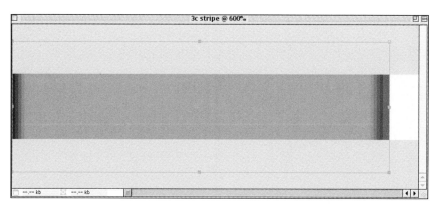

Figure 2.18
What do you get when you place a 40-pixel-high beveled object on a 20-pixel-high canvas? A perfect trim.

Here are the steps to make the stripes pop:

1. *Pop the first stripe.* Select the color stripe, open the 3D palette, and select the Emboss effect. Set Depth to 3, Softness to 1, Lighting to 100, Edge to Straight, Light to Dark Only, and Angle to 0.

2. *Oversize the stripe.* Use the Transform palette to make the stripe object 40 pixels high. Set the Y coordinate to -10.

3. *Pop (and oversize) the out-of-bounds stripe.* Apply similar settings to the out-of-bounds object.

4. *Get ready to export.* With the Export Settings palette open, set the format to GIF and the number of colors to 16. Make sure that the Transparency option is not chosen.

5. *Generate the background file.* Choose File|Export As. Name the file and click on Save.

Try placing the new seamless tile into a new LiveMotion composition.

3D Stripes: The Manual Way

Of course, you can always build 3D stripes the old-fashioned way: by creating each chunk of the gradation by hand. Why would you want to do this? Here are a number of reasons:

- *To take complete control over the effect*—LiveMotion's 3D effects require some tweaking. If you're working with a tight background, you may be able to knock out a nice 3D look with just a handful of objects.

- *To constrain colors to the Web-safe palette*—Automatically generated 3D effects often use colors from outside the Web-safe palette. By assigning colors manually, you can restrict color use and maintain control over the palette.

- *To keep file size to a minimum*—When you're creating every chunk of an image, you'll give each one careful consideration. The fewer the chunks, the smaller the file.

It isn't really that difficult to build 3D stripes manually. The best method is to zoom *way* in on the image. You can easily see what's going on when you're zoomed 800 percent—those single-pixel chunks are highly visible and effortless to manipulate. To build a 3D effect by hand, you'll want to start with a copy of the flat two- or three-color stripe, as completed earlier. Then, zoom in on the area where the colored stripe meets the body at the left side of the composition, as shown in Figure 2.19.

Use rectangles that are one, two, or three pixels wide—and the same height as the stripe rectangles—to manually build the gradation from light to dark (or dark to light). Stick with Web-safe colors to avoid the possibility of dithering in the browser. Be sure you vertically align (or bleed) all the objects to ensure a gap-free export.

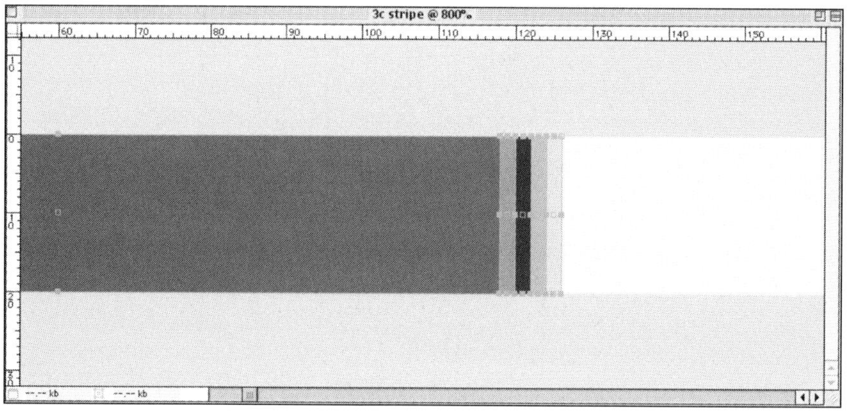

Figure 2.19

Building vertical 3D stripes one chunk at a time can fall just short of being a painstaking task. Always ensure that every chunk lines up with the same Y coordinates—otherwise, you may end up with artifacts in the vertically tiled pattern.

PROJECT Building Textured Stripes

Textured-stripe backgrounds can make a distinctive statement. The trick to implementing textures within vertically striped Web backgrounds is to select textures that are seamless from top to bottom. The texture tiles should be tall enough to avoid an obvious repeating pattern, yet the files should be small enough to ensure a reasonable download time. Consequently, the height of a textured-stripe background is governed by the height of the seamless texture itself. Here's a step-by-step project to create a textured-stripe background:

1. *Open a new LiveMotion window.* Choose File|New.

2. *Place the seamless tile.* Choose File|Place. Navigate to the Chapter 2 folder on the *Adobe LiveMotion In Depth* CD-ROM, select granite6.jpg, and click on Open to place the seamless texture.

3. *Position the tile.* Choose Window|Transform to open the Transform palette (if it isn't already open). Note that this texture's width and height are 116 pixels. Set the X and Y coordinates to 0.

4. *Set the background color.* Select the Document Background Color swatch on the toolbox, then select a light color from the Color palette.

5. *Set the composition dimensions.* Select Edit|Composition settings. Set the Width to 1024 and the Height to 116. Select Entire Composition from the Export menu.

6. *Pop the texture stripe.* You may want to add a few one-pixel-wide lines between the texture and the body to create a subtle 3D effect. You can use the Eyedropper tool to select the single-pixel object colors from the texture itself, as shown in Figure 2.20.

7. *Get ready to export.* Open the Export Settings palette by choosing File|Export Settings. Set the format to JPEG and Quality to 20 or 30.

Want More Page Definition?

Try adding an out-of-bounds stripe to the right side of the textured-stripe design.

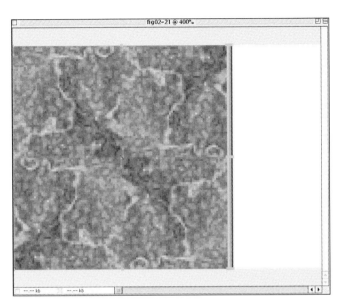

Figure 2.20
The manual 3D technique works well with textured stripes.

8. *Generate the background file.* Choose File|Export. Name the file and click on Save.

9. *Place the background.* Open the file that's going to use the new background. Choose File|Place As Texture. Select the background file and click on Open to place the background.

Let's take a look at some common textured-stripe designs. Each technique illustrated in the following section uses background-filled buttons within the texture bar to create a carved effect.

Elegant Woodgrains

How about an elegant woodgrain look? Quite honestly, you don't see a heck of a lot of woodgrain-textured Web graphics. And why not? Designers use woodgrain finishes on everything from automobile interiors to expensive pen and pencil sets. Three D Graphics Texture Creator is a wonderful source of procedurally rendered woodgrain patterns, like the one shown in Figure 2.21. Of course, you can find scores of woodgrain textures in commercially available seamless-texture collections.

Exquisite Marbles

Aiming for a cool, sophisticated look? Marble finishes are some of the most popular organic textures in Web and multimedia design. You can find marble tiles in a huge variety of colors and variations—from handsome dark greens and grays to creamy yellows and blushing pinks. You might also use a program such as Three D Graphics Texture Creator to generate a customized marble texture similar to the example shown in Figure 2.22.

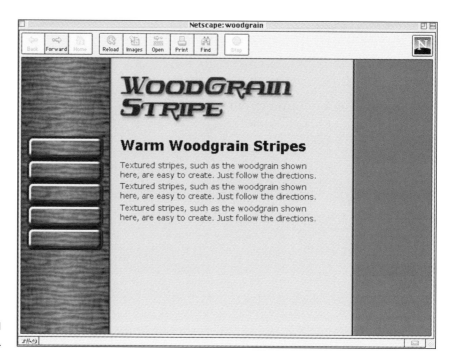

Figure 2.21
Woodgrains add a warm touch.

Figure 2.22
Well executed marble-textured graphics convey a refined air. Pass the Grey Poupon, please.

Enchanting Abstracts

Abstract patterns offer the widest array of possibilities. The CD-ROM that accompanies this book contains thousands of original abstract seamless patterns, such as the example shown in Figure 2.23. Xaos Tools Terrazzo is one of your main allies—you can use this Photoshop plug-in to create scores of unique seamless patterns from one original image.

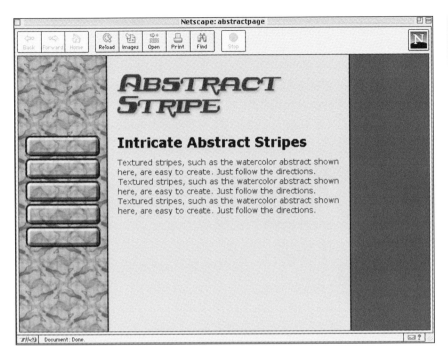

Set the Background Color *and* the Pattern

Sometimes you may want to set both the background color and the pattern. When? If a page uses a dark-colored background pattern and light-colored text, the text may not be legible until the background downloads. By specifying a dark background color in addition to a background pattern (in the HTML <BODY> tag), the text will be instantly readable.

Figure 2.23
Abstract patterns can invoke the feel of textile prints.

Fading Stripes

Are you looking to blend a vertical stripe into the body of your Web page? Build the composition as you would a three-color stripe, but use gradients, rather than solid colors. You can create fading stripes with a single gradient-colored object or with a collection of individually colored objects, as with the manual 3D effect. Figure 2.24 demonstrates one of the possibilities.

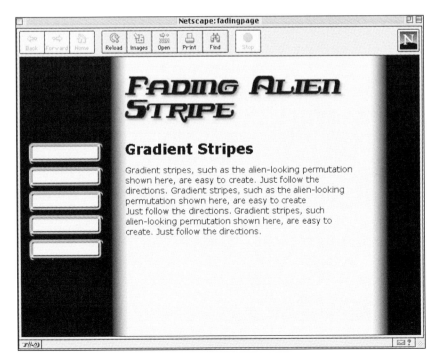

Figure 2.24
Fading gradient stripes can take on a 3D-like appearance.

Curving Edges

Want to add a curvaceous look to your Web designs? Curved-edge Web-page borders can be difficult to create, but when properly executed, they'll lend an unexpected and playful air. I've included a bunch of curved-border objects on **www.geekbooks.com** in EPS format—you can resize these vector objects at will. If you want to create your own curved-border objects, you probably should use a vector-drawing package, such as Adobe Illustrator, Macromedia FreeHand, or CorelDRAW.

Curve a Little

Try a subtle wave. I used CorelDRAW to generate the EPS object in the design shown in Figure 2.25. After I exported the simple object from CorelDRAW, I placed the EPS file into my background composition. Then, I duplicated (and rotated) the object to repeat the curve on the right side of the page. If you look closely, you'll see that I used a handful of duplicates to create the subtle 3D effect.

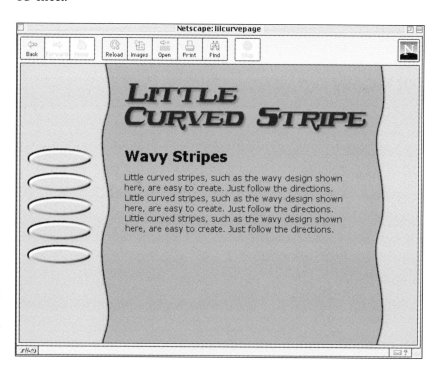

Figure 2.25

Hey, you must be working out. This unconventional design uses the same curved border on each side of the body.

Curve a Lot

Figure 2.26 shows another variation on the curved-stripe theme. I went for a bigger, bolder stripe. The result would feel at home in a bowling alley, or maybe in Las Vegas, circa 1962.

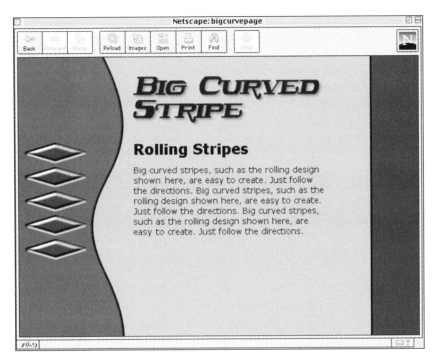

Figure 2.26

Uh-oh, those curves have put on weight.

Horizontally Striped Backgrounds

Although vertically striped backgrounds are the most popular on the Web, a horizontally striped background can be a stylish and distinctive choice. You can make your horizontally striped pages only so long. LiveMotion's maximum page depth is 1,024 pixels, which limits the height of the horizontally striped background tile. Repeating a horizontal stripe is a design faux pas. Consequently, you should use horizontal stripes only on short pages.

Solid Colors

Two solid areas of color are all you need to get started with a horizontally striped tile. The horizontal stripe serves as a clean backdrop for navigational and identification graphics, as demonstrated in Figure 2.27. Of course, you can always add a pinstripe rule or a touch of 3D to help pop the stripe from the page.

PROJECT Creating a Horizontally Striped Background

Creating horizontally striped background tiles is simple enough. Just take what you learned about vertically striped backgrounds and turn it on its side. Horizontal-stripe tiles are tall and skinny, as opposed to their wide and short vertical-stripe relatives. Here's a step-by-step:

Watch Out for Those Edges

When you place an EPS object into LiveMotion, the program may soften the object's edges through antialiasing. Keep an eye out for this softening if you're building seamless background tiles from the objects—the row of antialiased pixels will create a tiling artifact in the exported image. To avoid this problem, zoom way in on the tiling edges and create little rectangular strips of color to cover the (soft) antialiased edges *before* exporting.

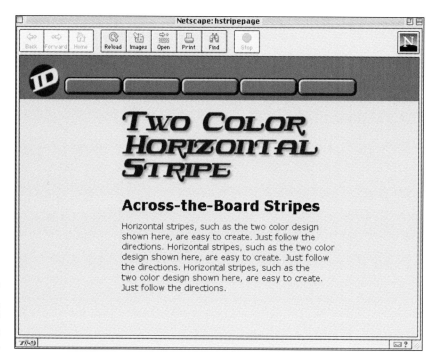

Figure 2.27
A horizontal stripe along the top edge of your Web page sets off the navigational elements from the body.

1. *Set the composition dimensions.* Select Edit|Composition settings. Set the Width to "36" and the Height to "1024". Select Entire Composition from the Export menu then click on OK.

2. *Set the background color.* Select the Document Background Color swatch on the toolbox, then select a light color from the Color palette.

3. *Draw the colored stripe.* Select the Rectangle tool. Draw a rectangle 36 pixels wide by 72 pixels high; it will represent the colored stripe. Use the Transform palette to set the width and height exactly. With the new rectangle selected, choose a dark color from the Color palette.

4. *Position the colored stripe.* With the new (stripe) rectangle selected, enter "0" in both the X and Y fields on the Transform palette. Doing so places the rectangle at the upper-left corner of the composition.

5. *Get ready to export.* Open the Export Settings palette by choosing File|Export Settings. Set the format to GIF and the number of colors to 4. Make sure that the Transparency option is not chosen.

6. *Generate the background file.* Choose File|Export As. Name the file and click on Save.

7. *Place the background.* Open the file that's going to use the new background. Choose File|Place As Texture. Select the background file and click on Open to place the background.

PROJECT Creating Pattern-Edged Stripes

You can place objects along the dividing line between the colored stripe and body area to create interesting sawtooth-edged designs. Patterned edges can run the gamut from sawtooth (triangles) to geartooth (rectangles), gingerbread (ellipses), and beyond. This step-by-step project creates a geartooth-edged, horizontally striped background image:

1. *Set the composition dimensions*. Select Edit|Composition settings. Set the Width to "24" and the Height to "1024". Select Entire Composition from the Export menu then click on OK.

2. *Set the background color*. Select the Document Background Color swatch on the toolbox, then select a light color from the Color palette.

3. *Draw the colored stripe*. Select the Rectangle tool. Draw a rectangle 24 pixels wide by 60 pixels high; it will represent the colored stripe. Use the Transform palette to set the width and height exactly. With the new rectangle selected, choose a dark color from the Color palette.

4. *Position the colored stripe*. With the new (stripe) rectangle selected, enter "0" in both the X and Y fields on the Transform palette to position the rectangle at the upper-left corner of the composition.

5. *Create the sawtooth*. Select the Rectangle Tool. Draw a 12-by-12-pixel square. Use the Eyedropper tool to assign the same color fill as the colored stripe. With the 12-by-12 square selected, enter "0" in the X field and "60" in the Y field on the Transform palette. Doing so butts the top of the square to the bottom of the colored stripe.

6. *Get ready to export*. Open the Export Settings palette by choosing File|Export Settings. Set the format to GIF and the number of colors to 6. Make sure that the Transparency option is not chosen.

7. *Generate the background file*. Choose File|Export As. Name the file and click on Save.

8. *Place the background*. Open the file that's going to use the new background. Choose File|Place As Texture. Select the background file and click on Open to place the background.

You can add some depth to the design by combining the two objects at the top of the composition (with Unite). Then, add a layer to the combined object and offset the new layer by two pixels; doing so creates a thin black line along the bottom horizontal edges of the combined object. Add two rectangles 1 pixel wide and 12 pixels tall along the vertical edges of the geartooth to finish the design. Figure 2.28 demonstrates the result.

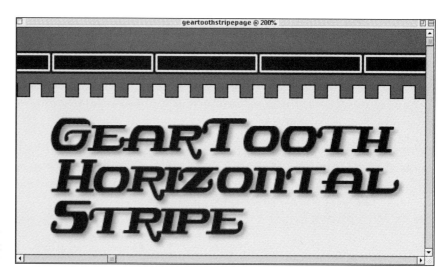

Figure 2.28

Okay, so this is pretty ugly—but you get the idea, right?

Deckle-Edged Stripes

To create a torn-edge design, you can use the rough-edged LiveMotion shapes or even try scanning some torn paper to create a dramatic effect. Figure 2.29 shows a deckle-edged, horizontally striped background image I created with a distressed square shape. I cropped the sides and top of the shape to square them and then dropped the shape into the top of the horizontally striped composition described earlier. I added a second layer with a two-pixel Y offset.

Figure 2.29

Rip it up. You can create deckle-edged designs in minutes.

Full-Page Backgrounds

Sometimes you may want to use one large (non-tiling) background image. In order for a background image not to tile, it must be larger than the contents of the Web page in both dimensions. Although LiveMotion is limited to a maximum image size of 1,024-by-1,024 pixels, this should be more than enough image. Remember, the larger the dimensions, the bigger the file—and the longer the download time.

The most successful full-page backgrounds consist of just a handful of colors. Don't entertain the idea of a photographic full-page background—the file size would be impracticably large. Instead, stick with limited palette images. Watermarked and ghosted images are the most common non-tiling background images. Figure 2.30 demonstrates a highly graphic two-color background.

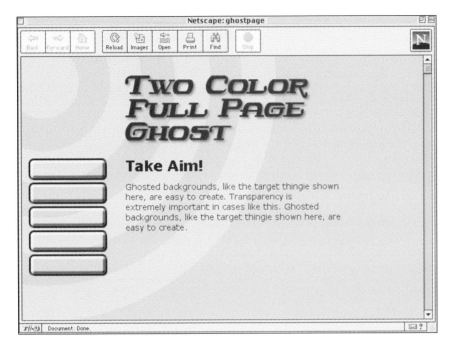

Figure 2.30
On target? If you're going to use a full-page background, keep it simple.

Background Bits

Although LiveMotion makes it easy to work with Web-page backgrounds, you'll want to watch out for a handful of situations. Let's touch on a trio of the most topical items.

Transparency and Backgrounds

"How do I get rid of the fringe and jaggies around my transparent graphics?" is one of the most frequently asked questions among neophyte Web-graphics designers. The answer, my friends, is to render your transparent GIF graphics on the same background on which they will be displayed in the Web page. By doing so, you'll be assured that the graphic will blend smoothly (through *antialiasing*) into the background, as the word "CLEAN" does in Figure 2.31. (The words "FRINGE & JAG" were rendered on a white background.)

Patterned backgrounds can be a bit problematic. You may want to try rendering the graphic on a solid color, rather than on the background tile. If you choose to use this method, you probably should select the dominant color in the pattern as your background color.

It Isn't Transparent

Wracking your skull trying to figure out why you aren't creating transparent GIFs? (The JPEG format doesn't support transparency.) Be sure the Transparency option is checked on the Export palette.

Figure 2.31
If you render your graphic on a light background and then place it on a darker background in the Web page, you'll end up with a ghostly, fringy, jaggy mess.

The Background Offset Dilemma

Ever notice how browsers push your Web graphics and text around? Netscape Navigator 4 and Microsoft Internet Explorer 3 and 4 push page contents down and to the right by eight pixels. This movement can create image-alignment problems, especially with transparency. LiveMotion avoids this problem by *automatically* offsetting page contents eight pixels. And, because Explorer actually lets the page designer set the offset by using **TOPMARGIN** and **LEFTMARGIN** attributes within the **<BODY>** tag, LiveMotion sets both attributes to eight pixels by default when exporting in AutoLayout mode.

When you place an image as a background texture, LiveMotion slides the image up and to the left by eight pixels. *That's* why your colored vertical stripe looks thinner in LiveMotion than it does in your Web browser. When you export your composition with AutoLayout, those eight pixels will reappear. Don't go crazy trying to align objects to the center of that background stripe. Keep those eight pixels in the back of your mind and you'll do just fine.

Backgrounds for Framed Sites

HTML frames allow for a wide range of advanced interfaces. In order to successfully build a framed Web site, you should have a thorough understanding of how frames work. Building a successful framed background scheme can take a great deal of forethought and careful planning. Chapter 5 goes into the topic of frames and Web-site interface issues.

Moving On

This chapter covered the topics of 3D effects, textures, and backgrounds. With a thorough understanding of these techniques, you'll be able to build graphics and backgrounds to your exact specifications. You'll never be stumped by a "How do I create a background that looks like..." question. The more time you spend with LiveMotion, the more you'll realize just how powerful this tool is. And as you continue to progress through this book, you'll find yourself adopting a new methodology for Web page creation. In the next chapter, I'll cover the subject of creating, altering, and managing styles, as you take your texture and 3D skills to the limit.

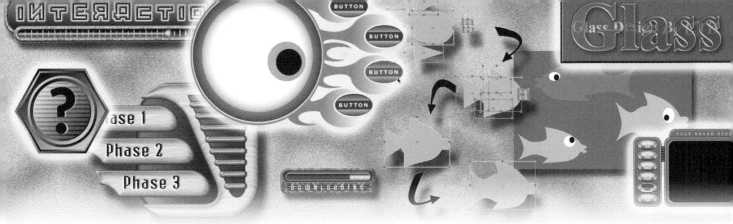

Chapter 3

Alpha, Style, and Image Magic

Ready for some more magic? LiveMotion's bag of tricks
includes powerful alpha channel and timesaving styles,
as well as handy image tweaking capabilities and
Photoshop plug-in support.

So Cool, so Fast

This chapter tackles the subjects of LiveMotion's alpha channel and style features, which provide a huge, timesaving advantage and ease of use. *Alpha channel* image mattes add distinctive forms and edges to placed images, whereas *styles* allow you to quickly assign intricate treatments to any object. The combination of these two features packs a serious punch; effects that are painstaking to produce in a conventional image editing environment can be applied instantaneously in LiveMotion.

Think of this chapter as a cookbook of sorts. You may find a style here that satisfies your needs, or you may take one and tweak it to suit your taste. I'll start with a discussion of alpha channel image mattes before covering style basics and management issues. Then, I'll get into LiveMotion's distortion effects, filters, and opacity controls. The chapter wraps up with "The Style Depot" (a sampling of my original styles). You'll find all the styles I talk about on the *Adobe LiveMotion f/x and Design* companion CD-ROM, along with dozens of additional original styles and a host of image mattes.

Let's begin the tour with LiveMotion's alpha channel capabilities.

Working with Alpha Channel Image Mattes

Image mattes are created from shapes, which in turn, can be created from any vector or bitmap file that can be placed into LiveMotion. (See "Importing Shapes" in Chapter 1 for a list of importable file formats.) This provides a huge amount of flexibility. Alpha channels carry only opacity information; they do not carry any color data. Vector image mattes can create crisp and smooth edges, whereas bitmap image mattes can create soft and variable edges. Figure 3.1 shows an image before and after applying a pair of image mattes. Notice how the vector example uses a hard edge (albeit antialiased), whereas the bitmap example demonstrates interesting opacity effects.

When an image comes into the LiveMotion environment, the Properties palette allows you to use alpha channel information in one of four ways: No Alpha, Use Alpha Channel, Build Alpha From Image, and Active Matte.

You can apply alpha channel image mattes in several ways. Let's take a look at the various procedures. Start by placing a photograph or other scanned image (this is the image that will receive the image matte) into your LiveMotion composition, then choose one of the following methods:

- *If the matte object is already in the Library palette*—With the photograph or object selected, choose an interesting shape from the Library palette. Click

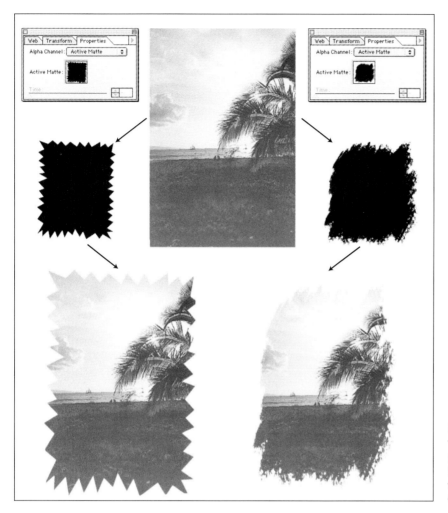

Figure 3.1
The original image above two image matte variations. The image matte on the left uses a vector shape; the image matte on the right uses a bitmap shape.

on the Make Active Matte button to apply the shape as the photograph's or object's active matte. (You can also drag the shape from the Library palette to the Properties palette.)

- *If the matte object is not in the Library palette*—You can add the object to the Library palette by dragging it to the palette. Then, with the photograph or object selected, choose the new shape in the Library palette, and click on the Make Active Matte button to apply the shape as the photograph's or object's active matte.

- *To apply an image matte without adding the shape to the Library palette*— With the photograph or object selected, drag and drop the file you want to use as the image matte from the desktop into the Properties palette's Active Matte preview to apply the shape as the photograph's or object's active matte.

- *If you want to use an object in your composition as the image matte (without adding it to the Library palette)*—Place the object you want to use as the image matte into your ImageStyler composition. Select the object and copy it to the clipboard. Select the photograph or object that will receive the image matte, then select Edit|Paste Special|Paste Active Matte to apply the object as the photograph's or object's active matte.

Now, let's take a look at LiveMotion's powerful style feature.

Style Basics

Styles are actually LiveMotion documents that (most often) contain just one object, which can include myriad attributes. When you apply a style to an object, LiveMotion assigns those attributes to the object. Although styles allow you to create a ton of cool effects, they don't let you do *everything*. Let's take a look at what styles can and can't contain.

Styles can include up to 99 layers of object attributes, including:

- Color

- Distortion

- Filters

- Gradients

- Layer information

- Opacity

- Texture

- 3D effects

- Photoshop filters

- Animation (layer, rollover, and object)

Viewing Styles

The four buttons at the lower-left side of the Styles palette provide a convenient means to view and sort styles, based on attributes. Selecting a button will cause styles with that attribute to be displayed. The attributes are:

- Animations
- Rollovers
- Layers
- Photoshop filters

Styles can't include:

- Typographical specifications (such as typeface, size, leading, and alignment)

- Web URLs

- Object type properties (ellipse, rectangle, rounded rectangle, and type)

- Outline specifications

Styles are cross-platform creatures. This means you can use a style created on a Macintosh on a PC, and vice versa. And, you don't have to jump through any hoops to make it happen. The only caveat is that you must name the file with LiveMotion's .liv file extension. (Windows relies upon the file extension, and the Macintosh recognizes files by creator type.)

Styles are stored in the Styles folder, within the LiveMotion folder. Active Styles (those in the Styles folder) are displayed in the Styles palette. LiveMotion refreshes the Styles palette when it scans the Styles folder:

- Upon launch

- When a style is added to the Styles palette

- When a style is deleted from the Styles palette

Creating Styles

You can add a style to the Styles palette in a number of ways:

- Drag the styled object to the Styles palette.

- Select the styled object and click on the Styles palette's New Style button.

- Drag and drop a LIV file into the Styles folder in the Finder (Mac) or Windows Explorer (PC). This method does not refresh the Styles palette automatically; it's best to drag and drop before starting LiveMotion.

When you save a style with the Styles palette, LiveMotion automatically appends the .liv file extension.

Altering Styles

Let's say you've located a style you really like, except for one or two nagging little attributes. No problem. You can tweak that style and save it as an updated (or new) style. In short, altering existing styles is a straightforward task. To alter an existing style:

1. Apply the style to an object.

2. Tweak the object to perfection.

Just One Object?

If you drop a LIV file that contains more than one object into the Styles folder, the resulting style will draw its attributes from the topmost object in the file.

3. Save the style either by dragging the styled object to the Styles palette or by selecting the styled object and clicking on the Styles palette's New Style button (as described earlier).

4. When the Name dialog box opens, give the style the same name as the existing style (to update and overwrite the existing style) or give it a new name (to leave the original style untouched).

If you mess up one of the original LiveMotion styles, fear not. You can always reinstall the style from the LiveMotion installation CD-ROM.

Deleting Styles

You can delete a style from the Styles palette in one of two ways:

- Select the style in the Styles palette and click on the Delete Style (trash can) button.

- From the Finder (Mac) or Windows Explorer (PC), drag and drop a LIV file from the Styles folder into the Trash (Mac) or Recycle Bin (PC).

That takes care of the basics. Now, let's look at some style attributes in depth.

Managing Styles

If you're a style junkie like me, your Styles folder can quickly get out of hand. This section lays out some simple solutions for dealing with a burgeoning collection of styles, and for facilitating moving styles between workstations.

Thin and Organize

If you're serious about your styles, the first thing you should do is to thin out your Styles folder. Move all the junk you don't use to a storage folder *outside* the Styles folder. Once you've cleaned out the debris, you can begin to organize your styles. Here are a handful of style-organization tips:

- *Name your styles (and layers) descriptively*—Keep the names short, sweet, and vivid. You don't want to have to guess what you named a style—and neither do your associates.

- *Pay attention to the starting character*—The Styles palette displays style names with numbers first and letters second. If you want your most frequently used styles to appear at the top of the list, the first character of the style name should be numeric.

- *Keep project styles in their own folder*—If each of your projects or clients has several styles, you might want to keep those styles in a folder *inside* the Styles folder. You can also use folder aliases (Mac) or shortcuts (PC) to accomplish this task.

Need to Unstyle an Object?

Select the object and then use the Styles palette to apply the Plain Style. Be warned: This turns off visibility on all but the top layer. It does not remove the extra layers.

- *Put away your master styles for safekeeping*—Copy your important styles and store them on another computer, file server, or removable media. Don't be a victim: Hard drives crash, and files are accidentally deleted all the time. (Backing up your hard drive every night is a great idea that's often overlooked.)

Passing Styles

Once you've created a style, you may need to share the file with a co-worker, friend, client, or associate. Here are a number of ways to pass files back and forth:

- *Email attachments*—This is the easiest way to pass styles. Just attach them to an email message and fire away.

- *Sneakernet*—Styles are small files by nature. Copy a bunch onto a floppy disk and away you go.

- *Point-to-point file transfer*—This is the fastest way to move files. Mirabilis ICQ is an immensely popular way to pass files back and forth over the Internet.

- *File server*—If your organization uses a file server, you can place files into a shared storage folder. Don't use a shared folder for your live Styles folder, unless you want everyone to be able to alter existing styles.

- *Web site or FTP server*—By posting your files, you'll let folks download the styles with their Web browser. Note that not all browsers may know what to do with a LIV file—use StuffIt (Mac) or WinZip (PC) to compress the file(s) into an archive before uploading.

> **Using ImageStyler Styles in LiveMotion**
>
> Because LiveMotion reads ImageStyler files, using Image-Styler styles in LiveMotion is as easy as dragging the Image-Styler IST style documents into the LiveMotion Styles folder. Some ImageStyler styles may not function properly in Live-Motion. If an IST style acts up, open the style as a file (File| Open), tweak it, and then resave it as a LIV style in the Styles folder. (Don't forget to move the original IST style out of the Styles folder.)

Distort, Adjust, and Opacity Palette Fun

The Distort, Adjust, and Opacity palettes enable you to exert considerable pixel-tweaking influence on placed textures and images. These controls make it possible to create exciting images far removed from the appearance of their original component images. This section will go into detail about each effect.

Using Distortion Effects

LiveMotion's *distortion effects*—displace, lens, twirl, spherize, quantize, and radial quantize—are most effective when you use them on a layer that's been assigned a gradient, texture, background, or image fill. (They will work on objects that have been outlined with these attributes, as well.) Generally speaking, the distortion effects are pixel pushers that work their magic on anything but flat color. (Flat color doesn't give the effects anything to sink their teeth into.) Figures 3.2 through 3.4 provide side-by-side examples of the basic differences among the distortion effects. Next, you'll take a closer look at each of the distortion effects.

Figure 3.2

Gradient distortions. From the top: no distortion, lens/radial gradient, twirl/burst gradient, spherize/linear gradient, quantize/linear gradient, and radial quantize/double burst gradient. (All backgrounds are linear.)

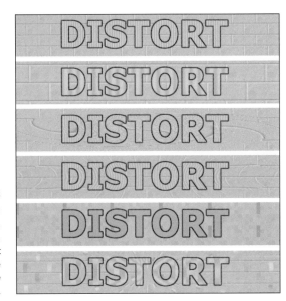

Figure 3.3

Texture distortions. From the top: no distortion, lens, twirl, spherize, quantize, and radial quantize. Notice how the quantize effect falls flat on the striped text; the original texture doesn't include enough randomness.

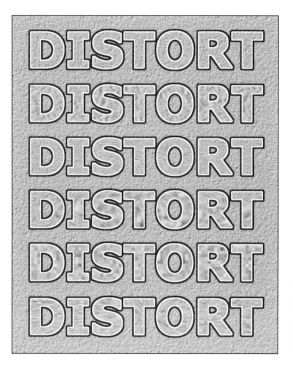

Figure 3.4
Background distortions. From the top: no distortion, lens, twirl, spherize, quantize, and radial quantize. Here the twirl effect falls flat; the background texture could use a bit more contrast to enhance the twirl.

The Displace Effect

The displace effect pushes pixels as much as 20 pixels from their original location. You'll use this effect most often in conjunction with a background fill, because it enhances the three-dimensional illusion. Figure 3.5 shows the displace effect in action. (The wacky patterned background image is from the "noodl" series, which you can find on the *Adobe LiveMotion f/x and Design* CD-ROM.)

The Lens Effect

The lens effect emulates a magnifying glass. Figure 3.6 demonstrates the lens effect when used with a background fill. Notice how the 75 percent lens actually makes the background pattern smaller. This effect is pretty cool, but ultimately you may be limited by the width of the background image. If you try to set the lens at too low a percentage, white will show around the edges of the lensed object. (The incredibly busy background image is from the "purp" series, which you can find on the *Adobe LiveMotion In Depth* CD-ROM.)

Mix It Up

You can use the displace filter to slide a textured pattern around an object. Careful use will help to avoid a series of identically patterned buttons. This method is more suited to JavaScript rollovers. With Flash rollovers, you'll want to have identical buttons to help shave file size.

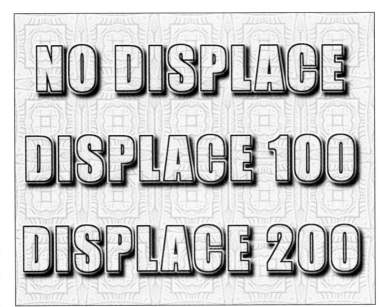

Figure 3.5
Just a little more pop. From the
top: background fill/no displace-
ment, background fill/displace
100 (10 pixels), and background
fill/displace 200 (20 pixels).

Figure 3.6
Get a closer look. From the top:
75 percent lens, no lens,
125 percent lens, and
175 percent lens.

The Quantize and Radial Quantize Effects

The quantize and radial quantize effects impart a digital appearance. Low quantize settings add a slightly jaggy look. The image will appear more and more chunky as you push the slider higher. Quantize effects can add a "digital age" appearance when you use them within JavaScript rollovers. Figure 3.7 demonstrates a handful of quantize effects.

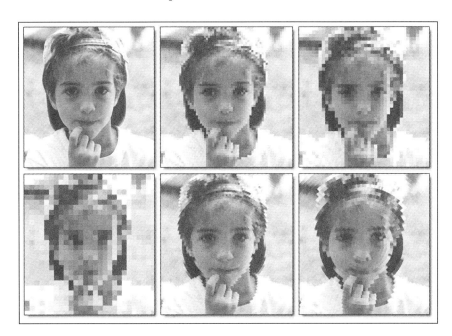

Figure 3.7

He's a digital dude: Colt gets quantized (and radial quantized). From left, top row: original, quantize 5, quantize 8. Bottom row: quantize 12, radial quantize 5, and radial quantize 8.

The Spherize Effect

The spherize effect drops a magic crystal on your image. You can zoom in and out in a manner very different from the lens effect. Figure 3.8 demonstrates seven spherize effects, along with the original image for comparison. Notice how the outside edges of the image remain intact—only the inner elliptical-shaped area is affected. I created all the spherized examples in Figure 3.8 (except the last one) with a magnification factor of 100.

The Twirl Effect

The twirl effect lets you take your image for a spin. Positive settings twirl the image clockwise, whereas negative settings twirl counter-clockwise. Figure 3.9 demonstrates seven twirl effects, along with the original image for comparison. I created all the examples in Figure 3.9 with a bandsize setting of zero. At this level, the twirl is completely smooth. The higher the band size setting, the chunkier the twirl will become.

Figure 3.8

Colt and Ally get spherized. Top row, from left: original, magnification 100/amount 33. Second row: magnification 100/amount 66, magnification 100/amount 100. Third row: magnification 100/amount -33, magnification 100/amount -66. Fourth row: magnification 100/amount -100, magnification 200/amount -100.

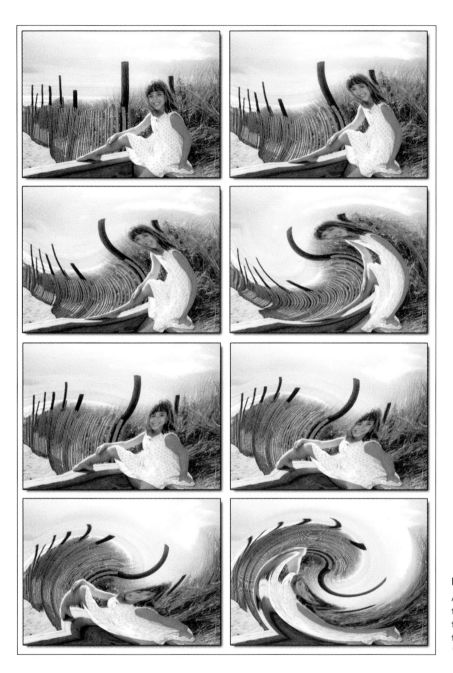

Figure 3.9
Ally gets twirled (in both directions). Top row, from left: original, twirl –8. Second row: twirl –16, twirl –32. Third row: twirl 8, twirl 16. Fourth row: twirl 32, twirl 64.

Adjust

Although they're no substitute for Photoshop image optimization plug-ins, LiveMotion's adjustment functions—brightness, contrast, saturation, tint, posterize, and invert—let you perform basic adjustments to bitmap images. Don't think of them solely in conventional image-editing terms. When used within a rollover, these six controls can create some dynamic effects—dimming, popping, color shifts, and startling solarizations.

Brightness

Does your scanned image look a little light or dark? The brightness slider allows you to adjust the overall lightness or darkness of an image. Push the slider to the right to lighten an image; push it to the left to darken an image. Figure 3.10 demonstrates the effects of positive and negative brightness settings.

Figure 3.10
Do you want a 40-watt or a 150-watt light bulb? Brightness settings, from left: -50, 0, 50.

Contrast

Need to add a little more snap to your image? The contrast slider allows you to increase or decrease the degree of tonal change. Push the slider to the right to add contrast; push it to the left to decrease contrast. Figure 3.11 demonstrates the effects of positive and negative contrast settings.

Figure 3.11
Change your definition. Contrast settings, from left: -50, 0, 50.

Saturation

Does your image have too much color? Does it look washed out? The saturation slider allows you to pump color out of or into an image—another cool trick to use within rollovers. You can use this filter to create subtle grayscales from color originals by pushing the slider to the left. Or, punch up an image by pushing the slider to the right to oversaturate with color.

Tint

Want to see the world through rose-colored glasses? The tint slider allows you to color an image with the foreground color. This filter is especially powerful when you're creating sepia tones or other tinted images, such as simulated duotones. Try using the tint filter in conjunction with a reduced saturation level.

Posterize

Yes, you too can put Andy Warhol to shame. The posterize slider allows you to create basic posterization effects. (*Posterization* cuts down the number of colors in an image.) In addition to creating cool effects, posterization has the side benefit of making photographs more suitable for export as compressed GIF images. Figure 3.12 demonstrates three posterization settings.

Figure 3.12
What were you expecting, a picture of Marilyn (or perhaps a soup can)? Posterize, from left: 6, 9, 12.

Invert

The invert function is a one-trick pony: All it does is reverse the color in the image. Black becomes white, red becomes cyan, blue becomes yellow, green becomes magenta, and so on. Figure 3.13 demonstrates the effect. Invert works on solid-color objects, as well as images—it's a great way to instantly create a high-contrast color combination. (Set two objects with the same color, and then set one to invert.)

Figure 3.13
The invert filter creates a negative image, for that x-ray look.

Opacity

LiveMotion's Opacity palette provides total control over the transparency (or "seethroughness") of objects and layers. You can set opacity at a constant level or as one of four opacity gradient options: linear, burst, double burst, and radial. Figure 3.14 demonstrates a basic transparency effect on a piece of black (R0, G0, B0) filled type. (The background image is from the "summr" series, which you can find on the *Adobe LiveMotion f/x and Design* CD-ROM.)

Figure 3.14
See through. The smaller the opacity percentage, the more the background shows through the object.

The opacity gradient options work in a manner similar to that of the color gradients. You can adjust the starting and ending opacity level, as well as the padding from the edges of the opacity gradient. Figure 3.15 demonstrates four opacity gradients. I set the alpha channel to Build Alpha From Image to enhance the effect.

Ready for some heavy-duty image manipulation? Let's jump into the wonderful world of plug-ins.

Figure 3.15
A selection of opacity gradients. Clockwise from top left: linear (from top-left corner), burst (vertical), double burst (spun to the corners), and radial.

Working with Photoshop Plug-in Filters

LiveMotion allows you to apply Photoshop plug-in filters to placed bitmap images (and only images). Unlike most other image editing applications, LiveMotion applies the plug-in filters in a non-destructive manner. The filters never touch the underlying image—instead, they only change the way the image appears.

Filters are initially applied via the Object|Filters menu. Once a filter has been applied to a bitmap image, you can use the Photoshop plug-ins palette, to adjust, delete, or turn off visibility on each filter effect. (Double-click on the filter you want to adjust to gain access to its dialog box.) This allows you to build up intricate filter treatments while maintaining full control over the effects at any time. And even better, you can save your built-up effects as LiveMotion styles, so they can be instantly applied to other images. The photographs shown in Figure 3.16 demonstrate three multiple-filter effects.

Use the Photoshop filter palette to:

- *Adjust a filter*—Double-click on the filter listing to access the filter's dialog box, and then tweak the settings.

- *Turn off a filter's visibility*—Click on the filter's eye button.

- *Delete a filter*—Select the filter, then click on the trash can button.

Can I Apply Plug-ins to Other Objects?

Although you cannot directly apply plug-ins to any surface, other than an image (this includes textures), an easy workaround is possible. (Don't go looking for a "Convert to Bitmap" command. You won't find one.) To apply plug-ins to a non-image object, you must first convert the object into an image. Select the object, copy it to the clipboard with Cmd/Ctrl+C , then select Edit|Paste Special|Paste Image. This replaces the original object with a bitmap. Voila! You now have access to the plug-ins, via Object|Filters.

Figure 3.16
If I were the king of the forest.
Clockwise, from top left:
untouched image, Glass and
Crystalize filters, Sponge and
Spatter filters, Ink Outlines
and Grain filters.

The Style Depot

LiveMotion ships with a whole load of styles. But how could that ever be enough? True to form, I've included a slew of styles on the *Adobe LiveMotion f/x and Design* CD-ROM. The following 10 styles are just a sample of the more than 100 styles that you'll find on the disk. These are all two-state rollover designs. Chapter 10 delves into the topic of animated styles.

Black Leather Emboss

It's been years since I owned a leather jacket—seems like the jacket left my life at about the time I dumped my last motorcycle. This style gains its name from the texture used in the first and third layers. The leather texture was created with Alien Skin's Baked Earth plug-in (part of the Xenofex package). Figure 3.17 shows the Black Leather Emboss style as applied to text and a sampling of Web graphics.

Figure 3.17
The Black Leather Emboss style may look dark when viewed with Windows gamma—try fiddling with the brightness setting on the Adjust palette to suit your tastes.

Black Leather Emboss is a four-layer style:

- *Layer 1*—A texture fill and a slight emboss (depth of 2, softness of 2, lighting angle 135 degrees, straight edge, normal light, and width of -1).

- *Layer 2*—Solid black provides a 1 pixel outline for layer 1 (width of 0).

- *Layer 3*—Another texture fill and slight emboss (depth of 2, softness of 2, lighting angle 330 degrees, straight edge, normal light, and width of 2). Identical to layer 1, with the exception of the lighting angle.

- *Layer 4*—Solid black provides a 1 pixel outline around the entire object (width of 3).

Blue Lizard

When I was a little kid, I was bummed to find out that my chameleon wouldn't change its skin to match the hideous red plaid upholstery of my Dad's 1969 Ford Maverick. It never turned blue, either. The Blue Lizard style has a raised beveled appearance that may make it appropriate for use on bizzaro button bars. Figure 3.18 shows the Blue Lizard style in action.

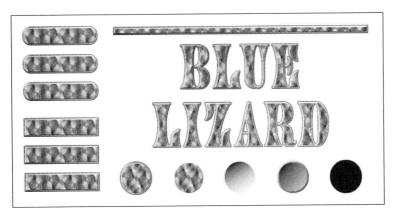

Figure 3.18
Blue Lizard has its roots in the KPT 5 Orb-it filter.

Blue Lizard is a four-layer style:

- *Layer 1*—A texture fill and a tiny bevel (depth of 1, softness of 0, lighting angle 135 degrees, button edge, normal light, and width of -1).

- *Layer 2*—Diagonal light aqua-to-black linear gradient (119 degrees) provides a bit of outline pop for layer 1 (width of 0).

- *Layer 3*—Diagonal black-to-dark aqua linear gradient (135 degrees), with a good sized bevel (depth of 3, softness of 1, lighting angle 135 degrees, straight edge, normal light, and width of 1).

- *Layer 4*—Solid black provides a 1 pixel outline around the entire object (width of 2).

Bubble Traction

It's not easy to come up with these wacky names, lemmetellya. The bubble texture (again, a product of KPT 5's Orb-it) is used on the first, second, and third layers of the style. Bubble Traction looks like a non-skid surface encased in acrylic resin. Figure 3.19 demonstrates the Bubble Traction style.

Figure 3.19
The inverted texture bezel creates a contrasting pattern.

Bubble Traction is a five-layer style:

- *Layer 1*—A shiny embossed texture (depth of 3, softness of 1, lighting angle 135 degrees, ripple edge, light only light, and layer width of -1).

- *Layer 2*—The inverted texture bezel emboss (depth of 3, softness of 3, lighting angle 135 degrees, button edge, dark only light, layer softness of 1, and width of 1). The invert option flips the texture to colors opposite of layer 1.

- *Layer 3*—A punch up emboss (depth of 3, softness of 3, lighting angle 135 degrees, button edge, dark only light, layer softness of 1, and width of 2). The invert option and a brightness setting of –209 pushes the texture to the darkest extreme.

- *Layer 4*—Soft emboss (depth of 1, softness of 3, lighting angle 135 degrees, straight edge, normal light, layer softness of 2, and width of 4).

- *Layer 5*—Solid black provides a 1 pixel outline around the entire object (width of 6).

Button Tuck

We're not done with the throwback car upholstery references. I mixed the KPT Orb-it filter with Xaos Tools Terrazzo and came up with this beauty. The Button Tuck style was inspired by the retro seat covers in a custom '57 Chevy I fondly remember from my youth. Figure 3.20 shows the Button Tuck style draped over a bunch of Web page doodads.

Figure 3.20
When's the last time you watched *American Graffiti*?

Button Tuck is a four-layer style:

- *Layer 1*—A texture fill, a subtle bevel (depth of 3, softness of 2, button edge), and a soft edge (softness of 2, width of –1) puff up the first layer.

- *Layer 2*—Solid black softly defines layer 1 (softness of 2).

- *Layer 3*—Medium blue provides a subtle bezel (bevel depth of 1, bevel softness of 1, lighting angle of 300, straight edge, layer softness of 1, width of 1).

- *Layer 4*—Solid black delivers a thin outline around the entire object (width of 2).

Crackle Rock

One good texture deserves another. Here's another style built from a cool texture generated with Alien Skin's Baked Earth filter. The bluestone and mortar effect looks like an old stone wall or driveway. Figure 3.21 shows the Crackle Rock style in action.

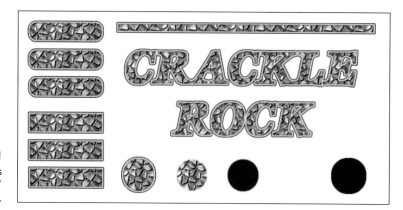

Figure 3.21
Alien Skin's corporate motto is "We Will Never Wear Suits." I can dig it.

Crackle Rock is a four-layer style:

- *Layer 1*—A texture fill and a soft (2) edge.

- *Layer 2*—Solid black provides a soft edge and emphasis around layer 1 (softness of 1, width of 1).

- *Layer 3*—Solid light aqua provides a complementary mortar bezel around the stone texture (softness of 1, width of 3).

- *Layer 4*—Solid black provides a substantial outline around the entire object (width of 5).

Electric Spiders

Well, this one's not subtle. Electric Spiders uses a high-voltage lime green pattern and a soft, almost pillow-like emboss. Not the kind of stuff you'd want to use for that insurance company Web site. Figure 3.22 shows the Electric Spiders style crawling all over a bunch of text and graphics.

Figure 3.22
If you think this one is bright, wait until you check out its rollover state.

Electric Spiders is a four-layer style:

- *Layer 1*—The Electric Spiders texture fill, a super soft emboss (depth of 2, softness of 10, button edge, dark only lighting), and a very soft edge (softness of 5, width of –2) puff up the first layer.

- *Layer 2*—Turn up the voltage with a lime green, super soft emboss (depth of 2, softness of 10, button edge, dark only lighting) and a hard edge (width of –1).

- *Layer 3*—Punch the pillow with a solid black and soft edge (layer softness of 2, width of 1).

- *Layer 4*—Soft black provides a fuzzy outline (width of 6, softness of 8).

Liquid Metal

It's all a (motion) blur. The base texture sprang from the tried and true combination of noise and the motion blur filter. Try this one as a rollover. The down state dims the surface with a brightness setting, while pushing the texture with a lesser displace setting. Figure 3.23 shows the Liquid Metal style wrapped around the usual suspects.

Figure 3.23
Three simple layers deliver the illusion of 3D.

Liquid Metal is a three-layer style:

- *Layer 1*—Take some noise, apply a motion blur, a nice soft emboss (depth of 6, softness of 5, plateau edge, dark only lighting), and a very soft edge (softness of 5, width of –3), then apply displace distortion (10 pixels at 122 degrees).

- *Layer 2*—A big, soft emboss on solid black (depth of 6, softness of 5, plateau edge, dark only lighting) and a soft edge (width of –3 and softness of 5).

- *Layer 3*—A slightly soft black outline blends subtly with the background (softness of 1).

Purple Circuits

This style is a cross between a circuit board and a flowery ground cover. Keep in mind that you don't have to stick with the original color scheme; the Adjust palette provides convenient control over tinting, saturation, contrast, and brightness. Figure 3.24 shows the Purple Circuits style growing on a number of buttons.

Figure 3.24
Don't like purple? Try tinting this one with the color of your choice.

Purple Circuits is a four-layer style:

- *Layer 1*—The soft purple texture fill (width of –1, softness of 4) is enhanced with a slight emboss (depth of 1, softness of 2, button edge, light only light).

- *Layer 2*—Dig that purple rippled bezel (ripple depth and softness of 1, straight edge, layer width of 1, softness of 2).

- *Layer 3*—A purple fill and a slight emboss (depth of 1, softness of 1, straight edge).

- *Layer 4*—A hard black outline snaps this style off the background (layer width of 4).

Purple Ghost

It's a poltergeist. No, it's a LiveMotion style. This style uses an ethereal texture generated with KPT 5's FraxFlame filter. Figure 3.25 shows the Purple Ghost style floating on a variety of text and Web graphics.

Purple Ghost is a four-layer style:

- *Layer 1*—A ghostly texture fill and a soft edge (softness of 2), twirled –15 turns.

- *Layer 2*—A fine violet outline separates the ghost surface from the bezel subtly with the background (width of 1, softness of 1).

Figure 3.25
Who ya gonna call?

- *Layer 3*—A lavender bezel stands out from the aura (width of 3, softness of 1).

- *Layer 4*—A soft blue-violet aura eases into the background (width of 5, softness of 8).

Soft Granite

The Soft Granite style looks like an expensive floor tile, albeit a tad fuzzy. (Have you seen my glasses?) If rocky styles are your bag, be sure to check out the Mr. Slate style (on the *Adobe LiveMotion f/x and Design* CD-ROM). Figure 3.26 shows the Soft Granite style, as applied to a sampling of buttons and text.

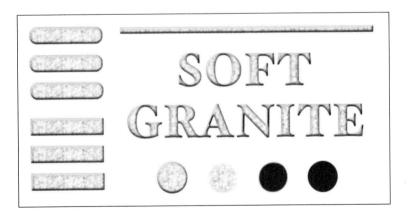

Figure 3.26
The Soft Granite style carries its weight.

Soft Granite is a three-layer style:

- *Layer 1*—The granite texture fill is softened (layer width of –3, softness of 5) and embossed (depth of 2, softness of 1, button edge, lighting angle of 85 degrees).

Check the CD-ROM

You can find all the styles (and more!) on the *Adobe LiveMotion f/x and Design* CD-ROM.

- *Layer 2*—A soft black fade (layer width of –1, softness of 2) and slight emboss (depth of 1, softness of 1, straight edge, lighting angle of 135 degrees).

- *Layer 3*—A slightly soft black outline blends subtly with the background (softness of 1).

Moving On

In this chapter, I spread a sampling of LiveMotion image manipulation and style recipes on the kitchen table for you to pick and choose. But like any good recipe, LiveMotion styles can always be improved upon and altered to fit individual tastes and specific needs. This chapter isn't the be-all and end-all of styles—it's merely a starting point for your own experimentation. In the next chapter, you'll learn how to make your Web pages sit up and bark with LiveMotion's amazing rollover capabilities.

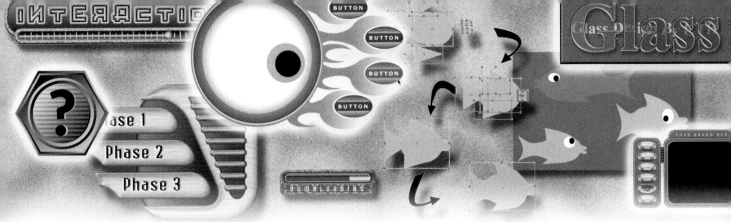

Chapter 4

Rollover, Sit Up, and Bark

This chapter delivers the goods on LiveMotion's ability to create JavaScript and Flash rollovers. Treat the program correctly and it'll be as faithful as a Labrador Retriever. Treat it the wrong way and it'll bite you in the rear.

It's a Very Good Dog

Have rollovers become a thorn in your side? Are your clients asking for more and more functionality under tighter and tighter deadlines? LiveMotion can slash production time and increase your design capabilities. The program uses an innovative point-and-shoot interface to quickly create from the simplest to the most complex rollovers in either JavaScript or Flash format.

Let's take a quick look back at the progression of Web design. In the beginning, there were plain old hypertext pages. Graphics were soon added to the equation, in the form of GIF and JPEG files. These early text and graphic pages delivered the functional equivalent of a newspaper page. You could read the news and see the pictures, but nothing jumped off the page. You could click on (what looked like) a button, and you'd be whisked away to another location. But something was missing.

The introduction of GIF animation capabilities in version 2 of the Netscape Navigator browser changed the way Web pages behaved. With GIF animation, images could move and dance. The images did this without any interaction from the visitor, however, so that old "ghost in the machine" feeling lingered.

Netscape also introduced Web page scripting to the world in Navigator version 2. What we now know as *JavaScript* was initially called *LiveScript* (Netscape renamed it to hook into the Java buzz). With the introduction of this exciting new technology, Web graphics entered the realm of true interactivity. JavaScript is often used to create what are commonly called *rollovers*.

This chapter, like a number of other chapters, contains a design cookbook. The Rollover Depot, later in this chapter, provides a ready source of examples and ideas that will help you create your own unique rollovers.

How Rollovers Work

Rollovers allow Web graphics to react to cursor movements in the browser. A button may glow when the cursor draws near and exhibit a depressed appearance when clicked upon. Such behavior enhances the visitor's experience by providing tactile feedback, as demonstrated in Figure 4.1. Technically, the rollover is accomplished by swapping one image for another, as dictated by the position of the cursor or a click of the mouse.

Figure 4.1
A typical combination of (from left) **normal**, **over**, and **down** states.

JavaScript rollovers moved Web pages from a static model into an interactive model that approached that of a multimedia CD-ROM. For a long time, the most common ways to create JavaScript rollovers involved hacking them out by hand or adapting an existing script. Eventually, software developers caught up with the trend and began producing tools that could create JavaScript rollovers without hand coding. ImageStyler was one example of this enabling technology. When properly instructed, the program produced all the code and graphics to create gorgeous JavaScript rollovers.

Macromedia Flash took rollovers to a whole new level. The format allowed for highly interactive rollovers that featured more than simple image swaps. With Flashed rollovers, the elements are not constrained by image slices—as with JavaScript rollovers—instead, they're free to move about the page.

Let's look at what makes a rollover roll over.

Rollover States

Rollovers are based on object *states*. These states represent the relationship between the browser's cursor and the object. As such, the object *reacts* to the cursor location. The four standard rollover states are:

- *normal*—The static, "untouched" rollover state

- *over*—Displayed when the cursor passes over the object

- *down*—Displayed when the object is clicked

- *out*—Displayed when the cursor moves away from the object

A rollover consists of at least two states: **normal** and **over** (the **down** and **out** states are optional). You'll use LiveMotion's Rollovers palette, shown in Figure 4.2, to assign up to four standard rollover states to an object (or group of objects). When you export the composition, LiveMotion will create a separate graphic for each specified state. The more states you add, the more graphics your visitors will have to download, so it's a good idea to keep the states to a minimum to maximize page performance. You'll learn how to use custom rollover states in the remote rollover project later in this chapter.

Rollovers and IE3.x

Unfortunately, Microsoft Internet Explorer 3.x doesn't display LiveMotion's JavaScript rollovers. If you know that your audience uses IE3.x extensively, you may want to hold off on implementing rollovers until they upgrade. Newer versions of the browser have no problem with LiveMotion's JavaScript.

Figure 4.2
Use the Rollovers palette to navigate object states.

Differences between JavaScript and Flash Rollovers

JavaScript and Flash rollovers can appear to be very similar to the viewer or they can appear to be very different. It's all in the implementation. Although you can sometimes export a composition in either format, more often you'll have a format in mind before you lay out the design. *JavaScript rollovers* are sliced into individual image chunks, in either GIF or JPEG format. *Flash rollovers* are contained within a Flash SWF file; they can be built from vectors (the fastest) or bitmaps (in either GIF, JPEG, or PNG formats).

Generally speaking, you might use JavaScript rollovers with sculpted, 3D interfaces. Flash rollovers are most often built from pure vector objects with flat color (although you certainly can use 3D bitmapped buttons, you'll pay a penalty in file size and download time). JavaScript rollovers work well when interactivity is limited. Flash is better for complex, animated interfaces.

Basic vs. Remote Rollovers

LiveMotion provides the ability to build both basic and remote rollovers. With a *basic rollover*, all of the image-swapping action takes place within a single image slice. With a *remote rollover*, cursor position can influence the action in a second slice; this allows for a high degree of interactivity. Moving the mouse over a button can display a product image or definition, as shown in Figure 4.3.

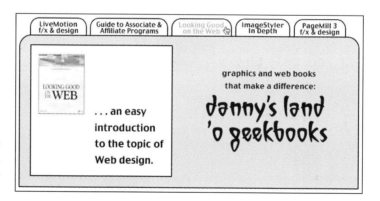

Figure 4.3
Remote rollovers can provide additional information *before* the visitor clicks through the link.

Creating Basic JavaScript Rollovers

In the following pages, you'll learn the basics of creating JavaScript rollovers—from simple to complex effects. Once you've conquered the basics, you can move on to the Rollover Depot for a smorgasbord of cool rollover effects. It's important to first understand how LiveMotion treats the objects within a rollover composition.

Create a Simple Rollover

The most basic rollovers change the attributes of just one element—perhaps a string of text or a button object, such as a rectangle or rounded-corner rectangle. A simple rollover might consist of a color change, a 3D tweak, a glow, or a dim. Let's run through the steps you'll take to create a simple rollover:

1. Select Edit|Composition Settings. Select AutoLayout from the drop-down menu, and ensure that the Make HTML option is selected before clicking on OK.

2. Use the Rectangle tool to draw a 120-by-30-pixel rectangle. Assign the rectangle a solid medium-blue fill (R0, G0, B153). Position the rectangle at the upper-left corner of the composition.

3. Use the Text tool to type the words "click here" in 18-point Verdana Bold (or whatever typeface works for you). Assign a solid light yellow fill (R255, G255, B102).

4. Select both the text and the rectangle, and then choose the Object|Align|Centers menu item to roughly align the text to the rectangle. Use the arrow keys to nudge the text string and visually center it on the rectangle, as shown in Figure 4.4. (You may want to zoom in to get a closer look.)

Figure 4.4
Hey, I said it was simple.

5. Hold down the Shift key and click on the text string to deselect it (if it is selected). You need to assign a state only to the rectangle.

6. Open the Rollovers palette and click on the New Rollover State button; this creates an **over** state.

7. Assign a solid magenta fill (R204, G0, B153).

8. Click back and forth between the **normal** and **over** states on the Rollovers palette to get a feel for how the rollover operates. (It's ugly, yet obvious.)

9. Open the Web palette and assign a URL to the rollover.

10. Open the Export palette. Select GIF, 32 colors, and select the Preview option (to get a peek at what the exported graphics will look like).

11. Now for the fun stuff. Choose File|Preview In|Netscape Communicator (or your browser of choice). LiveMotion will build the rollover and launch your browser so you can check it out. Notice how the AutoLayout export places the rollover in the same location in the browser window as in the LiveMotion composition.

    And that's it. Once you like the way the rollover looks, you can duplicate it to create additional rollovers. Position the rollovers carefully, alter the text strings, change the individual Web addresses, and preview again.

12. Once you've tweaked the rollover to perfection, choose File|Export to create the graphic and HTML files (replete with JavaScript code).

Some Things to Watch Out For

As you create rollover graphics, you need to engineer your composition for optimum results. If you design haphazardly, the rollover operations will fail—LiveMotion will clump the objects together, and the rollovers just won't work the way they're supposed to.

Here are a handful of things to watch out for:

- Don't allow objects from one rollover to overlap a neighboring rollover. This is one of the most common problems. Pay attention to *all* the layers. Watch out for soft glows and the like.

- Don't group a rollover with a second rollover. (However, you can group objects within a single rollover.)

- Don't group a rollover with any underlying objects.

In general, LiveMotion treats any object that overlaps (or even touches) a rollover as part of that rollover. A rollover can sit on top of another object, as long as the other object isn't part of another rollover.

Influencing the Slices

Although other programs use drawn guidelines to control image slicing, LiveMotion is different, because it's the objects that control the image slicing. Although this can be disconcerting at first, you'll soon become accustomed to the custom. LiveMotion is capable of highly precise slicing. The operator is in charge, however.

Selecting View|Preview AutoSlice Area displays a set of green guidelines to represent the image slices. Once you (zoom in and) see where the slices fall, you can influence the cuts by altering the size and position of each chunk. Chapter 5 delves into the topic of precision slicing techniques.

More Intricate Rollovers

As your skill and confidence increase, you'll want to build more complex rollovers. With a little work (on your part), LiveMotion's capable of some really nice effects, like those shown in Figure 4.5. In this example, the gold metallic highlights change subtly as the cursor passes over the button. The red indicator light glows, as well. This example is more complex than the first example, but it still uses just two states—**normal** and **over**.

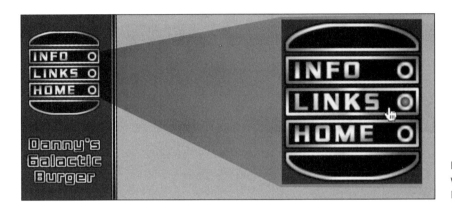

Figure 4.5
Welcome to Danny's Galactic Burger—please click through.

Each Galactic Burger rollover button contains three objects: the rectangular button, the text string, and the elliptical indicator light. This rollover effect involves four changes between the **normal** and **over** states. The highlights change on the text string, the button frame, and the indicator-light bezel. To achieve this effect, you rotate the gold double-burst gradients on each layer. The top layer on the indicator light changes from solid black to a red radial gradient.

Engineer your compositions so that the objects butt each other. Doing so requires careful use of the Transform palette and takes a good amount of patience, but, it's worth it.

Where It All Goes

When LiveMotion creates a rollover, the program exports all the necessary graphics and writes JavaScript code into a text file. LiveMotion places the exported graphics in the images folder within the folder where the HTML file resides. (Note that this folder name starts with a lowercase *i*.) The names of the graphics files are based on the individual rollover text strings; this naming convention makes the files easy to identify if you need to do any post-processing.

Exporting as an AutoLayout forces LiveMotion to create a complete HTML file. The program places the rollover script into the <**HEAD**> portion of the file. Let's examine the Galactic Burger example, where I used just two states (**normal** and **over**). Although you don't have to deal with the code on a regular

What About **down** and **out**?

In many cases, the **down** and **out** states are overkill. Adding a **down** state can heighten the interactive feel, but the effect plays so quickly it may not be worth the design effort or download time. And, because LiveMotion's code will recycle the **normal** state, a separate **out** state is largely unnecessary—until you start building complex or remote rollovers.

That's a Lot of Code

If you're familiar with the JavaScript code generated by ImageStyler, you'll note that the LiveMotion code is far more verbose. It's also thoroughly commented. (I've added a handful of my own comments, as well).

basis, you may be interested in how it all works. If you could care less about the code, you don't have to read too closely—as long as you understand where everything goes.

```
<Html>
<Head>
<Title>
galactic burger
</Title>
```

The script starts by setting up the functions:

```
<Script Language="JavaScript">

<!--Adobe(R) LiveMotion(TM) 1.0 Generated JavaScript.
Please do not edit.

function NewState(id, action, fileName)
{
        // Check if there is not an object for this state
        if (gzimages[id] == null)
                // Create an object for this state
                gzimages[id] = new Object();

        // Create a new image for this state
        gzimages[id][action] = new Image();

        // Set the new image source to the given filename
        gzimages[id][action].src = fileName
}

function NewAction(id, action)
{
        // Check if there is not an actions object for
this state
        if (gzimages[id].actions == null)
                // Create an actions object for this state
                gzimages[id].actions = new Object();

        // Check if there is not an actions array for
this state object
        if (!gzimages[id].actions[action])
                // Create an actions array for this state object
                gzimages[id].actions[action] = new Array();
}

function ExecuteActions(id, action)
{
        // Make sure that the browser can do JavaScript rollovers
        if (document.images)
        {
```

```
                      // Make sure that the actions array has
been created
                      if (gzimages[id].actions)
                      {
                              // Loop through the array of actions
                              for
(anAction in gzimages[id].actions[action])
                              {
                               // Execute the action
                               gzimages[id].actions[action][anAction]();
                              }
                      }
              }
}

function ChangeImageAction(id, action, depId, depState)
{
        // Make sure the action array is properly initialized
        NewAction(id, action);

        // Insert a new function pointer for the action
      gzimages[id].actions[action][gzimages[id].actions[action].length]
= new Function("SwapImage(\"" + depId + "\", " + depState + ");");
}

function SwapImage(id, action)
{
        // Make sure that the browser can do JavaScript rollovers
        if (document.images)
        {
                sourceImage = eval("gzimages." + id +
"[" + action + "]");
                sourceName = sourceImage.src;
                sourceImage.src = "";
                document.images[id].src = sourceName;
                sourceImage.src = sourceName;
        }
}
```

Then, the script preloads all the images as it defines the objects:

```
function Initialize()
{
        NewState("object", 0, "images/galactic_burgerinfo.gif");
// "Default"
        NewState("object", 1,
"images/galactic_burgerinfoov.gif");
// "OnMouseOver"
        ChangeImageAction("object", 0, "object", 0);
        ChangeImageAction("object", 0, "object", 0);
        ChangeImageAction("object", 1, "object", 1);
```

```
        NewState("object1", 0,
"images/galactic_burgerlinks.gif");
// "Default"
        NewState("object1", 1,
"images/galactic_burgerlinksov.gif");
// "OnMouseOver"
        ChangeImageAction("object1", 0, "object1", 0);
        ChangeImageAction("object1", 0, "object1", 0);
        ChangeImageAction("object1", 1, "object1", 1);

        NewState("object2", 0,
"images/galactic_burgerhome.gif");
// "Default"
        NewState("object2", 1,
"images/galactic_burgerhomeov.gif");
// "OnMouseOver"
        ChangeImageAction("object2", 0, "object2", 0);
        ChangeImageAction("object2", 0, "object2", 0);
        ChangeImageAction("object2", 1, "object2", 1);
}

// Make sure that the browser can do JavaScript rollovers
if (document.images)
{
        gzimages = new Object();
        Initialize();
}

// end generated JavaScript. -->

</Script>
</Head>
```

That's it for the script. The background is loaded next. Notice how the file name is based on the original (LIV) file name, with a *bg* modifier:

```
<Body Background="images/galactic burger_bg.gif"
LeftMargin="8" TopMargin="8">
```

This line is followed by a disclaimer about formatting and the layout table. This code is as follows:

```
<!-- The table is not formatted nicely because some browsers
cannot join images in table cells if there are any hard
carriage returns in a TD. -->

<Table Border="0" CellSpacing="0" CellPadding="0" Width="182">
        <Tr>
                <Td Width="16" Height="38"></Td>
                <Td Width="5" Height="38"></Td>
                <Td Width="155" Height="38"></Td>
                <Td Width="6" Height="38"></Td>
        </Tr>
```

Here's the first chunk of image:

```
<Tr>
        <Td Width="16" Height="34"></Td>
        <Td Width="5" Height="34"></Td>
        <Td Width="155" Height="34"><Img Src="images/
galactic_burgerimage.gif" Border="0" Height="34"
Width="155" Name="" Alt=""></Td>
        <Td Width="6" Height="34"></Td>
</Tr>
<Tr>
        <Td Width="16" Height="2"></Td>
        <Td Width="5" Height="2"></Td>
        <Td Width="155" Height="2"></Td>
        <Td Width="6" Height="2"></Td>
</Tr>
```

And here come the rollovers. The base image is set up in the <IMG SRC> tag, whereas the **onMouseOut** and **onMouseOver** states are defined within the <A HREF> tag. Because I didn't specify an **onMouseOut** action in the Rollovers palette, the **normal** and **onMouseOut** images are one and the same. (As you may surmise, **onMouseOver** is the **over** state, whereas **onMouseOut** is the **out** state.) The following table rows set up the three rollovers, separated by one-pixel-high rows:

```
<Tr>
        <Td Width="16" Height="34"></Td>
        <Td Width="5" Height="34"></Td>
        <Td Width="155" Height="34"><a Href="info.html"
OnMouseOut="ExecuteActions('object', 0)"
OnMouseOver="ExecuteActions('object', 1)" >
<Img Src="images/galactic_burgerinfo.gif"
Border="0" Height="34" Width="155" Name="object"
Alt="INFO"></a></Td>
        <Td Width="6" Height="34"></Td>
</Tr>
<Tr>
        <Td Width="16" Height="1"></Td>
        <Td Width="5" Height="1"></Td>
        <Td Width="155" Height="1"></Td>
        <Td Width="6" Height="1"></Td>
</Tr>
<Tr>
        <Td Width="16" Height="34"></Td>
        <Td Width="5" Height="34"></Td>
        <Td Width="155" Height="34"><a Href="links.html"
OnMouseOut="ExecuteActions('object1', 0)"
OnMouseOver="ExecuteActions('object1', 1)" ><Img Src="images/
galactic_burgerlinks.gif" Border="0"
```

```
Height="34" Width="155" Name="object1" Alt="LINKS"></a></Td>
            <Td Width="6" Height="34"></Td>
    </Tr>
    <Tr>
            <Td Width="16" Height="1"></Td>
            <Td Width="5" Height="1"></Td>
            <Td Width="155" Height="1"></Td>
            <Td Width="6" Height="1"></Td>
    </Tr>
    <Tr>
            <Td Width="16" Height="34"></Td>
            <Td Width="5" Height="34"></Td>
            <Td Width="155" Height="34"><a Href="home.html"
OnMouseOut="ExecuteActions('object2', 0)"
OnMouseOver="ExecuteActions('object2', 1)" ><Img
Src="images/galactic_burgerhome.gif" Border="0" Height="34"
Width="155" Name="object2" Alt="HOME"></a></Td>
            <Td Width="6" Height="34"></Td>
    </Tr>
    <Tr>
            <Td Width="16" Height="2"></Td>
            <Td Width="5" Height="2"></Td>
            <Td Width="155" Height="2"></Td>
            <Td Width="6" Height="2"></Td>
    </Tr>
```

Here's the bottom of the burger:

```
    <Tr>
            <Td Width="16" Height="34"></Td>
            <Td Width="5" Height="34"></Td>
            <Td Width="155" Height="34"><Img Src="images/
galactic_burgerimage1.gif" Border="0" Height="34"
Width="155" Name="" Alt=""></Td>
            <Td Width="6" Height="34"></Td>
    </Tr>
    <Tr>
            <Td Width="16" Height="43"></Td>
            <Td Width="5" Height="43"></Td>
            <Td Width="155" Height="43"></Td>
            <Td Width="6" Height="43"></Td>
    </Tr>
```

And here's the logo slice:

```
    <Tr>
            <Td Width="16" Height="105"></Td>
            <Td Width="166" Height="105" ColSpan="3"><Img
Src="images/galactic_burgerburger.gif" Border="0" Height="105"
Width="166" Name="" Alt="Burger"></Td>
    </Tr>
```

LiveMotion places a single-pixel GIF placeholder image into the last line of the table to hold the column widths. This common trick prevents the table from collapsing. The single-pixel GIF is transparent—your visitors will never know it's there:

```
        <Tr>
                <Td><Img Src="images/is_single_pixel_gif.gif"
Alt="" Width="16" Height="1"></Td>
                <Td><Img Src="images/is_single_pixel_gif.gif"
Alt="" Width="5" Height="1"></Td>
                <Td><Img Src="images/is_single_pixel_gif.gif"
Alt="" Width="155" Height="1"></Td>
                <Td><Img Src="images/is_single_pixel_gif.gif"
Alt="" Width="6" Height="1"></Td>
        </Tr>
</Table>

<!--Adobe(R) LiveMotion(TM) DataMap1.0 DO NOT EDIT
end DataMap -->
</Body>
</Html>
```

Of course, every table will be different, but this one should give you a good idea of what's happening when you export rollovers. Once you've exported the JavaScript and images, you'll probably have to move them into a host HTML file. Chapter 11 provides details on moving the rollover code with a handful of popular What You See Is What You Get (WYSIWYG) Web page editing applications.

Now that the rollover basics have been covered, let's take a look at how LiveMotion creates remote rollovers.

Creating Remote Rollovers

LiveMotion's approach to the creation of remote rollovers is stunningly sweet. The program uses a point-and-shoot methodology to specify the secondary rollover and state. This allows you to quickly and logically build complex remote rollovers. In short, the procedure goes something like this:

1. Build the primary rollover states.

2. Build the remote rollover states.

3. Target the primary rollover states to the remote rollover states.

Let's take a closer look at how it's done.

PROJECT Building a Remote Rollover

In this project, you'll create a simple remote rollover. Begin by creating a new composition (Cmd/Ctrl+N). At the Composition Settings dialog box, set the Width to 580 and the Height to 350. Select AutoLayout from the drop-down menu, select the Make HTML checkbox, and then click on OK.

To make things as straightforward as possible, the design for this project is extremely simple. You will have three primary rollovers, linked to a single remote rollover with four states. You'll begin by creating an outlined ellipse, as a design element:

1. Select the Ellipse tool and draw an ellipse 480 pixels wide by 316 high. Use the Transform palette to dial in the precise size. Set the fill to black. Position the ellipse in the middle of the composition.

2. Select the Outline checkbox on the Properties palette and set the Width to 12.

3. Use the Transform palette to rotate the ellipse 352 degrees, so that it appears as in Figure 4.6.

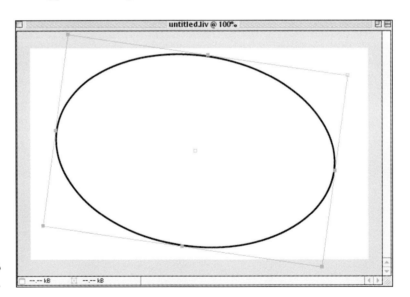

Figure 4.6
The outlined ellipse.

4. At the Opacity palette, select Linear from the drop-down menu, and set the angle to 299 degrees. Move the starting and ending Opacity level sliders so they appear as in Figure 4.7.

5. Select the Type tool. In the Type Tool dialog box, specify 36-point Times Roman Bold Italic. Select left alignment, type "digital dream drives" in the text area, and click on OK. Position the text at the lower right side of the composition, as you'll see in Figure 4.8.

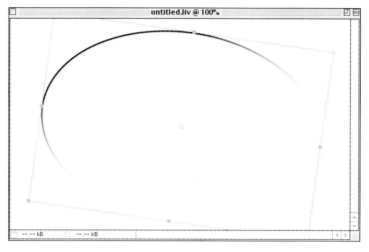

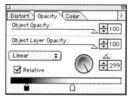

Figure 4.7
The outlined ellipse becomes a design element.

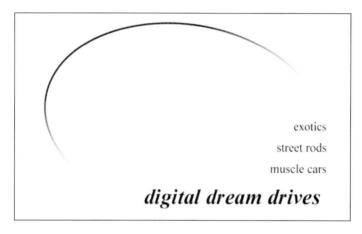

Figure 4.8
Where do I draw my inspiration? Let's just say that the Civic has 140K on the clock, and leave it at that.

Build the Primary Rollovers

The static elements are out of the way. Let's create the primary rollover elements:

1. Select the Type tool. In the Type Tool dialog box, specify 20-point Times Roman Regular. Select right alignment, type "exotics" in the text area, and click on OK. Position the text at the right side of the composition, as shown in Figure 4.8.

2. Repeat the previous step twice, using "street rods" and "muscle cars" as the terms.

3. Select exotics, street rods, and muscle cars, then select a medium gray fill from the Color palette. Use Object|Align|Right to right align all three pieces of text, then vertically space and position the text as shown in Figure 4.8.

4. With exotics, street rods, and muscle cars still selected, click on the New Rollover State button (on the Rollovers palette). This creates an **over** state.

5. Select black from the Color palette.

You now have three two-state rollovers. Take a look to see how they operate by selecting the Preview tool. As you move the Preview tool cursor over the rollovers, they should change from medium gray (**normal**) to black (**over**).

Build the Remote Rollovers

This next section gets a little tricky as you create three custom states:

1. Select the Type tool. In the Type Tool dialog box, specify 22-point Times Roman Italic. Select center alignment, and type:

    "the finest in

    european sports

    and super cars"

    in the text area, and click on OK. Position the text at the upper left side of the ellipse.

2. With "the finest in european sports and super cars" still selected, click on the New Rollover State button (on the Rollovers palette). This creates an **over** state. Select the **over** state, then select Custom State from the drop-down menu. In the Custom State dialog box, type "exotic" and click on OK.

3. Déjà vu time. With "the finest in european sports and super cars" still selected, click on the New Rollover State button. Once again, this creates an **over** state. Select the **over** state, then select Custom State from the drop-down menu. In the Custom State dialog box, type "muscle" and click on OK. Double-click on "the finest in european sports and super cars" to summon the Type Tool dialog box and replace the text with:

    "the baddest

    detroit iron"

    and click on OK.

4. Déjà vu one more time. With "the baddest detroit iron" still selected, click on the Duplicate Rollover State button to create an **over** state. Select the **over** state, then select Custom State from the drop-down menu. In the Custom State dialog box, type "street" and click on OK. Double-click on "the baddest detroit iron" to summon the Type Tool dialog box and replace the text with:

    "clean and

    mean machines"

    and click on OK.

You should now have a rollover with four states—**normal**, **exotic**, **muscle**, and **street**. The **normal** and **exotic** rollovers are identical at this point. In the next step, you'll make the **normal** state invisible.

5. Select the **normal** state from the Rollovers palette, then set the Object Layer Opacity level to 0 via the Opacity palette.

6. If necessary, select each of the other states and set their Object Layer Opacity levels back to 100.

Target the Remote Rollover States

Now that you have both the primary and remote rollovers in place, you can target the custom states. Targeting is fairly easy, once you get the hang of it. Just select the primary rollover's **over** state, then drag the **over** state's target icon onto the remote rollover. Once the remote rollover has been targeted, it will appear in the Rollovers palette, underneath the primary rollover. Select the appropriate state from the drop-down menu and you're set. Repeat this procedure for each of the remote rollovers. (If you can't see the **normal** state, don't fret. The object's bounding box will display when the cursor touches the object, as shown in Figure 4.9.)

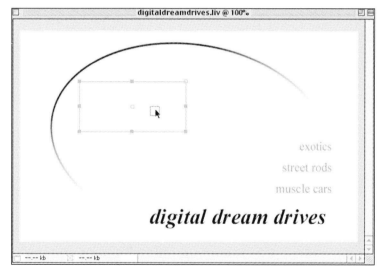
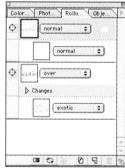

Figure 4.9
It can be disconcerting when you drag a target from a Rollover palette to an invisible state. It's like driving on a foggy night. Watch the lines.

Once you've set the rollovers for each of the **over** states, you'll need to target the **normal** states. If you fail to create and target a blank **normal** state for the remote rollover, it won't function properly. (The last mouseover state will be persistent.) Use the Preview tool (the pointer hand at the bottom right of the toolbox) to check out your composition after all of the states have been targeted. If everything looks good, preview the file in a browser by selecting File|Preview In|your browser of choice.

Although this is an extremely simple composition, you might want to preview different export options. Try tweaking the Export palette, if you're so inclined. (Note that Flash files should be exported with the Entire Composition option selected in the Composition Settings dialog box.) Figure 4.10 shows the digital dream drives composition in Netscape Navigator.

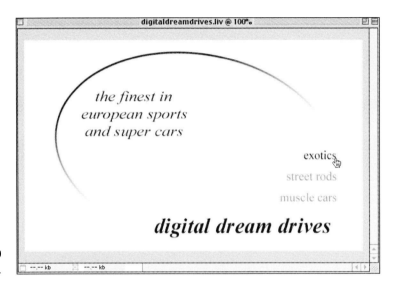

Figure 4.10
The finish line.

Rollover Depot

Looking for rollover ideas? You've come to the right place! In the Rollover Depot, I'll demonstrate many techniques you can use to build unusual and effective rollovers. This section begins with some basic rollover effects and works up to an intriguing array of advanced designs. To get a real feel for how it all works, warm up your CD-ROM drive—you can find the LiveMotion (LIV) and exported (HTML, GIF, and JPEG) files for each technique on the *Adobe LiveMotion f/x and Design* CD-ROM.

Basic Rollover Designs

I've assembled a slew of basic rollover designs for your browsing pleasure and design inspiration. These rollovers are best suited to sliced JavaScript layouts, because they use various shadow, glow, and three-dimensional effects.

Dim Bulb

The **normal** state of the Dim Bulb rollover uses text in a muted color similar to the background color. The **over** state changes the text to a color much brighter than the background color. This simulates the effect of turning on a light switch—hence the name. Figure 4.11 demonstrates how I used the SmileICG typeface along with MiniPics WhiteBread symbols to create the rollover groups.

From JavaScript to Flash

You can export all of the rollover designs featured in this section either as JavaScript or Flash files. Before exporting as JavaScript, ensure that the AutoLayout and Make HTML options are selected in the Composition Settings palette. Before exporting in Flash format, choose the Entire Composition option.

Some image treatments are better suited to the Flash format than others. If file size is a prime consideration, you'll want to stick with flat color objects, so that LiveMotion can export them as vector objects, rather than bitmap objects. I'll get into this topic in depth in Chapter 9, when I cover Flash exports.

Figure 4.11
Spacing is everything—don't let one button overlap the next.

Here's an overview of how to create the Dim Bulb buttons:

1. Use the Text tool to create each text string and symbol. Set the type in 28-point SmileICG with a 20-unit track. Set Alignment to Horizontal, Left. Set each symbol in 59-point MiniPics WhiteBread. Set the color to R51, G102, B51.

2. Spread the symbols vertically, select them all, and use the Object|Distribute|Vertical command to space them equally. (You'll probably need to nudge them a bit with the arrow keys to get the spacing just right.)

3. With all the symbols selected, choose Object|Align|Left. (Once the symbols are left-aligned, you may want to squish the symbol widths to make them a bit more consistent with each other.)

4. Select all the text strings. Choose Object|Distribute|Vertical and Object|Align|Left to space and align them in relation to their corresponding symbols.

5. Group each symbol with its corresponding text string. Be sure the bounding boxes don't overlap, as shown in Figure 4.11.

6. Create an **over** state for each group by clicking on the New Rollover State button on the Rollovers palette.

7. Choose each group's **over** state. Use the Subgroup Selection tool to select each element and assign an R102, G255, B102 color fill.

8. Use the Web palette to assign a URL to each rollover.

9. Once everything is looking good, take a gander at the finished page by choosing File|Preview In|your browser of choice. The rollover should operate as shown in Figure 4.12.

Figure 4.12
A hammock is everyone's favorite place to kick back with a cold one.

Why Use the Subgroup Selection Tool?

LiveMotion's Subgroup Selection tool—located at the top right side of the toolbox—allows you to select individual objects *within* a group. Choose the Subgroup Selection tool, and then click on the object you want to select. This isn't always easy. If you have a bunch of overlapping objects, it may take a handful of clicks to choose the right object.

You can also select individually grouped objects by drilling down into the Timeline. Keeping the Timeline open isn't a bad idea (given the monitor space), because it will always tell you exactly which objects are currently selected.

A Glow About You

The **normal** state of the Glow About You rollover starts with bright text that contrasts against the background color. (In fact, the text is the same color as the rolled-over text in the Dim Bulb design.) The **over** state adds a second layer that imparts a substantial glow. This rollover goes even further to simulate the effect of turning on a light switch—this is a halogen bulb design, not a 40 watter. Figure 4.13 shows the difference between the **normal** and **over** states. As you can see, the bounding box grows substantially between the two states. This design requires careful planning and spacing to avoid any button overlap. If the buttons overlap, the rollover will not export properly.

Figure 4.13
Check out the difference in bounding box size.

Here's an overview of how to create the Glow About You buttons:

1. Set the text and symbols in the Dim Bulb design, using an R102, G255, B102 color fill for the **normal** buttons.

2. Select all the icons and text strings.

3. Add a new layer to all the icons and text strings by pressing Command/Ctrl+L.

4. Give the new layer the same R102, G255, B102 color fill. Set the softness level to 9 on the Layer palette. Click on Layer 2's eye icon (in the Object Layers palette) to make the layer invisible while in the **normal** state.

Why Not Use a Rollover Style?

Although rollover styles can be huge timesavers, they can only be applied to individual objects, not to groups.

5. Group each symbol with its corresponding text string.

6. Select all of the groups. Create an **over** state for all the groups by clicking on the New Rollover State button on the Rollovers palette.

7. Choose each group's **over** state. Use the Subgroup Selection tool to select each element. Make the glow layer visible by clicking on Layer 2's eye icon on the Layer palette.

8. To accommodate that big fat glow, open up the vertical space between each button, as shown in Figure 4.13.

9. Use the Web palette to assign a URL to each rollover.

10. Take a look at the finished page by choosing File|Preview In|your browser of choice. The rollover should glow as shown in Figure 4.14.

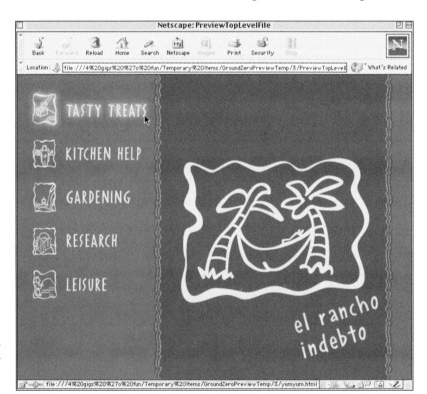

Figure 4.14
A spaced-out, glowing rollover gives this derivative design a different feel.

Get Depressed

The **normal** state of the Get Depressed rollover starts with a soft-embossed, rounded-rectangle button. The **over** state creates the appearance of a depressed button through careful manipulation of the emboss lighting and text color. Figure 4.15 compares the **normal** and **over** states.

I created the navigational graphic by combining a series of rounded-corner rectangles. I exported the graphic and placed it as a background image to

Figure 4.15
There's plenty of space between these rollover buttons.

Figure 4.16
Save me a slice. The buttons will overlay the structural background image.

minimize the number of slices in the final exported file. Figure 4.16 shows the background image. (This technique can greatly reduce the complexity of a full page.)

Let's take a look at the button specs:

1. Create buttons using 113-by-24-pixel rounded-corner rectangles with a radius of 42. The **normal** color is R51, G102, B102.

2. Set the button's **normal** state to a 4-pixel-deep emboss with a softness setting of 1, a straight edge, and normal light at a 135-degree angle.

3. Set the **normal** text in 12-point Charcoal regular with a 20-unit track. The first layer is white. The second layer is black with a two-pixel X and Y offset.

4. Select the **over** state, select Layer 1, and change the color so that it dims to R153, G204, B204. The rectangle's emboss lighting changes on the button's **over** state. By changing the lighting to dark only, LiveMotion darkens not only the embossed edges, but the face of the button, as well.

In this example, the text strings aren't grouped with their corresponding buttons. I created the first button in its entirety—with an **over** state—before I made four alias buttons. Using the alias feature with a series of buttons makes it easy to update colors and styles. Figure 4.17 shows the finished navigational structure.

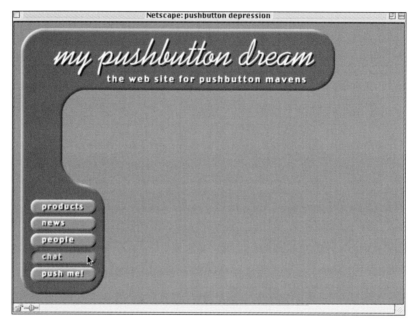

Figure 4.17
All you need to do is tweak the emboss settings to create a rollover button with a depressed appearance.

On The Side, Please

The Hidden Message is one of my favorite rollover techniques. When the visitor rolls over the button, a text string or image pops out. The trick, in some cases, is the same as that used in the simple glow—you simply hide the text string (or image) by deselecting the eye icon on that layer. Let's take a look at the first of the three Hidden Message techniques.

On The Side, Please text appears out of nowhere as it flies from the side of a vertical button bar. In this first variation of the Hidden Message technique, the flyout text is grouped with the main button and made invisible. Figure 4.18 shows the **normal** state in LiveMotion, with all the rollover groups selected.

Figure 4.18
The bounding box of each **normal** state group shows that the rollover text exists, although it isn't visible.

Let's take a gander at how to construct the buttons:

1. Create a background stripe pattern and place it in the composition as a texture. The background provides a place for the buttons to nest.

2. Create the button: a 129-by-20-pixel rounded rectangle with a radius of 13. The color is R51, G102, B102.

3. Set the **normal** button text to 15-point SevenSansICG, caps, with a track of 20. Set the color to white.

4. Set the flyout text to 14-point SevenSansICG, lowercase, the same color as the button (R51, G102, B102), with a track of 20.

5. Align the objects sequentially: Fit the buttons to the background, vertically center the button text to the buttons, left-align all button text, left-align all flyout text, and vertically center the flyout text to the buttons.

6. Group the corresponding button, button text, and flyout text for each button.

7. Select all of the button groups, and click on the New Rollover State button (on the Rollovers palette) to create **over** states for each button.

8. With all of the button groups still selected, click on the **normal** state in the Rollovers palette.

9. One-by-one, use the Subgroup Selection tool to select and make each chunk of flyout text invisible in each button's **normal** state. (Click on the eye icon in the Object Layers palette.)

Figure 4.19 shows the complete navigational structure and demonstrates the chat button's **over** state.

Figure 4.19
Don't forget to set a URL with the Web palette.

Depending on the page layout, text could also fly out from above or below a horizontal button bar. Although this technique is fairly versatile, it demands a certain amount of white space for the flyout text. The white space requirement imposes on the overall page design, but don't be afraid of it—white space can be a good thing. (For more complex designs, you'll probably want to build a remote rollover.)

A Change Of Face

Looking for a little Change Of Face? With this technique, all the magic happens on the face of the button; the **normal** text changes into the **over** text when the cursor passes over the button. Change Of Face works well in layouts with limited space. It provides a nice degree of interactivity without sacrificing any real estate.

Let's take a look at how to create these buttons:

1. Create a button bar consisting of two overlapping rounded corner rectangles—one filled, one outlined. (The outlined object creates the shadow-glow frame.)

2. Create a two-layer button: a 116-by-35-pixel rounded-corner rectangle with a radius of 13. Make the top layer white with a softness setting of 1. Make the bottom layer black with width and softness settings of 2. Doing so creates an unusual high-contrast embossed look. And, because it's an outlined object, the background color shows through the face of the button.

3. Set the **normal** button text to 18-point SevenSansICG, black, caps, with a track of 10.

4. Duplicate the button and **normal** text to create five buttons. Align them so the buttons butt each other, without overlapping. Set the button text as shown in Figure 4.20.

Figure 4.20
These buttons butt each other exactly. With precisely butted buttons, LiveMotion doesn't have to export that little chunk of "between button" image lint.

5. Drag-select each respective button with its text, then select Object|Align|Centers to align the text to the button.

6. Select just the button text and click on the New Rollover State button (on the Rollovers palette) to create **over** states for each button.

7. Set the **over** text to purple (R51, G0, B51), and change the text for each button. (Use "VISION!", "THE BIG LIST", "CALL US!", "FINEPRINT", and "NEED MORE?" as the **over** state text.) You may need to use extra spaces to nudge each chunk of **over** state text back into alignment with the button. The similar STUFF/need more? rollover is shown in Figure 4.21.

El Rancho Indebto Pop Up

Here's the most ambitious rollover so far: the El Rancho Indebto Pop Up. This example allowed me to revisit some photographs I shot a while back. The pictures come from my backyard in all its summertime splendor. The El Rancho Indebto Pop Up is notable not just for its magically appearing text, but for the unusual image effects, which use image adjustments, layers, and opacity gradients. Figure 4.22 shows the page—sans background—in the **normal** state. Although there seems to be a lot of space between the buttons, they move closer together in the **over** state, as demonstrated in Figure 4.23.

Figure 4.21
What does it all mean? I don't know—it's a hidden message.

Figure 4.22
It's easy to see the bounding boxes without the background image.

Figure 4.23
A series of three additional layers creates an interesting frame.

Let's take a look at what makes the El Rancho Indebto Pop Up rollover so unusual:

1. Set the **normal** state of each flower picture using a 100 percent radial opacity gradient, with the opaque (left) slider pushed to approximately 75 percent of scale. (Note: Opacity gradients affect object layers, not the entire object.)

2. Give the black button text a slight green glow in the second layer. Group the text with the flower photograph and make it invisible in the **normal** state.

3. The **over** state turns on the text and switches the flower photograph to a muted, square-framed button. The image adjustment settings are Brightness 92, Contrast -44, and Saturation -85.

4. Create the flower image's frame by adding three layers. The second layer is two pixels wider than the first and colored medium gray (R142, G142, B142). The third layer is four pixels wider than the first and colored light tan (R210, G196, B189). The fourth layer is six pixels wider than the first and colored the same medium gray as the second layer. Draw the frame colors from the muted flower photos using the Eyedropper tool.

Figure 4.24 demonstrates the Tiger Lily button in its **over** state. This one has to be experienced to be appreciated—load that file.

Figure 4.24
Switching from a radial opacity gradient to a square-framed image creates a tasty rollover effect.

Want a better look? You'll find another view of the El Rancho Indebto Pop Up in the color section, and the LIV file on the *Adobe LiveMotion f/x and Design* CD-ROM.

Take It For A Spin

You can accomplish a spinning or rotating rollover effect a couple of ways. Depending on the effect you're after, you might use the Twirl filter or just rotate the object itself. Remember the Half Moon exercise back in Chapter 1? Take It For A Spin uses the Twirl filter with the same technique to create a spun result. Figure 4.25 demonstrates the **normal** and **over** states.

Figure 4.25
In addition to the spinning buttons, the text dims on rollover.

Figure 4.26
Applied in this manner, Take It For A Spin delivers a subtle effect on this remote-controllish interface.

Notice how tightly this layout fits together. The buttons butt each other exactly. I used a dummy rectangle behind each button to prevent LiveMotion from chopping the interface to smithereens. (I'll detail this technique in the next chapter.) Figure 4.26 shows a clip of the interface as the Fun Stuff button is rolled over in the browser.

Now, let's move from the subtle to the unabashedly silly.

Swing That Hammer

In the midst of writing this chapter, I became involved in a home improvement project. My brother-in-law, who makes his living as a contractor, came over to do the drywall. One day, he popped into my home office to see what I was doing. I explained about the project and showed him some of the JavaScript rollovers I'd created. "You know what would be cool?" he said. "How about some swinging hammers?" And that's how this example came to be. Figure 4.27 shows Matt's **normal** and **over** states.

Together, the hammer rollovers, Spackle spots, and pseudo-blueprints create a whimsical motif, as shown in Figure 4.28. Here's a rundown on how I created the hammer rollover:

1. Start with a simple black hammer illustration in a drawing program. Export it in EPS format, place it in the LiveMotion composition, and color it with a purple fill with a second 1-pixel black layer (to create the outline).

2. Set the text in 24-point Humana Sans ITC Medium with 100 percent leading, set flush right. Create the hung punctuation effect by adding a space after the word *sheds*.

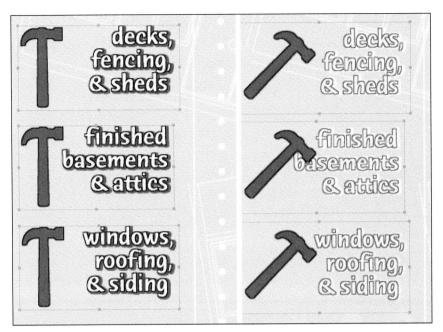

Figure 4.27
Notice how the dimensions of the rollover groups change between states.

Figure 4.28
I wanted to use a scan of the actual room addition blueprints for a background. When I couldn't find them, I faked it.

3. The **normal** text uses three layers: light yellow, black, and purple. The black layer is 1 pixel wide; the purple layer is 2 pixels wide, with an X offset of 2 and a Y offset of 1. These settings create a raised, cartoonish appearance.

4. Rotate the **over** hammer 315 degrees. The **over** text plays color and offset games to provide a hammered appearance. The first layer turns light blue with a Y offset of 4. The second layer has a Y offset of 4, and changes from black to purple. The third layer uses a Y offset of 4, along with an X offset of 2 and a lighter color.

Indicator Lights

Indicator lights are one of the most popular rollover motifs. These little critters light up unobtrusively when they're rolled over. For the most part, you can create them entirely within LiveMotion. And, because they're so small, you probably won't need to assemble them with anything other than primitive objects. Figure 4.29 shows 20-odd indicator lights I created one morning. You can find this file (littlegems.liv) in the Indicator Lights folder on the *Adobe LiveMotion f/x and Design* CD-ROM.

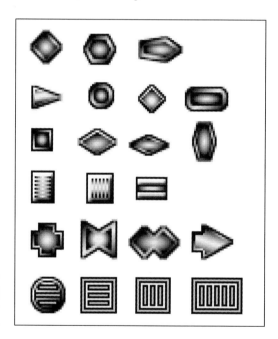

Figure 4.29
You can readily see the effects of antialiasing on anything other than a horizontal or vertical line.

Most of these examples use burst or radial gradients to achieve a glowing effect in the **over** state. The indicator lights in the littlegems.liv file haven't been assigned any actions, however. Tweak the colors to your liking, create a second rollover state, and then dim the color in the **normal** state.

Let's take a look at some examples of how you can use indicator lights in your rollover schemes. These three designs are based on the premise of light-emitting diodes (LEDs)—those tiny lights found on stereos, computers, and peripherals.

Little Arrows

Little Arrows point out the currently highlighted link without overwhelming the text. They provide instant recognition and deliver an elegant alternative to common bullets. The example shown in Figure 4.30—like all the indicator lights in the littlegems.liv file—uses a bezel design around the light itself. Although this design makes the indicator light invisible in the **normal** state, it would be just as easy to dim the light or ghost the entire object.

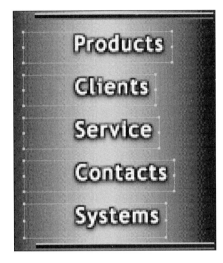 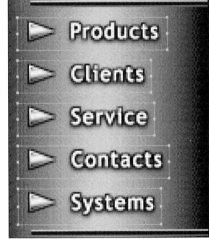

Figure 4.30
The invisible indicator is divulged by the bounding box of the Little Arrow design's **normal** state.

Here's the skinny on how to construct the Little Arrow design:

1. Create the arrow from a three-layer polygon. The first layer has a width of -1 and a light green-to-black burst gradient set at 279 degrees. The second layer has a width of 0 and white-to-medium gray linear gradient set at 274 degrees. The third layer is black, with a width of +1.

2. Set the text in 12-point Trebuchet MS Regular on 100 percent leading, with a tracking value of 10. Use three layers. The top layer is white. The second layer is black with a width of 1. The third layer creates a soft drop shadow—it's also black, with a width of 1 and a softness setting of 2.

3. Group each arrow with its corresponding text before creating the **over** state. Make the arrow invisible in the **normal** state by clicking on the respective eye icon on the Layer palette.

The Contacts link's **over** state is demonstrated in Figure 4.31.

Little LED

Ah, from whence do we draw our inspiration? It's an obscure—yet frightening—thought. I came up with this indicator light while staring at the flashing lights on my modem. The design has a markedly stereo component-like appearance, with metallic bars and simple aqua LEDs. Figure 4.32 displays the **normal** and **over** states side by side.

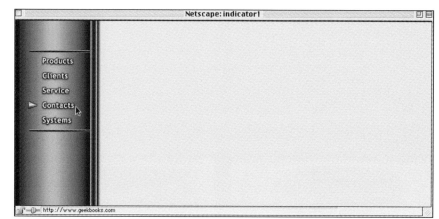

Figure 4.31
An arrow gets right to the point. There's no question which link is selected.

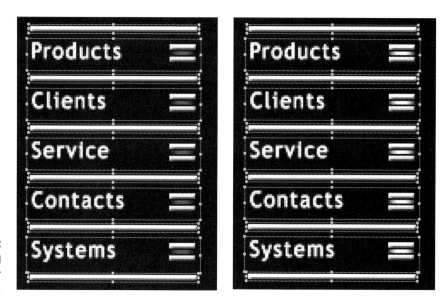

Figure 4.32
Although the rollovers are laid out closely in this design, their bounding boxes don't butt.

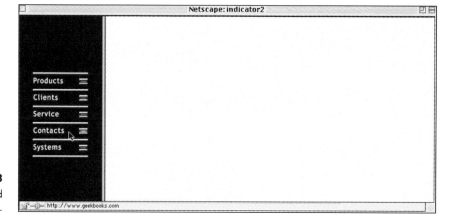

Figure 4.33
If only my CD player worked this well.

This design is very simple, but effective. Each indicator light consists of three little rectangles—two metallic bars surrounding an LED bar. Figure 4.33 shows how the navigational interface looks in the browser when you roll over the Contacts link.

Here's a rundown on how to create the elements:

1. Create each metallic bar from a 17-by-5-pixel, 2-layer rectangle. For the first layer, use a light gray-to-medium gray linear gradient at 270 degrees, along with a 1-pixel-wide bevel (softness setting of 1, straight edge, normal light at 135 degrees). Make the second layer black with a width of 1.

2. Create the LED bar from a simple 17-by-2-pixel rectangle. Use a dark green-to-black burst gradient in the **normal** state and a bright aqua-to-black burst gradient in the **over** state, both at 0 degrees.

3. Group each LED with its corresponding text before creating the **over** state. Set the text with the same specifications as the earlier Little Arrow example.

Big LED

The Big LED design takes a bigger, bolder approach, with a grill-covered indicator light many times the size of the Little LED. But, this design is different in a number of ways, in addition to its size. Figure 4.34 demonstrates the differences between the Big LED design's **normal** and **over** states.

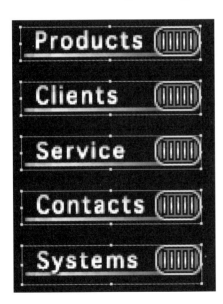 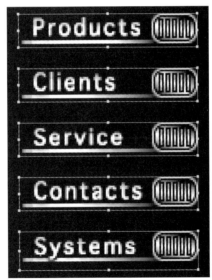

Figure 4.34
The highlight on the horizontal button bar adds a bit of flash to the **over** state.

Let's take a look to see what makes this design unusual:

1. Create the Big LED from a 27-by-17-pixel, 3-layer rounded rectangle with a corner radius of 28. Make the first layer solid olive green in the **normal** state and a lime green-to-black burst gradient at 258 degrees in the **over** state. Make the second layer black with a width of 1. Make the third layer medium gray with a width of 2.

2. Create the gridwork of vertical bars from 5 identical 3-by-11-pixel, 2-layer rectangles. Make the first layer a white-to-medium gray burst gradient at 270 degrees. Make the second layer black with a width of 1. Center the bars vertically and space them evenly horizontally with one pixel between them.

3. Set the text in 12-point Geneva Regular on 100 percent leading with a tracking value of 15. Use three layers. Make the top layer white. Make the second layer black with a width of 1. The third layer creates a soft black drop shadow, with a width of 1 and a softness setting of 2. The drop shadow falls subtly on the horizontal bar.

4. Assign the horizontal bar a medium gray-to-black linear gradient in the **normal** state and a white-to-black linear gradient in the **over** state, both at 0 degrees.

The Clients button's **over** state is demonstrated in Figure 4.35. But, be warned: The illustration doesn't do it justice. Load the indicator3.html page from the *Adobe LiveMotion f/x and Design* CD-ROM to check it out.

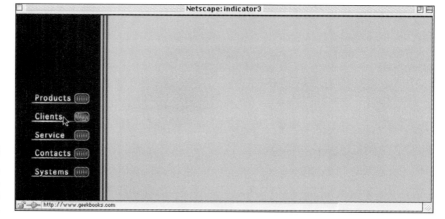

Figure 4.35

When viewed in the browser, the single pixel spaces blur, heightening the effect of the LED reflecting in the bezel.

Exclaim!

Various forms of this rollover design had been floating in my head for weeks. I wanted something to portray movement and excitement, but I was looking for the right way to express these concepts. One day, I was poking around in the MiniPics MardiGras Hop typeface, when I came across a whimsical illustration of a Wild West sheriff—and that's when this design happened. Within 10 minutes, I came up with a rootin' tootin', straight-shootin' rollover. Figure 4.36 shows the **normal** and **over** states.

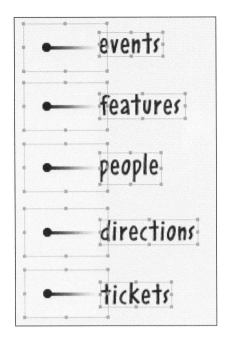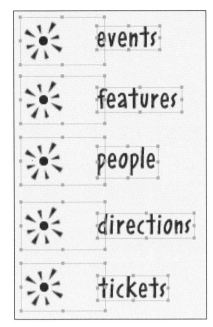

Figure 4.36

These rollovers work their magic as objects are made invisible with the Object Layer palette.

I created this page entirely in LiveMotion, without the aid of any other programs. Here's a blow-by-blow:

1. Create the deckle-striped background by arranging and exporting a bunch of triangles and rectangles.

2. Create the sheriff illustration from a 359-point *F*, set in MiniPics MardiGras Hop. Set the page title in 23-point Blackoak on 140 percent leading. Set the button text in 29-point Smile ICG Medium.

3. Construct the rollovers with LiveMotion's Polygon, Ellipse, and Rectangle tools. Make the impact triangles invisible in the **normal** state. Make the dark blue-to-light blue linear gradient velocity trail invisible in the **over** state.

4. Group the triangles, circle, and rectangle. Note that they aren't grouped with the corresponding text, as they overlap cleanly.

This is a fun rollover to play with, as demonstrated in Figure 4.37. I highly recommend that you look this one up on the *Adobe LiveMotion f/x and Design* CD-ROM, if only as an inspiration to create your own whimsical designs.

Figure 4.37
Ready, aim, fire!

Moving On

It would be nice to say that this chapter taught you all there is to know about the subject of creating rollovers with LiveMotion, but that would be an unfair statement. There's *always* more to learn: new techniques, new styles, new workarounds, and a new means to an end. In the next chapter, I'll talk about image slicing, exporting, and creating full-page layouts with LiveMotion. Chapter 10 dives into the topic of full-page Flash interfaces (complete with rollovers, of course).

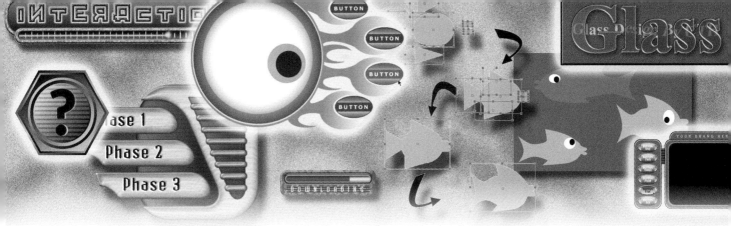

Chapter 5

It Slices, It Dices, It Builds HTML Layouts

This chapter ties it all together by discussing image slicing, exporting, and full-page HTML layouts, in addition to covering the fine points of LiveMotion's tasty batch image-replacement feature.

It Doesn't Peel Potatoes

But LiveMotion *does* create slick graphic and HTML exports, *if* you've prepared your compositions properly. The trick lies in understanding what to export and how to engineer your designs. In this chapter, I'll disclose the proper settings and formats, as I explain how to build compositions that exploit LiveMotion's potential.

Complex graphic Web page design is based on *image slicing*—carving large images into smaller, more manageable chunks. These chunks are then loaded into an HTML table to reconstruct the original appearance of the graphic. Once sliced and tabled, individual table cells can contain Flash ornaments (or larger animations), JavaScript rollover information, animation, Java applets, and other goodies.

Export and Slicing Methods

LiveMotion differs from Web graphic applications in that it slices images based on *object boundaries*. (Other programs—such as Macromedia Fireworks—rely on individually drawn slice lines.) LiveMotion's unique method of *clumping* objects together during sliced exports begs you to become familiar with the logic behind its slicing. In general, LiveMotion draws slicing boundaries around rollovers and individually compressed objects.

Where Do the Slices Fall?

LiveMotion's View|Preview AutoSlice Area (Cmd/Ctrl+7) shows exactly where the boundaries force the slices to occur. Through careful object positioning, you can minimize the number of slices in your composition. One pixel can make all the difference.

What's clumping all about? LiveMotion assumes that any objects falling entirely within the boundary are part of the clump and exports them in the slice. Any objects that are partially overlapped (rather than completely covered) by the boundary may be carved into pieces; the portion of the object within the boundary is exported with the slice, whereas the portion(s) of the object outside the boundary are exported as a separate slice (or slices).

The Composition Settings dialog box (Edit|Composition Settings) provides four ways to export a page: Entire Composition, Trimmed Composition, AutoSlice, and AutoLayout. Let's see when you might need to use each of these methods.

Why Use Entire Composition?

The Entire Composition method exports the entire LiveMotion canvas area as one image. You'll want to use this option when you're designing:

- *Flash exports*—Whether for full-page interface designs or diminutive ornaments, Entire Composition gets the nod.

- *Banner ads*—Fix dimensions at an exact size. (You'll find a chart of popular banner ad sizes in Chapter 6.)

- *Backgrounds*—Eliminate unwanted antialiased artifacts at the top and bottom of the seamless tile.

- *Other fixed-dimension graphics*—Ensure an exact height and width.

Want a perfect example of why you might want to use the Entire Composition method? Let's say that your banner ad design includes soft drop-shadowed text that exceeds the 468-by-60-pixel banner area boundary. If you export the banner as a trimmed composition, the export will include the overlap. But, if you build the banner on a 468-by-60 canvas and export the entire composition, you'll have a neatly trimmed banner. Figure 5.1 shows the original LiveMotion composition (on an oversized canvas). Figure 5.2 shows the placed results from an Entire Composition (468-by-60 canvas) export, along with a Trimmed Composition export (from the oversized canvas). The Entire Composition method ignores anything outside the image area; it ignores object clumping as well.

Figure 5.1
The overlapping image areas created by soft drop shadows can be troublesome.

Figure 5.2
The Entire Composition export (top) is correct, whereas the Trimmed Composition export is a blobby mess. Check out those edges.

Selecting the Make HTML option in conjunction with Entire Composition places all the graphics and code into an HTML page. Use this option to include image map information when you're exporting the entire composition. Deselect the Make HTML option if all you need is an image file (and not an HTML file).

Why Use Trimmed Composition?

The Trimmed Composition method exports the smallest area that encompasses all the objects within the composition. Because all objects are exported with this method, object clumping doesn't come into play. You may want to use the Trimmed Composition option when designing:

- *Individual transparent GIFs*—Render graphic chunks on a specific background color for smooth antialiasing.

- *Other bits and pieces*—Create them fast.

Trimmed Composition works in a manner similar to the File|Export Selection command, although the objects don't have to be selected. Figure 5.3 shows the bounding boxes surrounding a typical composition, and Figure 5.4 shows the result as exported with the Trimmed Composition option.

Figure 5.3

This is an ungrouped composition. If you group it, the bounding box echoes that of the file created with the Trimmed Composition export method.

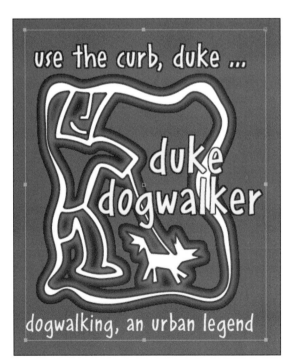

Figure 5.4

Here's the exported transparent GIF graphic, placed on a lighter background in LiveMotion.

Selecting the Make HTML option in conjunction with Trimmed Composition places all the graphics and code into an HTML page. Use this option to include image map information when you're exporting a trimmed composition. Deselect the Make HTML option if all you need is an image file (and not an HTML file).

Why Use AutoSlice?

The AutoSlice method exports all the objects within the composition, complete with any link and JavaScript information, to an HTML page. This method slices the composition into individual chunks, although it doesn't always create HTML layout tables. AutoSlice may create tables, however, if the composition includes JavaScript rollovers. The tables generated by AutoSlice are neatly formatted and indented—this may lead to the dreaded "table-grouting problem" with certain browsers. The spaces created by the table formatting result in gaps between the graphics; these gaps can look like the grout lines in a ceramic tile floor. If you need tables, it's best to use the AutoLayout method. (Unlike AutoSlice, AutoLayout does not include carriage returns within the table rows.)

In short, you'll want to use the AutoSlice option when designing:

- *Hand-crafted tables*—When LiveMotion-generated tables don't cut it, you can reassemble AutoSliced images in an HTML layout application (or text editor).

- *HTML without tables*—Simple pages often use sliced graphics and code without resorting to complex tables.

LiveMotion relies on object clumping and groups to determine slicing boundaries when you use the AutoSlice export method. Figure 5.5 shows the original LiveMotion design, and Figure 5.6 shows the graphics as exported with the AutoSlice option. Notice how the AutoSlice export does not maintain the composition's horizontal and vertical distance from the edges of the browser.

Why Use AutoLayout?

The AutoLayout method goes one step further than AutoSlice. It exports all the objects, links, and JavaScript information to a formatted HTML page. The composition is contained in an HTML table to maintain the proper spacing. You'll want to use the AutoLayout option when designing:

- *Full-page layouts*—You can create some pretty amazing pages, straight out of LiveMotion. The latter part of this chapter delves into the subject of full-page layouts.

- *Complex structures*—Let LiveMotion build intricate tables for your navigational graphics and other involved images. You can simply cut and paste the LiveMotion-generated code into your existing layout.

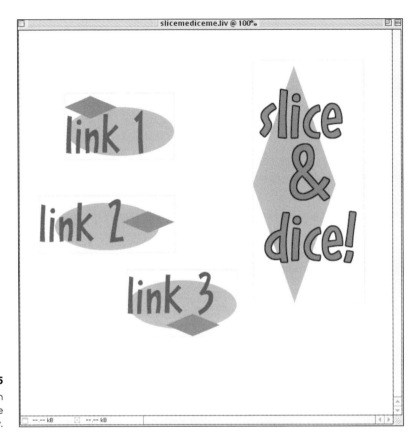

Figure 5.5

The graphics as laid out in LiveMotion, with Active Export Preview.

Figure 5.6

The graphics as they appear in a browser after being exported with the AutoSlice option.

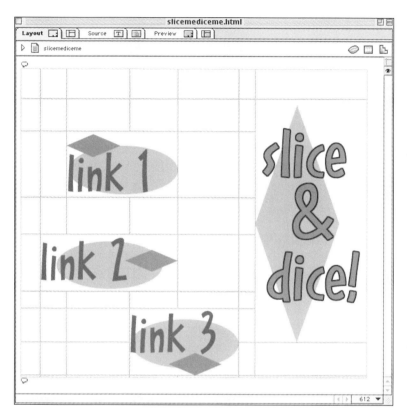

Figure 5.7
Here's a telltale view of a table exported using Auto-Layout, as displayed in Adobe GoLive's Layout view. (GoLive makes it easy to see the table cell boundaries.)

LiveMotion relies on object clumping to determine slicing boundaries when you use the AutoLayout export method. Figure 5.7 demonstrates a table generated with AutoLayout. Although this table appears to be unnecessarily complex, it points out that the program needs a bit of persuasion to generate the cleanest tables.

With some careful engineering, LiveMotion will generate tight code. I'll dive into that topic in the "Building Full-Page Layouts" section, right after a review of graphic-file exports.

Export Format Tweaks and Techniques

LiveMotion takes a simplified approach to exporting optimized images. Although the program doesn't provide all the bells and whistles of programs such as Equilibrium DeBabelizer, Macromedia Fireworks, and Adobe's own ImageReady, it delivers what you need to get the job done with a minimum of hassle. If you're really into squeezing the last possible byte out of your compositions, you can always post-process your graphics.

The Active Export Preview option (View|Active Export Preview) is a great boon to productivity. By selecting Active Export Preview, you'll get a relatively accurate idea of how your composition will appear once it's been exported. And, just as important, you'll have a good estimate of the file size. This power comes

Hold That Shift Key

If you hold down Shift while you click on the Export palette's GIF Colors slider, the slider will jump between 4-, 8-, 16-, 32-, 64-, 128-, and 256-color palettes. Do the same with the JPEG Quality slider, and it will jump in 10-percent quality increments.

at a price, however: Screen redraw speed is significantly slower when you're using the Active Export Preview option. On a fast machine or with a small composition, you might not feel the speed hit. But on a slower box or with a large composition, you'll find yourself waiting. For this reason, you'll probably want to turn Active Export Preview off until you need to throw an eyeball on the export.

In general, you'll weigh exported file size against overall image quality. This judgment doesn't happen automatically—you'll have to play with the options to strike an acceptable balance between the two. Let's take a look at some methods you can use to optimize your exported images.

GIF Techniques

In GIF mode, LiveMotion's Export palette provides a number of key options, including Transparency, Dithering, Interlacing, and six palette choices (Perceptual, Selective, Web Adaptive, Web, Mac OS, and Windows). For most Web work, you'll likely use the Web Adaptive or Web palettes.

Stay Small

To keep your GIF files tight, stick with a small palette. As always, a tradeoff exists between image quality and file size. You don't want to negatively affect image quality if you can avoid it. But, a certain amount of compromise is often necessary. With Active Export Preview chosen, I like to decrease the number of colors until degradation is obvious and then push the slider up to the equilibrium point at which the tradeoff disappears. Once I'm at that point, I'll try turning the Dither option on and off. Dithering can increase the image quality in *some* situations, but most often it will lead to a larger file. In other cases, dithering can actually make the image look worse than its undithered equivalent.

Flat's Where It's At

The manner in which you choose your color schemes and shading will greatly affect the exported file size. As I mentioned earlier, the GIF format is most appropriate for flat-color images. For the smallest file sizes, you'll want to design with a limited palette and large contiguous areas of similar color.

Get Horizontal

Long horizontal rows of similarly colored pixels exhibit the highest levels of GIF compression. With this in mind, you may want to design your graphics so that they contain long horizontal runs of flat color. Choose a solid color, rather than a texture.

Stay Web-Safe

If you design your LiveMotion compositions with Web-safe colors (by choosing colors with the color cube selected on the Color palette), you'll be ahead of the game. Select either the Web Adaptive or Web palettes from the Export palette and LiveMotion will automatically push the exported GIF colors toward the Web-safe palette. If the colors start Web-safe, they should stay Web-safe. When you begin using gradients and special effects (such as 3D), however, LiveMotion will have to work to create the exported colors. This extra effort can lead to shifted colors in the exported file.

JPEG Techniques

If you're building lush, continuous-tone Web interfaces with lots of photographs, you'll find the JPEG format to be most appropriate. I use the same technique with JPEG compression that I do with GIF compression—that is, I back the slider down to the point of visible degradation. (An old mechanic's joke comes to mind. The apprentice asks the journeyman mechanic how much to tighten a bolt. "I usually tighten the bolt until it starts to strip," answers the senior mechanic. "Then I back off a quarter-turn.")

Here are a handful of JPEG pointers:

- *Take a close look*—JPEG compresses in a different manner than GIF. GIF images look grainy and then posterized when over-compressed. On the other hand, JPEG images become blurry and then blotchy, with an "underwater" appearance.

- *Don't JPEG a JPEG*—The JPEG format is lossy. Each time you save an image in JPEG format, it loses a certain amount of quality. Repeatedly resaving an image in JPEG format will turn the image into mud. Use the Photoshop (PSD) format as an intermediary, if necessary.

- *Avoid JPEG for flat-color files*—Solid colors can be difficult for JPEG compression to handle. These areas may display lots of visible artifacts.

Not for Pros Only

LiveMotion exports both Progressive and Standard JPEG format files. Progressive JPEGs shouldn't be a problem with modern browsers (those designed after the Stone Age), although the earliest browsers didn't support the Progressive JPEG format. If you know that a significant percentage of your audience is using Lame-O browser version 0.1, you *might* want to stick with nonprogressive JPEG images.

Optimized

The Optimized option can reduce file size when used with Standard JPEG exports, by building a special compression table for the image.

AOL Browser Woes

Have you viewed your Web site with the America Online (AOL) browser? This browser may have problems when you try to view certain JPEG graphics. The difficulty arises from AOL's image-compression scheme. AOLers will have no problems with JPEGs if their browsers are properly configured. To turn off the compressed graphics option, select My AOL|Preferences|WWW|Web Graphics and deselect the Use Compressed Graphics option.

Reduce Chroma

The Reduce Chroma option gives you one more chance to squeeze a few more bytes out of your JPEG files by discarding redundant color information in the exported image. You can often choose this option without a noticeable effect, other than a reduction in file size.

No Transparency

Unfortunately, the JPEG format doesn't support transparency. If your composition contains transparent images, your best bet is to use the GIF format for compatibility's sake.

Per-Object Compression: Mixing GIFs and JPEGs

Want the best option for a mixed continuous-tone and flat-color design? You *can* get the best of both the GIF and JPEG worlds, but you'll have to work at it. LiveMotion's per-object compression function allows you to assign different format settings to individual objects. If the bulk of the composition would export best as a GIF, with the exception of a photograph, you can select the photograph and set it to export as a JPEG image.

Here's an example of a hybrid layout. Figure 5.8 shows the mythical Pixelpush Industries Web page in LiveMotion with all the objects selected. Figure 5.9 shows the AutoLayout exported page in Adobe GoLive. Replacing the GIF elephant with the JPEG elephant results in a better-looking page with a faster download, to boot. The area where the text overlaps the flower photo can be problematic, because the JPEG photo looks good, but the solid color around the text gets blotchy. In such cases, you may want to use the GIF flower and text image, rather than the JPEG image.

Figure 5.8
This layout will create a clean export. The individual elements align with each other and the buttons butt.

What about PNG?

The Portable Network Graphics (PNG) format is very cool. It compresses well and provides transparency in both in-dexed and TrueColor modes. But, it isn't a ubiquitous format. Although the Windows version of Microsoft Internet Explorer has supported the PNG format since version 4, PNG is not supported in the Mac version (through 4.5). The Netscape Navigator browser prior to version 4.04 doesn't support the PNG format without a plug-in. As the PNG format support becomes universal in the installed base of browsers, designers will start to switch. (The Flash format supports PNG graphics.)

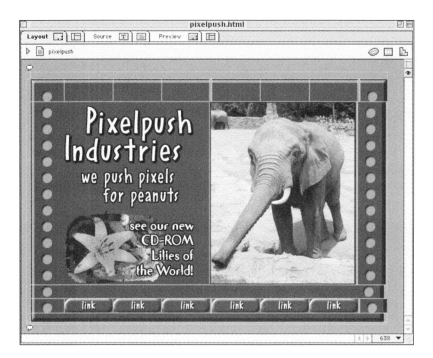

Figure 5.9
When viewed in Adobe GoLive's Layout mode, the hard work shows off.

To assign per-object compression settings to a specific object, select the object, then:

1. Select Object from the drop-down menu at the bottom left corner of the Export palette.

2. Click on the Export palette's Create Object Settings button.

3. Set the image format and compression settings, as required.

LiveMotion doesn't allow you to assign per-object compression to a group of objects, although you can assign per-object compression to multiple selected objects (that are not grouped).

Building Full-Page Layouts

Although LiveMotion can create remarkably complex full-page HTML lay-outs, the program also makes it easy to create a horribly splintered mess. To gain the program's full benefit, you must understand how LiveMotion makes its slicing decisions. Once you grasp the methods, your layouts will benefit.

Creating Structure

You must begin with a blueprint on which to build your design. Think of the exported HTML table as a grid. Each element must fall logically within that grid. The more uneven your designs, the more complex the table grid—and the more splintered the resulting export. Start with a mental picture of the grid, whether you begin your design work on a piece of scrap paper or on your computer. Figure 5.10 shows a rough drawing of the Pixelpush Industries design, with drawn guidelines.

Figure 5.10
A framing contractor starts with blueprints. You should, too.

Careful Alignment

Want to know the surest way to turn your sliced exports into a splintered mess? Don't bother to align or butt your objects. Let them sit willy-nilly. You'll be rewarded with a frightening melange of image fragments. Figure 5.11 shows a less carefully engineered layout in LiveMotion, and Figure 5.12 demonstrates the exported abomination in PageMill 3. Refer back to Figure 5.9 to get a feel for how the composition should be sliced.

Grids, Guides, and Alignment Tricks

LiveMotion's grids and guides are a big help for object alignment. But they're not the be-all end-all. In addition to grids and guides, I use three methods for precise object placement:

- *The Transform palette*—Know *exactly* where objects lie, because the Transform palette provides X and Y coordinates accurate down to the pixel.

- *Object|Align*—Use this function to quickly align elements along their horizontal and vertical boundaries.

- *Straight edges*—Create a skinny rectangle and drag it around for visual alignment. Always align via the bounding box. (This method, though it's not for everyone, can be faster than using the guidelines.)

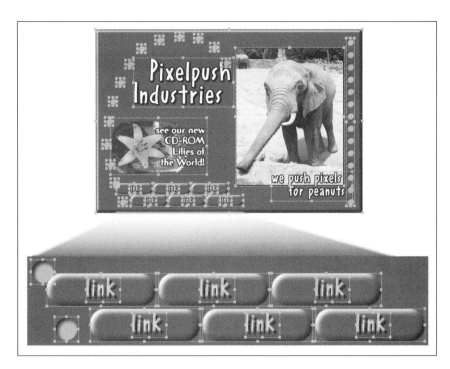

Figure 5.11
The big problem here is the manner in which the rollover buttons are placed.

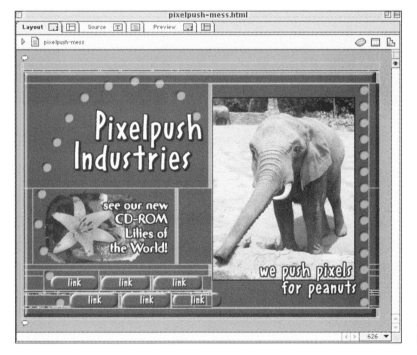

Figure 5.12
Is that a Web page or a train wreck? Check out the slivers between the buttons.

Using Space

Open space is a crucial element of design. The eye needs places to stop and rest, and a Web page crammed to the gills is hard to digest. Too many Web designers ignore this simple fact and try to stuff as much as they can into as little space as possible. Don't let yourself fall into this trap. Pages that must be dense with content will benefit the most from open space.

The effective use of open space benefits more than just readability. It can also help make your HTML tables work properly. When you design using such page elements as text blocks, graphics, logos, buttons, and photographs, you should think of open space as an element, as well.

The HTML Text Tool

LiveMotion's HTML Text tool comes in handy when creating full-page layouts. You drag out a text area in the same manner as drawing a rectangle. Once the HTML text area is on the page, you have the option of adding HTML text to the layout from within LiveMotion. Double-click on the HTML text area to summon the Edit HTML dialog box.

The Edit HTML dialog box displays raw HTML—it does not provide any formatting or preview features. Likewise, LiveMotion does not display any HTML attributes in the composition. The HTML text area will be exported as a table cell within an AutoLayout exported document. You can use LiveMotion's Edit|Edit Original command to move HTML text between your HTML editor and LiveMotion.

Effective Slicing

Slicing a graphic is akin to carving the Thanksgiving turkey. You'll shred your first attempts until you get the hang of it, as shown back in Figure 5.12. Once you've learned the subtle nuances, you'll slice those graphics with the precision of a brand-new set of late-night-TV Ginsu knives.

Here are some of my favorite techniques.

Use Dummy Objects for Spacing

LiveMotion has only so much built-in intelligence. Sometimes, it needs a helping hand. If the program doesn't slice the way you want it to, you can always fake it out. When an exported LiveMotion layout has been splintered to smithereens, I take a long, cold look at how the image is built. I begin by optimizing object alignment. Then, I devise a scheme to add dummy objects to carry the slicing information.

A *dummy object* is an object with a background fill, drawn to exact proportions. It's often grouped with other objects, perhaps as part of a JavaScript rollover. Dummy objects are transparent and serve only to influence LiveMotion's slicing decisions. Because they are transparent, you can use dummy objects to create butting buttons that *appear* to have space between them—thus solving one of the thorniest slicing issues. Figures 5.13 and 5.14 show the original composition, along with an optimized version—with views of the individual objects and slicing. (I left a slight tint on the dummy objects.)

SWF and the HTML Text Tool

Unfortunately, LiveMotion doesn't export SWF compositions with HTML text areas. You'll have to piece these elements together in an HTML editor.

See-Through First, Then Invisible

When working with dummy objects, you may want to set their opacity levels low. This makes it easy to see through the objects to achieve precise alignment. Once all the dummy objects are in position, assign them with a Background fill (on the Layer palette).

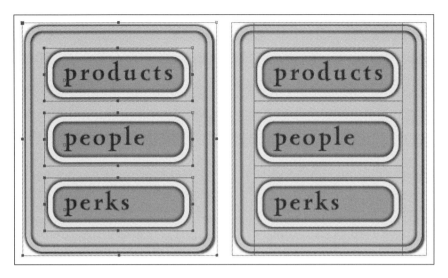

Figure 5.13
View|Preview AutoSlice Area (at right) shows where the chunks fall.

Figure 5.14
Dummy objects help carve the navigational structure into five chunks, instead of nine.

Precision Carving with Selected Dummy Objects

Have you ever wanted LiveMotion to carve conventional slices? Here's one of the slickest—yet least obvious—tricks you can pull. You can use dummy transparent objects in conjunction with the File|Export Selection command to carve a composition chunk by chunk. This method is a bit kludgy, but it works. Create a dummy rectangle for each chunk, ensuring that all the dummies butt. Methodically select each dummy object and use the File|Export Selection command to save the individual slices.

Stuff It into the Background

Does that object have to be an object? Or can you stuff it into the background? You can often cure troublesome layouts by carefully constructing a background to carry certain elements. Doing so makes LiveMotion's job easier, because you reduce the complexity of the exported layout. Fewer clumps generally result in less-splintered exports.

Use a canvas height of 1,024 pixels, but limit the number of colors and detail in the background to hold down the file size. Use this method only on short pages—you don't want the background to repeat.

OJECT Try a Slice

Ready to try the precision slicing method now? Open the preciseslice.liv file from the *LiveMotion f/x and Design* CD-ROM's Chapter 5 folder. This file contains the three button navigational structure, as shown in Figure 5.13, sans rollovers and dummy objects.

1. Draw three dummy rectangles, with a width of 219 pixels—matching that of the navigational structure—and a height of 70 pixels. Assign an object opacity of 30% with the Opacity palette. (Color doesn't matter.)

2. Position the rectangles so that their horizontal edges butt, as shown in Figure 5.14.

3. Select all three rectangles, along with the navigational structure, and select Object|Align|Left.

4. Use Object|Arrange to place each dummy rectangle *behind* its corresponding button (and in front of the navigational structure).

5. Set the opacity level of each dummy rectangle to 0% with the Opacity palette.

6. Select the first dummy rectangle, along with its corresponding button. Select Object|Group to group the rectangle with the button. Repeat this procedure for the second and third buttons (and their corresponding dummy rectangles).

7. Assign rollovers to each of the buttons with the Rollovers palette.

8. Select the over state of each rollover, then select the button text with the Subgroup Selection tool. Assign a white fill to the text.

9. Select View|Preview AutoSlice Area to check the slicing. It should appear as in Figure 5.14.

10. Select Preview mode at the bottom right corner of the Toolbox (or press Q), then pass the cursor over the buttons to preview the rollovers.

Cooking Up a Batch

Batch image replacement is one of LiveMotion's most powerful features. The batch function lets you quickly and easily build text headings, buttons, and other text graphics by applying a defined look to a list of text strings. Before

LiveMotion existed, each graphic had to be painstakingly assembled by hand. Thankfully, those days are over! LiveMotion's batch image replacement has turned a time-consuming, laborious procedure into an instantaneous point-and-shoot affair.

The batch operations are fairly straightforward, but you must know a handful of ins and outs. This chapter goes above and beyond to provide you with the recipe for success. I'll begin by covering the batch basics; then, I'll slide into another cookbook and introduce my Batch Button Depot.

Batch Basics

When you set out to create a batch of Web graphics, you'll need two items: a *look* and a *list*. The look can merely consist of some styled text or it can include text on top of a button or other graphic. The list consists of an HTML file with specifically tagged text strings. Figure 5.15 demonstrates the before and after effects of a lightning fast batch replacement.

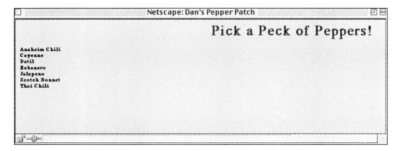

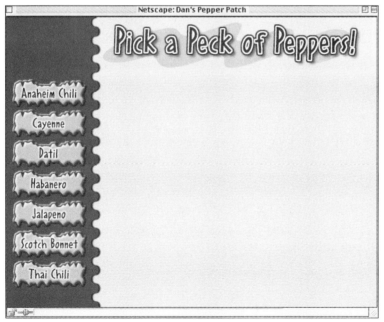

Figure 5.15

Hot cha cha! A quick batch replacement created both the heading and the button graphics.

You've Got the Look

You'll probably begin by developing the look of your batch replacement. The first steps are as follows:

1. Spice up the sample text.

2. Place the text on a tasty button object (if desired).

3. If you're using a button, group the text with the button and assign the Object|Maintain Alignment option (if desired).

4. With the group selected, assign an HTML heading or class code via the Replace menu on the Web palette.

It's a good idea to create your batch-replacement look on the background the target Web page uses. This is true for a couple of reasons. First, LiveMotion will place the background from the LIV file into the batch-processed page. Second, doing so ensures that the exported graphic antialiases smoothly into the finished page (which is essential when you're creating soft-edged objects). If you render a transparent GIF graphic on a background that's the wrong color, you may end up with a jaggy halo surrounding the image.

Maintain Alignment (or Not)

The Maintain Alignment option allows a button to grow or shrink to fit the text string. Figure 5.16 illustrates the effect. Many folks get confused by this option. Don't be one of the unenlightened. Here's the skinny:

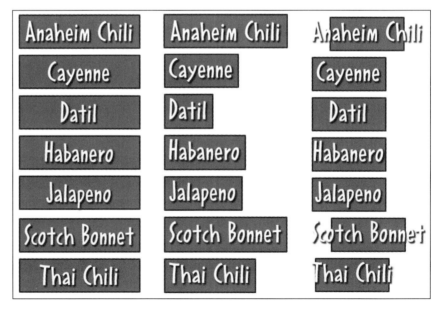

Figure 5.16
From the left: wide button, Maintain Alignment not selected; wide button, Maintain Alignment selected; narrow button, Maintain Alignment not selected.

- If you want your button to adjust itself (to fit the length of the text string), be sure you select the Maintain Alignment option.

- If you want the button's size to remain constant, don't select the Maintain Alignment option.

You can use Maintain Alignment only on grouped objects that contain a text element. To activate the Maintain Alignment option, select the group and then choose Object|Maintain Alignment.

Making a List, Checking It Twice

You can run a batch replacement against a live HTML page or a simple HTML page that you've dummied up with text strings. Let's start with a dummied page prepared with an ASCII text editor or a What You See Is What You Get (WYSIWYG) Web page design application, such as Adobe GoLive or PageMill, Macromedia Dreamweaver, or Microsoft FrontPage.

Set up the HTML file so that each chunk of text sits on its own line. Assign a consistent heading level (**<H1>**, **<H2>**, **<H3>**, **<H4>**, **<H5>**, or **<H6>**) or class attribute to each line, and then save the file. Each heading level or class attribute should match the one(s) specified via the Replace menu in LiveMotion's Web palette.

The text might look something like this:

```
<HTML>
<HEAD>
<TITLE>Dan's Pepper Patch</TITLE>
</HEAD>
<BODY>
<H1 ALIGN=RIGHT>Pick a Peck of Peppers!</H1>
<H6>Anaheim Chili</H6>
<H6>Cayenne</H6>
<H6>Datil</H6>
<H6>Habanero</H6>
<H6>Jalapeno</H6>
<H6>Scotch Bonnet</H6>
<H6>Thai Chili</H6>
</BODY>
</HTML>
```

You can also set up your text strings with the lines separated by **
** codes, like this:

```
<HTML>
<HEAD>
<TITLE>Dan's Pepper Patch</TITLE>
</HEAD>
<BODY>
<H1 ALIGN=RIGHT>Pick a Peck of Peppers!</H1>
```

Can I Replace More Than One Type of Graphic?

Of course. LiveMotion lets you render multiple batch replacements. Just don't let the individual looks overlap in the LiveMotion file, or you'll end up banging your head against the wall. Repeatedly.

```
<H6>Anaheim Chili<BR>
Cayenne<BR>
Datil<BR>
Habanero<BR>
Jalapeno<BR>
Scotch Bonnet<BR>
Thai Chili</H6>
</BODY>
</HTML>
```

What About Links?

You can add links either before or after you run the batch replacement. If the text is linked before you run the replacement, LiveMotion automatically links the graphics with the corresponding links. If the text isn't linked, you can link after running the batch—either manually or with a WYSIWYG Web page application.

When you separate the text-string lines with heading or class codes, the resulting graphics are individually tagged. Consequently, they're separated by horizontal space. If you separate the text strings with **
** codes between lines, the graphics will be stacked tight with no space. Figure 5.17 demonstrates the effects of each method. I coded the column on the left with individual heading tags and the column on the right with **
** codes between the lines.

Figure 5.17
Spaced out? If you want your buttons to stack without space, use **
** codes between the lines.

PROJECT Sit Back and Let LiveMotion Go to Work

Once you've created your look and saved the HTML file containing the tagged text strings, it's time to let LiveMotion do the cooking. Here's the chain of events:

1. Set the file format options with the Export palette.

2. Deselect the object.

3. Choose File|Batch Replace HTML to open the File Open dialog box.

4. Select the HTML file containing the tagged text strings and click on Open.

LiveMotion will parse the HTML file, create the images, and update the code to reflect the changes. When LiveMotion runs the batch replacement, it creates an images folder (if it doesn't already exist) within the folder where the original HTML file resides. The program places all the batch-generated graphics into this images folder.

In addition to updating the HTML code to include the new images, LiveMotion adds some extra code to the end of the file. The program also creates a backup of the original file with the .old file extension. Here's how the HTML code for the sample page appears after you run the batch replacement:

```
<HTML>
<HEAD>
<TITLE>Dan's Pepper Patch</TITLE>
</HEAD>
<BODY BGCOLOR="#ffffff">
<H1 ALIGN=RIGHT>Pick a Peck of Peppers!</H1>
<H6><IMG SRC="images/anaheim_chili.jpg" BORDER="0"
NAME="peppertest" ALT="Anaheim Chili"><BR><IMG SRC="images/
cayenne.jpg" BORDER="0" NAME="peppertest1" ALT="Cayenne"><BR>
<IMG SRC="images/datil.jpg" BORDER="0" NAME="peppertest2"
ALT="Datil"><BR><IMG SRC="images/habanero.jpg" BORDER="0"
NAME="peppertest3" ALT="Habanero"><BR><IMG SRC="images/
jalapeno.jpg" BORDER="0" NAME="peppertest4" ALT="Jalapeno">
<BR><IMG SRC="images/scotch_bonnet.jpg" BORDER="0" NAME=
"peppertest5" ALT="Scotch Bonnet"><BR><IMG SRC="images/
thai_chili.jpg" BORDER="0" NAME="peppertest6" ALT="Thai Chili">
</H6>

<!--Adobe(R) LiveMotion(TM) DataMap1.0 DO NOT EDIT
<?FPPI  ObjId="peppertest" IsOrigTag="H6"IsOrigText=
"Anaheim Chili" ?>
<?FPPI  ObjId="peppertest1" IsOrigTag="H6"IsOrigText=
"Cayenne" ?>
<?FPPI  ObjId="peppertest2" IsOrigTag="H6"IsOrigText=
"Datil" ?>
<?FPPI  ObjId="peppertest3" IsOrigTag="H6"IsOrigText=
"Habanero" ?>
<?FPPI  ObjId="peppertest4" IsOrigTag="H6"IsOrigText=
"Jalapeno" ?>
<?FPPI  ObjId="peppertest5" IsOrigTag="H6"IsOrigText=
"Scotch Bonnet" ?>
<?FPPI  ObjId="peppertest6" IsOrigTag="H6"IsOrigText=
"Thai Chili" ?>
end DataMap -->
</BODY>
</HTML>
```

Take a look at how the **<IMG SRC>** tags are created and how the individual graphic files are named. LiveMotion uses each text string as the basis for both the file name and the **ALT** text. The program assigns a border width of zero. It doesn't assign any image height or width attributes—in a moment, you'll see why this is extremely important.

LiveMotion embeds its **DataMap** information in the end of the HTML file for internal record keeping. Because this information is encased in a comment tag, it won't display in the browser (although anyone looking at the HTML source code for your pages will know that you use Adobe LiveMotion).

You can easily read the data at the end of the HTML file. It provides the details on each of the batch-replaced graphics:

- *ObjId*—The object identifier, which ties the **DataMap** string to the **<IMG SRC>** tag
- *IsOrigTag*—The original HTML heading or class tag
- *IsOrigText*—The original text string

Can I Go to Jail for This?

Have you ever torn the *DO NOT REMOVE UNDER PENALTY OF LAW* tag from a pillow or piece or furniture? Although the **DataMap** section carries a frightening *DO NOT EDIT* warning, there are times that you'll want to edit it.

Making Adjustments

Everything may not be rosy the first time you run a batch replacement. Certain text strings may be too large for their buttons. In general, you'll want to base the dimensions of your buttons on the longest line of text they will contain.

If you want to edit the text strings after you run the batch replacement, you'll need to open either the original HTML file (which LiveMotion saved with the .old file extension) or the HTML file that contains the graphic links (which LiveMotion created). Each time you rerun the batch replacement, LiveMotion creates a new backup (OLD) file. These backup files are numbered sequentially—the highest number indicates the most recent backup.

Here are some pointers on editing the HTML files:

- Editing the original file is straightforward. Simply change the .old file extension back to .htm or .html. (LiveMotion won't recognize files with other file extensions as valid HTML files.)

- Editing the file that contains the graphic links requires that you work with the extra code at the bottom of the HTML file, as mentioned earlier. This **DataMap** section tells LiveMotion how to handle any changes to existing graphics. To edit the text, you'll need to alter the

```
IsOrigText="Make Those Changes Here!"
```

section of each line. Note that this technique will change the graphics, but it will not change the ALT text strings to match the new text.

- Adding text strings is simple in either scenario. Just plug in the new text strings, enclosing them with the proper heading or class tags.

LiveMotion doesn't include any height or width attributes within the <IMG SRC> tags when it writes the HTML code to insert the batch images into the updated file—for a very good reason: If you were to alter the width or height of the look within LiveMotion, the changes would create havoc when you reran the batch. LiveMotion would generate the batch graphics with the new width or height, but the code embedded in the Web page would distort the graphics to fit the original dimensions.

Such distortion isn't usually a problem, because LiveMotion doesn't include height or width information within the tags. You will have a problem, however, if you open and save the generated HTML file with a WYSIWYG Web page editor, such as Adobe PageMill. The height and width attributes may be added as the page editor parses the code, looks at the graphics, and rewrites the <IMG SRC> tags. If you try to rerun the batch after PageMill has fiddled with the page, your graphics may end up being distorted in the browser—and that isn't a pretty sight.

Now that you have a basic understanding of how LiveMotion's batch-replacement scheme operates, let's look at how you might put it to work with the Batch Button Depot.

The Batch Button Depot

In this chapter, it's my distinct pleasure to present the *Batch Button Depot*—a repository of button examples and ideas for your dining, dancing, and Web-page-building pleasure. On the *Adobe LiveMotion f/x and Design* CD-ROM, you'll find LiveMotion and EPS files for the buttons I discuss in this section, and a whole lot more.

Let's start with the most basic buttons of all: simple rectangles.

Simple Rectangle Buttons

Purists and download speed demons love plain and simple buttons, like those shown in Figure 5.18. Export these buttons with just enough colors in the GIF palette to ensure that the text antialiases smoothly. Separate the text strings in the HTML file with heading commands, rather than <BR> commands, lest the graphics run together.

> **Can I Make Two-Line Batch Buttons?**
>
> Nope. LiveMotion can create only one-line buttons. The ability to create two-line batch buttons is on our wish list for version 2.

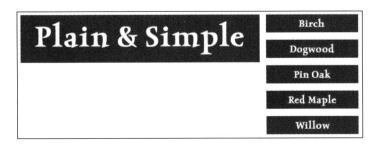

Figure 5.18
Simple rectangular buttons are the fastest route.

Outlined Rectangle Buttons

Outlined buttons, like those shown in Figure 5.19, are one step up from plain and simple buttons. Your buttons will take on a tad more definition when you add a second (rearward) layer with a width of +1 or +2. For the most pop, choose a color that contrasts with the first layer color. With an outlined design, you can use **
** commands between the text strings to stack the buttons tightly. (However, the horizontal rules between stacked buttons will appear twice as thick as the vertical rules—in such cases, it may be more appropriate to use a variation of the thin-rule button technique presented in the following pages.)

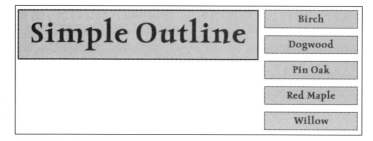

Figure 5.19
Outlined rectangular buttons stand out without frivolity.

Drop-Shadowed Text Buttons

Buttons with drop-shadowed text, like those shown in Figure 5.20, can be a simple and elegant solution. Set the drop-shadowed text on top of transparent rectangles to achieve precise horizontal and vertical spacing. The higher the X and Y shadow-layer offset, the more the text will appear to float above the surface of the page. Fiddle with the shadow layer's opacity and raise the softness setting to heighten the effect.

Figure 5.20
When they're done right, buttons with drop-shadowed text take on a soft, floating appearance.

Beveled Buttons

Here's where LiveMotion starts to work its 3D magic. The beveled buttons shown in Figure 5.21 are just a simple example. Try to keep the bevel depth relatively small, or you'll lose precious button-face real estate. Bevel highlights can be a bit overwhelming—add a second layer with a width of +1 or +2 for more definition.

Figure 5.21
Don't let those bevels get
too large.

Embossed Buttons

When compared to their beveled brethren, embossed buttons provide a softer, squishier look. The embossed buttons shown in Figure 5.22 provide a simple example. As with beveled buttons, try not to use too large an emboss depth or too high a softness setting. And again, a second layer with a width of +1 or +2 helps to better define the button edges.

Figure 5.22
Embossed buttons deliver a
softer look.

Cutout Buttons

Cutout buttons, like those shown in Figure 5.23, are often used in conjunction with beveled or embossed buttons to represent the pushed-down JavaScript **onMouseOver** state. Raise the softness setting to more closely emulate the embossed look. Chapter 4 covers the topic of JavaScript rollovers extensively.

Figure 5.23
When used in conjunction
with beveled rollover buttons,
cutout buttons call for lower
softness settings.

Thin-Rule Buttons

Thin-rule buttons provide another elegant solution that conserves bandwidth. I right-aligned the text in the example shown in Figure 5.24, but you can use whichever alignment method suits your needs. You can create thin-rule buttons several ways, but the fastest method uses a cutout. Set the color to match

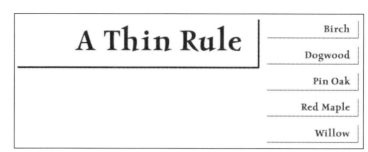

Figure 5.24

Try this technique on some
rounded-corner rectangles,
ellipses, polygons, or placed
EPS artwork.

the background and then apply the cutout with a depth of 2 and a softness of 0.
Set the light to dark only and the angle to 315 degrees. Bingo—instant rules!

If you want to create a thin-rule button the hard way, you can draw two skinny
rectangles—a long horizontal and a short vertical—and butt them at the bot-
tom-right corner. If you want to waste even more time, draw an outlined
rectangle and block out the top and left sides with two skinny rectangles. Take
it from me—the cutout method is the coolest route. Altering the depth, softness, and angle can yield attractive results, as well.

Gradient Buttons

Gradient buttons are another popular choice. The horizontal gradient buttons
shown in Figure 5.25 illustrate one example. I used a slight glow behind the
text (with a soft white layer) to help pop it from the gradient. (I did so only for
the purposes of this grayscale illustration.)

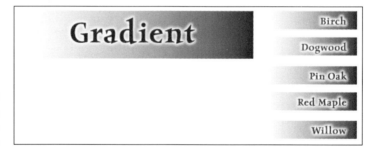

Figure 5.25

When enough contrast exists
between the gradient and the
text, the glow is optional.

Fast Metallic Buttons

The fast metallic example shown in Figure 5.26 builds on the basic gradient
button. It uses a bevel over a burst gradient (set at 90 degrees). A slight twirl
distortion adds movement to the highlight, and I added a soft white layer to
the text to give it a glow. (Be careful not to use too soft a glow.) Notice that the
buttons in Figure 5.26 aren't spaced evenly. This is the case because the descenders in the words *Dogwood* and *Maple* extend the bounding box, thereby
adding vertical (yet transparent) height to the images.

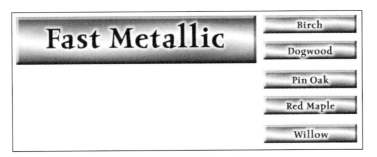

Figure 5.26
It's a virtual Fort Knox. Just don't put too much shine on it.

Jaggy Buttons

Placed EPS objects can lend a new dimension to your button work. Figure 5.27 demonstrates a modern prehistoric effect created with a jaggy EPS rectangle from the *Adobe LiveMotion f/x and Design* CD-ROM. A large emboss on the first layer and slightly smaller emboss on the second layer (which is four pixels wider) form an interesting gasket around the jaggy shape. A third layer adds a touch more definition to the gasket.

Take a gander back at Figure 5.15 for a slightly different take on the jaggy button look.

Figure 5.27
If Fred and Barney designed Web pages, they'd dig these jaggy buttons.

Firecracker Buttons

I dubbed these shapes *firecrackers*, for lack of a better name. The example shown in Figure 5.28 mates an EPS firecracker shape with a rounded rectangle. The firecracker shape uses a double-burst gradient and a twirl distortion on the first layer (shades of the fast metallic effect), along with a +2-pixel-wide, basic black second layer. The rounded rectangle uses the same double-burst gradient (without the twirl) and black second layer. A slightly offset white second layer creates an embossed appearance behind the text. You'll find quite a few firecracker and burst shapes on the *Adobe LiveMotion f/x and Design* CD-ROM.

Leaf back to Figure 5.17 for another variation on the firecracker look.

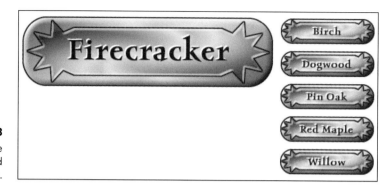

Figure 5.28
A firecracker shape lies at the heart of this pineapple-edged button.

Cigarband Buttons

The button shown in Figure 5.29 uses a curved EPS shape and a gradient-filled rectangle to create a metallic cigarband. Like the firecracker and fast metallic designs, this design uses burst gradients to create luminosity. The curved shape features a ripple-edged emboss, whereas the text uses a glow layer above and a shadow layer below. Together, these effects heighten the embossed foil appearance.

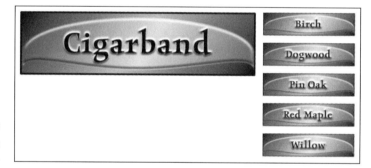

Figure 5.29
Fidel would never let these out of the country.

Doodle Buttons

Placed objects offer scores of opportunities for creative and unique buttons. The doodle button shown in Figure 5.30 is a simple example. If you can scan or create a shape, it can become a button.

Figure 5.30
When is a doodle a button? When it's a doodle button, of course.

Stupid Batch Tricks

After you've built your pages and initial batch graphics, the biggest gains come when you update existing pages. The trick lies in engineering your pages so you can quickly and easily update them. The methods you use will depend on the tools at hand. Here are some batch ideas to think about.

Comment Your Source

Want to make batch replacement easier? Begin by annotating your HTML source code. Although doing so isn't entirely necessary, you should consider adding <!—**COMMENT**—> tags before and after the major sections where the batch graphics reside (such as button bars). Annotations will help you easily find the section when you're scrolling through the code.

Easy Horizontal Button Bars

Here's a quick trick for those times when you want to batch-create a bunch of buttons in a horizontal bar. Set up the text strings as you would for a vertical button bar, with <**BR**> commands separating the lines. Run the batch replacement and then remove the <**BR**> commands with your text editor. Voilà—the vertical button bar turns into a horizontal bar. This trick works exceptionally well with a variation of the thin-rule (hard-edged cutout) button to delineate the individual buttons.

Batch Headings with a Kiss

You can use the batch-replacement feature to instantly build stylized page or section headings, such as the "Pick a Peck of Peppers" shown way back in Figure 5.15. Batch headings are best kept simple. Don't fall into the trap of creating too ornate a heading—keep things clean and straightforward.

Plain Old Text Works, Too

Although I've shown a good number of more involved examples, your buttons don't have to include anything other than styled text. Set the background, pick a distinctive typeface, tweak the typographic attributes, and let LiveMotion do the (unadorned) typesetting for you.

Image Maps

LiveMotion turns the creation of image maps into child's play. You can assign URLs to any object, shape, block of text, or group. The Web palette provides the means to specify the linked URL, the all-important **ALT** text tag, the frame target, and the file name (for sliced images). You'll need to expand the Web palette into Detail view to gain access to all of these options.

Open the button bar.liv composition you created in Chapter 1. (If you didn't save it, you can find a copy in the Chapter 1 folder on the *Adobe LiveMotion f/x and Design* companion CD-ROM.)

PROJECT Creating the Image Map

Here are step-by-step instructions to turn your button bar into an image map:

1. Select the products button. In the Web palette, enter the URL value "products.html" and the **ALT** value "Our Products".

2. Select the company button. In the Web palette, enter the URL value "company.html" and the **ALT** value "Our Company".

3. Select the support button. In the Web palette, enter the URL value "support.html" and the **ALT** value "Support You Can Depend On".

4. Select the contacts button. In the Web palette, enter the URL value "contacts.html" and the **ALT** value "Contact Us".

5. Select the partners button. In the Web palette, enter the URL value "partners.html" and the **ALT** value "Our Partners".

6. Select all the buttons and their text.

7. Group all the buttons and text by pressing Cmd/Ctrl+G.

8. Select the 520-by-35 rectangle. Use the Transform palette to set the width to 530.

9. Choose Object|Arrange|Send To Back to send the 530-by-35 rectangle to the back of the composition.

10. Hold down the Shift key and select the group of buttons.

11. Choose Object|Align|Centers to horizontally and vertically align the 530-by-35 rectangle with the group of buttons.

With a flat-color GIF graphic such as this, you can use just 16 colors to help minimize the size of the exported file. Select Active Export Preview in the Export palette to see the effects of fewer (and more) colors. Try turning the Dithering option on and off to see how it changes the quality of the image and size of the file. The Transparency option is insignificant in this case, because this is a totally rectangular composition. (If the light gray rectangle had rounded corners, you'd want to select the Transparency option.) Either the Entire Composition or Trimmed Composition export will work for this artwork, because you don't need to slice the image. Select Make HTML in the Composition Settings dialog box to have LiveMotion create a complete HTML page.

Go ahead and export the file now. Then, open up the HTML file with a text editor to have a look at the image map code—it's not that hard to understand, but it sure is nice not to have to hack it out by hand. Note that the **IMG SRC** command calls the GIF image and tells the browser which map to use. The individual hotspot definitions describe the shape, size, and coordinates of the hotspot, along with the

HREF link and **ALT** text. It's more than polite to include **ALT** text within an image map. With the newer version browsers (version 4 and higher), the **ALT** text is displayed as a definition when the cursor passes over the hotspot. Don't overlook the **ALT** tags.

The Trimmed Composition method works well when you're exporting small compositions. You can also select portions of a (larger) composition and use File|Export Selection to export just those pieces. When your designs grow more complex, you'll graduate to the AutoSlice and AutoLayout methods.

Moving On

LiveMotion's object-clumping methodology is one of the program's most daunting traits. In order to take total control over your compositions, you need to understand how clumping affects image exports. As such, this chapter has provided you with much of the knowledge you'll need to slice and dice with the pros. LiveMotion's powerful batch image-creation capabilities are an incredible timesaver. Once you've mastered its subtle nuances, the batch replacement function will supercharge your Web graphics productivity.

The next chapter introduces the topic of animation. Get your soda and popcorn, the movie's about to begin!

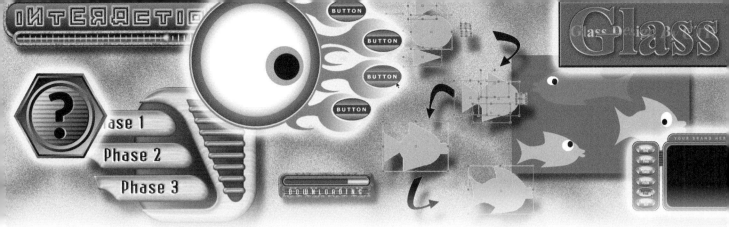

Chapter 6

LiveMotion
Animation Basics

*This chapter introduces the Timeline and touches on the
topics of Time Independent Groups and GIF animation.*

Meet the Timeline

Ready to put your designs into motion? In this chapter, you'll learn about the basics of LiveMotion's Timeline-based animation functions. The *Timeline* provides a treasure chest of animation features. Unlock its mysteries and you'll gain access to a world of possibilities. Make no bones about it; the Timeline *is* mysterious to the uninitiated. The more familiar it becomes, however, the better you'll fare as a budding animator. And if you're already familiar with LiveMotion's big brother, AfterEffects, you have a big leg up—the LiveMotion Timeline is largely inspired by the AfterEffects Timeline.

LiveMotion delivers *keyframe-based* animation on an object attribute basis, allowing each attribute of an object to be animated over time. This allows for the highest levels of control. The occurrence of each attribute change (the keyframe) is shown in the Timeline, whereas the specific change to the attribute is shown in the pertinent palette. When you see a diamond appear in one of the attribute timelines of an object, you'll know that *something* has changed. You'll have to look at the pertinent palette to see exactly *what* has changed.

Subsequent chapters focus largely on the creation of Flash (SWF) files. This chapter starts with the simple stuff—things that relate to animation in any format—before it covers the topics of animated GIFs and nested animation.

The Timeline Interface

Let's take a close look at the Timeline in order to put a name to each piece of its user interface. Figure 6.1 provides an annotated view of the Timeline of an empty composition. At the top left, you'll see the current time and VCR controls, followed by the Composition/Object menu. The Behaviors timeline sits between the Composition and Object listing. (Click on the Edit Behaviors button to add a timeline behavior with the Edit Behaviors dialog box.)

Moving to the bottom of the Timeline window, you'll find the Loop and Lifetime buttons at the bottom left side. When the Loop button is depressed, the animation of the selected Timeline Independent Group(s) or composition will loop continuously (click the Loop button again to turn off looping). Clicking the Lifetime button will extend an object lifetime to the full composition length (click the Lifetime button again to retract the object lifetime).

At the bottom center of the Timeline window, the Time Zoom controls provide the ability to display more (or less) of the animation's frames in the Timeline window. Push the Time Zoom slider all the way to the left, and the Timeline will display only seconds. Push the Time Zoom slider to the right, and it will display both seconds and frames. (You can also use the Time Zoom Up and Down buttons on either side of the slider.)

Navigation through time and elements is straightforward. The horizontal and vertical scrollbars allow you to scroll through a composition's duration and

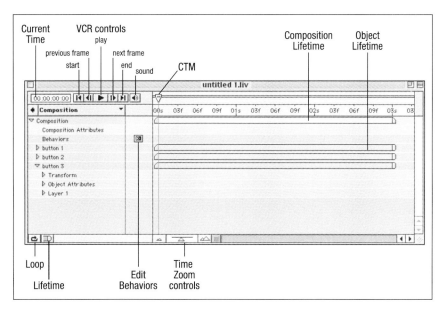

Figure 6.1
An empty Timeline with the composition selected.

objects, respectively. The widget that slides along the top of the Timeline is known as the Current Time Marker (CTM). The vertical red line that extends downward from the CTM allows you to pinpoint the time for each attribute.

Adding an Object

When an object is added to the composition, it appears in the Timeline with a starting point at the current time. The object's duration automatically extends to the end of the composition. New objects are added to the top of the stack of objects. (You can alter object order via Object|Arrange.) Objects are automatically named by attribute or placed file name, as shown in Figure 6.2.

When an object is first added to a composition, the object's attributes are not immediately displayed in the Timeline. To display an object's attributes, click on the twist-down arrow (or *twisty*) to the left of the object. The Timeline will then display entries for Transform, Object Attributes, and object layers (in this case, just Layer 1). Click on the Transform, Object Attributes, or Layer twisties to gain access to the individual characteristics, as shown in Figure 6.3.

Renaming Objects

To rename an object, select the object in the Timeline and press Enter to summon the Name dialog box (or select Timeline|Edit Name). Type a custom name in the text field and click on OK.

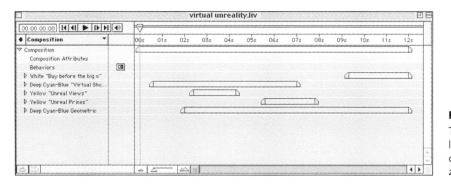

Figure 6.2
The order of objects in the Timeline reflects the object stacking order (often referred to as the *z-order*) in the composition.

> **What's Hiding under the Twisties?**
>
> The twisties conceal a raft of information. Here's a rundown of where you'll find the various attributes:
>
> - *Transform attributes*—Includes Position, Object Opacity, Rotation, Skew, and Scale.
> - *Object attributes*—Includes Replace, Outline Width, Corner Radius, Anchor Point, Shape, and Crop.
> - *Layer attributes*—Includes Color, Gradient (including start and end), Distortion, Object Layer Opacity, 3D Effects (including Type, Depth, Softness, Angle, Edge, Lighting, and Lighting Type), Texture, Offset, Width, and Softness.

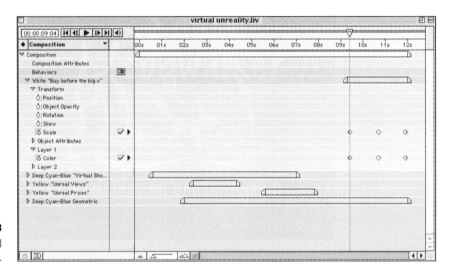

Figure 6.3

Turn down the twisties to reveal the hidden attributes.

LiveMotion tries to keep Timeline clutter to a minimum. Certain characteristics will not be displayed in the Timeline until they've been altered from their default settings. This is most evident in the Layer attributes, where only the Color is displayed at first.

Setting a Keyframe

To set a keyframe, do the following:

1. Select the object.

2. Turn down the applicable twisty to gain access to the attribute you wish to animate.

3. Set the CTM to the time where you want the first keyframe to be set, then, click on the stopwatch button to the left of the attribute you wish to animate. When you click the stopwatch, a checkmark will appear to the right of the attribute and a diamond will appear in the Timeline at the current time.

You *must* set the first keyframe for each attribute (that you wish to animate) with this method—all of the subsequent keyframes for the attribute will be set automatically.

Tweening

LiveMotion's keyframe-based animation function will automatically create *tweens* of most object attributes. These "in-between" objects allow for the smooth transition between object size, color, opacity, and many other attributes.

Unfortunately, LiveMotion does not tween the actual object shapes (other than scaling and the like). Instead, you'll have to rely on manual techniques. The following chapters demonstrate a number of methods for more intricate character animation.

Setting Additional Keyframes

Although LiveMotion sets additional keyframes automatically—when an attribute is changed—sometimes you'll want to manually set an additional keyframe without changing the attribute. This is often the case when you want to prevent *tweening* over a period of time.

Table 6.1 lists five handy keyboard shortcuts to create specific keyframes.

Table 6.1 New keyframe keyboard shortcuts.

New Keyframe	Shortcut
Anchor Point	Option/Alt+Shift+A
Opacity	Option/Alt+Shift+T
Position	Option/Alt+Shift+P
Rotation	Option/Alt+Shift+R
Scale	Option/Alt+Shift+S

Moving between Keyframes

You can move between keyframes in a number of ways. The most obvious is to simply drag the CTM to the specific time on the Timeline. Once a number of keyframes have been set for an attribute, you can pop between keyframes with the attribute keyframe arrow buttons.

Two handy keyboard shortcuts are available to move to the previous and next keyframes, on a per-object basis:

• To move to the previous keyframe, press Option/Alt+K.

• To move to the next keyframe, press Option/Alt+J.

Let's put the Timeline to work in a quick little project.

PROJECT The Bouncing Ball—Animating Position, Size, and...

In this exercise, you'll see how easy it is to animate object position, size, and other attributes by creating a bouncing ball. The exercise will begin with a simple object position animation before altering the object size:

1. Start out by creating a new composition (File|New).

2. In the Composition Settings dialog box, set the Width to 400 pixels and Height to 300 pixels. Select a Frame Rate of 12, then set Export to Entire Composition, select Make HTML, and click on OK.

3. Open the Timeline window with Ctrl/Cmd+T. Drag the composition time end (right) handle to 03s. This sets the composition time to three seconds.

4. Select the Ellipse tool, then draw a 70-by-70-pixel ellipse at the lower left corner of the composition. (Hold down the Shift key to constrain the ellipse to a perfect circle.) Select a medium blue (R153, G153, B255) from the Color palette.

5. Press V to return to the Selection tool.

6. In the Timeline, set the CTM to 00s, turn down the Medium Blue Ellipse twisty and the Transform twisty, then, click on the Position stopwatch. This sets a position keyframe at 0 seconds. The ball will begin its trajectory from this position (X: 20 Y: 220), as shown in Figure 6.4.

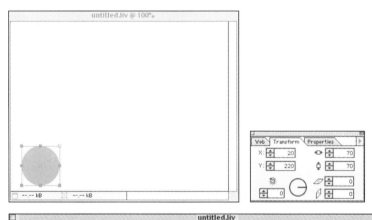

Figure 6.4

The ball at its starting position. Note the Timeline and Transform palette.

7. Move the CTM to 06f. Select the medium blue ellipse in the composition and drag it upward and slightly to the right (X: 90 Y: 35).

8. What comes up must come down. Move the CTM to 01s. Drag the medium blue ellipse downward and slightly to the right (X: 160 Y: 220).

    At this point, the ball has completed one bounce. You can preview the action with the Play button on the Timeline. (Set the animation back to the starting point—00s—by clicking on the Rewind button [at the far left] or by dragging the CTM.) When the animation plays, the medium blue ellipse will bounce once, then sit at X: 160 Y: 220 for the duration of the animation.

    In the following steps, you'll set up two more bounces—one more to the right and one back to the left. The ending bounce will place the ball at the exact starting point of motion path. As you move the CTM from frame to frame, try setting the object position with the Transform palette, rather than dragging the object.

> **Motion Path Preview**
>
> To see the motion path, select View|Preview Motion Path. LiveMotion will show a trail of little blue breadcrumbs for each selected object.

9. Move the CTM to 01s 06f. Drag the medium blue ellipse upwards and slightly to the right (X: 230 Y: 70).

10. Move the CTM to 02s. Drag the medium blue ellipse downward and slightly to the right (X: 300 Y: 220).

11. Move the CTM to 02s 06f. Drag the medium blue ellipse upwards and to the left (X: 160 Y: 130).

12. Move the CTM to 03s. Drag the medium blue ellipse downward and to the left (X: 20 Y: 220). Figure 6.5 shows the completed motion path.

    Try previewing the animation again, this time using the VCR Play button. The ball should bounce twice to the right, and then back once to the left. In the next section, you'll animate the size of the ball, making it appear as if it's bouncing first into the distance, then forward.

13. With the medium blue ellipse still selected, move the CTM to 00s, then, click on the Scale stopwatch to set a keyframe.

14. Move the CTM to 02s, then, set the medium blue ellipse's width and height to 40 with the Transform palette. This will make the ball smaller as it appears to bounce into the background.

15. Move the CTM to 03s, then, set the medium blue ellipse's width and height back to 70 with the Transform palette. This will make the ball larger as it appears to bounce back into the foreground.

16. Save the file (Cmd/Ctrl+S) as bouncingball.liv. You'll reuse it at the end of this chapter.

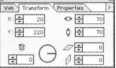

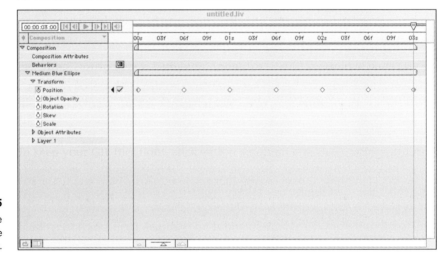

Figure 6.5
The larger blue squares in the motion path denote the keyframes.

Figure 6.6
Position, Scale, and Opacity animations are often used in countdown intros.

Take another look at your handiwork with the VCR Play button. You've created a simple position and scale animation. Try animating some additional attributes, such as color and opacity. These are the building blocks of many common animations. Figure 6.6 provides one such example, and you'll find other examples on this book's companion CD-ROM.

Creating GIF Animation

Much of the buzz that swirls around LiveMotion is focused on the program's ability to create animated Flash files. It's easy to overlook that LiveMotion is very competent in the creation of good old animated GIFs. As cool as the Flash format is, animated GIFs are going to be with us for a long, long time. LiveMotion adds a wealth of possibilities to your animated GIF repertoire.

When I worked with Adobe to develop the tutorials that come with the original Adobe LiveMotion CD-ROM, I made sure to include a simple animated GIF banner exercise. (If you haven't checked out those original Adobe exercises, you should. Take a look in LiveMotion's Training/Exercises folder.) In the following section, I'll lay out some techniques you can use to create animated GIF banners with LiveMotion.

Planning GIF Animations

Great little GIF animations take careful planning. You want to pack the maximum amount of punch into the minimum number of frames and the smallest file possible. Whereas Flash animations can indulge in smooth movement and fades, GIF files deliver their impact primarily through sharp transitions. And unlike the JPEG format, the GIF format isn't well-suited to display deeply colored textures and crisp photographs. With GIF, big, bold, and basic gets the nod.

Here are some pointers for LiveMotion GIF animations:

• *Set the exact size*—Use the Composition Settings dialog box to create your GIF animation at its exact height and width. Be sure to select Entire Composition from the Export menu.

• *Limit the number of colors in the composition*—Don't go hog wild with a huge range of colors. Using LiveMotion's Color Scheme feature helps you to create a tight complementary set of colors.

• *Aim for large areas of contiguous color*—The larger the area, the smaller the resulting GIF file.

• *Convey the feeling of motion in a concise manner*—GIF animations don't offer the luxury of SWF animations; you can't provide the illusion of movement over a large number of frames. Instead, try to create the effect with just a frame or two.

• *Use the least number of frames*—It's all about file size and download time. Keep your GIF animations to a bare bones minimum number of frames. Plan your keyframes carefully.

Exporting GIF Animations

The Export palette's Frame Rate menu has a Keyframes Only option that's well suited to the creation of animated GIFs. When you select Keyframes Only, LiveMotion will export just the keyframes—without any tweened frames. When properly executed, this results in a nice, tight export. Other Frame Rate options will export frame-for-frame. You definitely don't want to export your GIF animations frame-for-frame—the resulting file would be far too large.

Here are some additional animated GIF export pointers:

• *Use the Web Adaptive palette*—Don't let your colors dither in the browser.

• *Reduce the number of exported colors*—This goes hand in hand with limiting the number of colors in the composition itself. Use the Export palette's Colors slider to dial the number of colors down as far as possible. With the Preview option selected, you'll be able to get a feel for what's happening before you export. Use File|Preview In to see exactly how the exported file will appear.

- *Use transparency only if you must*—And you'll avoid the possibilities of fringed and jaggy edges. And most importantly, always render the animation on the same color background as it will appear on the Web page.

- *Avoid dithering*—The less you have to dither, the tighter the resulting exports. If you must dither, consider doing so on an object-by-object basis.

- *Don't interlace*—Whereas interlacing is cool for static graphics, it's usually not desirable for animated graphics. The underwater effect just doesn't cut it.

PROJECT Creating an Animated GIF Banner

Let's create an extremely simple animated GIF banner that applies some of the principles covered previously. As you build the banner, notice how few keyframes you'll have to set:

1. Create a new composition (File|New).

2. In the Composition Settings dialog box, set the Width to 468 pixels and Height to 60 pixels. Select Entire Composition from the Export menu, and set the Frame Rate to 8. Select Make HTML and click on OK.

3. Select the Document Background Color on the toolbox, and select black from the Color palette.

4. Select the Current Fill Color on the toolbox, and select a medium orange (R255, G204, B102) from the Color palette.

5. Select the Text tool and click in the middle of the composition to summon the Text dialog box. Type "All That Glitters" in the text field. Set the type size to 36 point Helvetica Bold (or a similar sans-serif typeface, such as Arial), set the tracking to 5, and the alignment to horizontal center. Click on OK. Press V to switch to the Selection tool and position the text in the middle of the composition.

6. Open the Timeline (Cmd/Ctrl+T). Drag out the composition time to 07s.

7. Turn down the twisty next to "All That Glitters", then, turn down the Object Attributes twisty. With the CTM set to 00s, click on the stopwatch next to Text. This sets a Text keyframe at 00s.

8. Move the CTM to 02s. In the composition window, double-click on "All That Glitters" to summon the Text dialog box. Replace the text with "Isn't Gold" and click on OK. This automatically sets a Text keyframe at 02s. Note that the object's name changes in the Timeline.

9. Move the CTM to 04s. In the composition window, double-click on "Isn't Gold" to summon the Text dialog box. Replace the text with "sometimes..." and click on OK. This automatically sets a Text keyframe at 04s. Once again, the object's name changes in the Timeline.

10. Drag the "sometimes…" end time handle to 05s. This makes the text disappear at the five-second mark.

11. Move the CTM to 05s. In the composition window, double-click on "sometimes…" to summon the Text dialog box. Replace the text with "…" and click on OK. (This sets one last keyframe for the text block.)

12. With the CTM still at 05s, select the Rectangle tool and draw a rectangle 468 pixels wide by 60 pixels high. Select a pale blue (R204, G204, B255) from the Color palette. Use the Transform palette to position the rectangle at X: 234 Y: 0. (You'll probably want to use the Transform palette to set the object size before setting the position.)

13. In the Timeline, turn down the twisty next to the Pale Blue Rectangle, then, turn down the Transform twisty. Click on the stopwatch next to Position; this sets a Position keyframe at 05s.

14. Move the CTM to 05s 01f (one frame over). With the Pale Blue Rectangle still selected, type "0" in the Transform palette's X field and press Enter.

15. Select the Text tool and click in the middle of the composition to summon the Text dialog box. Type "It's Silver" in the text field. Set the type size to 30 point Helvetica Bold Oblique (or a similar sans-serif typeface, such as Arial Bold Italic), set the tracking to 5, and the alignment to horizontal center. Click on OK. Select black from the Color palette, and position the text in the middle of the composition. The Timeline should appear as shown in Figure 6.7.

16. Save the file (Cmd/Ctrl+S) with the name "allthatbanner.liv". Preview the composition with the Preview tool.

17. At the Export palette, start by selecting GIF from the drop-down menu. Then, make sure that the Transparency, Dithering, and Interlacing options are not chosen, and select Preview. Set the Frame Rate to Keyframes Only.

18. Next, move the Colors slider to the left until you can see a visible degradation in image quality. As you move the Colors slider, watch the edges of the text. Drag the CTM around to preview different frames. You should be able to set this simple animation to 16 colors or so. Try turning the dithering option on and off.

Use the File|Preview In feature to test your composition before exporting. This is a fairly simple composition. Figure 6.8 shows the animation's keyframes. You may want to try some variations in timing and transitions.

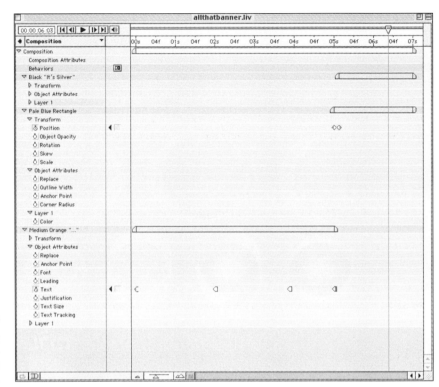

Figure 6.7
Synchronize the keyframes in your GIF animations—as at 05s—to keep the number of frames to a minimum.

Figure 6.8
GIF animations use a minimum number of frames for maximum impact.

GIF Banner Ad Pointers

The most effective GIF animations are the result of careful planning, diligent execution, precise timing, and a big dollop of creative genius. Although the same could be said for any kind of animation, the GIF medium is ultra-restrictive in terms of file size and creative effects.

More with Less

GIF banners need to be very tight little files. Most of the Internet advertising networks provide tight restrictions on banner file size. Stuffing all you can into just 12K (or so) can prove to be a daunting task. Going large is not an option. If you use photographic images, they should be limited to a fraction of the animation area. The Posterize function (on the Adjust palette) can help to reduce the number of colors in a photographic image, allowing for the maximum amount of compression.

Ad Banner and Button Sizes

In the bad old days of the Web, no standards existed for ad banner sizes. Each Web site dictated what it thought were appropriate sizes. This lack of guidelines led to many wrinkled brows, because banner sizes weren't consistent from site to site. Thankfully, the Internet Advertising Bureau (IAB) and the Coalition for Advertising Supported Information and Entertainment (CASIE) jointly developed a set of voluntary standards for advertising banners, thus ending the confusion. Table 6.2 lists these common sizes.

Easy on the Cheese

Every seasoned designer has a flaming rotating logo story to tell. You know, the one where the client wanted a ridiculously cheesy animation or piece of artwork—much to the designer's dismay. When I worked in print design, my favorite adage was, "The client is always right, especially when they're wrong." This went hand in hand with my next favorite, "The client never knows what they want, until you give them exactly what they ask for."

As designers, it's our responsibility to temper the client's enthusiasm and lack of sophistication with our expertise and real-world aesthetics. They're going to ask for cheese—no, they're going to *insist* on cheese. But there's cheese, and then there's *cheese*. It's our role to make sure that the client doesn't end up with the Limburger.

Table 6.2 IAB/CASIE standard ad banner sizes.

Ad Type	Size (in pixels)
Full banner	468x60
Full banner with vertical navigation bar	392x72
Half banner	234x60
Vertical banner	120x240
Button 1	120x90
Button 2	120x60
Square button	125x125
Micro button	88x31

Nested Animation—Time Independent Groups

TIGs and Interactivity

Time Independent Groups (TIGs) aren't just for cartooning. They're an essential part of LiveMotion's ability to create interactive interfaces. By nature, every rollover is a TIG—functioning independently of the composition timeline.

LiveMotion allows for *nested animation* (animation within animation) through *Time Independent Groups*. Why would you want to create nested animations? Let's say that your animated scene is a living room. While the main action takes place with the actors in the foreground, a nested fish tank animation might be off to the side. As your actors play out the scene, the fish are happily swimming back and forth in their tank, as shown in Figure 6.9. The fish tank is a nested animation (in LiveMotion's terminology, a Time Independent Group).

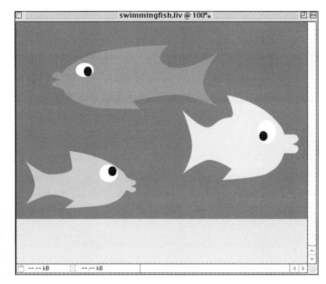

Figure 6.9
Time Independent Groups often nest within each other. This allows for highly complex animations.

Creating a Nested Animation

To create a nested animation, select the object or group of objects, then, select Timeline|Make Time Independent Group. A checkmark will appear next to the Time Independent entry in the Timeline menu, and a Time Independent icon will also appear in the group's Timeline listing. (You can rename the group to your liking by selecting it in the Timeline. Press Enter and rename the group with the Name dialog box.)

Editing a Nested Animation

To edit a Time Independent Group, double-click on it in the Timeline. The Timeline will change to show only the objects within the group. Select individual elements within the group (right from the Timeline) and make alterations to their attributes. To switch the Timeline back to Composition display, click on the left facing arrow button or select Composition from the flyout menu (next to the arrow button).

Looping a Nested Animation

Many times, you'll want a nested animation to loop continuously, so that it plays over and over. To loop a Time Independent Group, simply select the group, then, select Timeline|Loop (or click on the Loop button at the lower left corner of the Timeline). Once a Time Independent Group is set to loop, it will loop continuously throughout its lifetime.

PROJECT Creating a Swimming Fish (Using a Time Independent Group)

In this project, you'll apply a motion path to a vector-drawn fish. You'll start by drawing the fish using LiveMotion's Combine features and Pen Selection tool. You'll turn him into a Time Independent Group and shrink him down before adding the motion path.

Drawing the Fish

This project is a confidence builder—even if you have no drawing skills, whatsoever. By combining objects, you'll quickly create a rough fish shape. Fine-tuning with the Pen Selection tool will enable you to create a gorgeous aquatic creature. A word of advice: don't go for perfection—just have fun.

1. Create a new composition (File|New).

2. In the Composition Settings dialog box, set the Width to 500 pixels and Height to 400 pixels. Select a Frame Rate of 12, then, set Export to Entire Composition, select Make HTML, and click on OK.

3. Select the Polygon tool, then, draw a 100-by-100-pixel polygon at the left side of the composition. (Hold down the Shift key to constrain the polygon to symmetrical proportions.) Use the Properties palette to make the new polygon a triangle (set the Sides slider to 3). Select a green (R51, G255, B51) from the Color palette.

4. Select the Ellipse tool, then, draw a 125-pixel wide by 100-pixel high ellipse in the center of the composition.

5. Select the Rounded Rectangle tool, then, draw a 30-pixel wide by 15-pixel high rounded corner rectangle at the right side of the composition. Set the Radius slider (on the Properties palette) to 20. Duplicate the rounded corner rectangle (Cmd/Ctrl+D) and drag the duplicate just below the original. The pieces should appear as in Figure 6.10.

6. Draw a couple of fins with the Polygon tool. Drag everything together as shown in Figure 6.11.

Looping an Entire Composition

To loop an entire composition, select Composition in the Timeline, and then, click on the Loop button at the lower left corner of the Timeline. This is most often used with compositions that are to be exported as animated GIF files.

174 Chapter 6

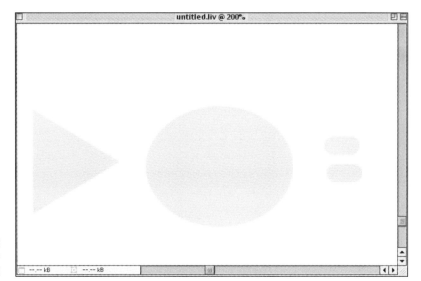

Figure 6.10
This is going to make a fish? Just wait!

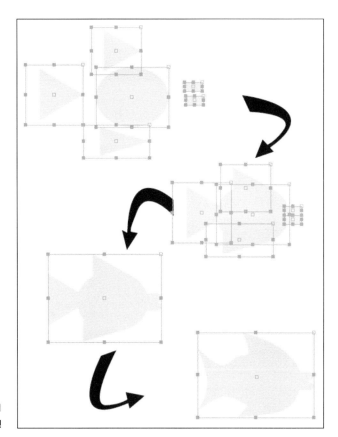

Figure 6.11
That's a good bit more fishy!

7. Select all of the pieces (Cmd/Ctrl+A), then, select Object|Combine|Unite. This fuses all of the objects into one single vector object.

8. With the new object selected, select the Pen Selection tool and use it to reshape the fish. Push and pull at the barnacles to get a nice smooth fishy shape.

9. Use the Ellipse tool to add an eye to the fish. Create two ellipses: The back-most ellipse will be white, and the top (pupil) will be black. Position the pupil at the lower left side of the eye, and take note of its X and Y position in the Transform palette.

Animate the Fish Eye

Next, you'll animate the fish eye and turn it into a Time Independent Group. It's not a complicated animation—just a handful of frames, with the pupil darting back and forth—nonetheless, it should be enough to give you an idea of what you can do with nested animation:

1. Open the Timeline (Cmd/Ctrl+T). Extend the composition time end handle to 02s.

2. Turn down the twisty next to "Black Ellipse", then, turn down the Object Attributes twisty. With the CTM set to 00s, click on the stopwatch next to Position. This sets a Position keyframe at 00s.

3. Move the CTM to 01s. Use the cursor keys to nudge the "Black Ellipse" to the top right corner of the fish eye. A Position keyframe will automatically be set.

4. Move the CTM to 02s. Use the Transform palette to put the "Black Ellipse" back at the lower left corner of the fish eye (use the same exact coordinates as 00s). A Position keyframe will automatically be set.

5. Select all three of the objects (Cmd/Ctrl+A). Group the objects (Cmd/Ctrl+G). Turn the group into a Time Independent Group by pressing Shift+Cmd/Ctrl+G.

6. Select "Group of 1 objects" (the fish) in the Timeline. Press Enter to summon the Name dialog box. Rename it "The Fish" and click on OK.

7. Click on the Loop button at the lower left corner of the Timeline. This turns The Fish into a looping Time Independent Group. The pupil will dart back and forth continuously.

If you're feeling ambitious, you can add some additional items, such as bubbles, to the group.

Create a Motion Path for the Entire Group

Use the technique you learned earlier in the chapter (in the Bouncing Ball project) to assign a motion path to the entire (fish) group. Make the fish swim from the left side of the composition to the right side. Then, try taking it a step further, and have the fish swim from off-screen left to off-screen right.

If you'd like to make the fish swim continuously, make it a Time Independent Group (a second time) and loop again.

Moving On

This chapter provided an easy introduction to the LiveMotion Timeline and the topics of GIF animation and Time Independent Groups (nested animations). As you become more familiar with LiveMotion's keyframe-based animation capabilities, the possibilities will unfold like a magical map. The next chapter goes full-bore into the topic of Flash and SWF file creation.

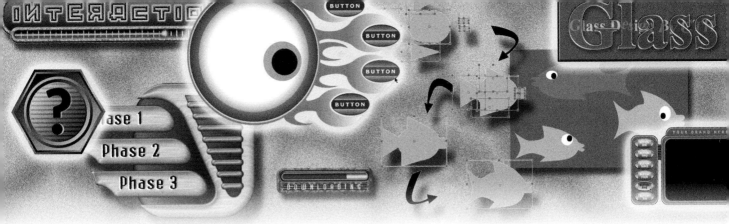

Chapter 7

SWF Animation Basics

With the Flash plug-in loaded in the client's browser,
you can deliver an engrossing environment far beyond
what's possible with HTML and JavaScript.

Why Flash?

At some point, HTML and JavaScript just became, oh so last century. The Flash file format changed the game in interactive Web page design. But is this it? Is Flash the future of Web design technology? Or is it just another step along the way?

Flash was originally known as *FutureSplash Animator*. In early 1997, FutureSplash was purchased by Macromedia, which relaunched the product as Macromedia Flash. Macromedia wisely saw the value in an Internet-targeted, vector-based animation format. At the time, developers could only dream of a fast way to deliver animation and interactivity.

Although Macromedia had made significant progress transforming Director, their flagship product, into a Web tool (with Shockwave), the marketing push couldn't disguise the fact that bitmaps just weren't the way to go for fast downloads and instant interactivity. To a certain extent, the move to vector graphics on the Web world echoed what happened more than a decade earlier in the print world, when Adobe released Illustrator. Smaller, faster, and scaleable were the battle cries then, as they are now. Then, as now, the vector zealots trumpeted the advantages of designing with objects, rather than with pixels.

Justifying Flash

Once your clients or coworkers have seen their first great Flashed page, they'll be hooked. No longer will they be satisfied by mere HTML pages; they'll just have to have Flash. This puts a lot of responsibility on you as the designer. Your creations must please their palettes, as they serve their needs. (What they *think* they want isn't always what they *need*.) You have to temper the desire to build a way cool Flash site with the reality of what ultimately works best.

Adoption Rate

Macromedia press releases happily boast of the Flash plug-ins extraordinarily high adoption rate. Although the Flash plug-in *is* extremely popular, and has been bundled with major browsers for some time, it's not loaded in every browser. And more importantly, the latest version of the plug-in may not be loaded. The version is crucial.

LiveMotion creates Flash 4 format files. This means that the SWF files created by LiveMotion may not play (or play properly) on computers that are equipped with older versions of the Flash plug-in. For this reason, it's a good idea to install browser-sniffing code to see which version of the plug-in is loaded. If the current version isn't loaded, you can give folks the choice to download it. (This is discussed further in Chapter 9.)

What About SVG?

When LiveMotion was in development—and just a rumor, code-named "Ground Zero"—the buzz had it that the program would be a *Scalable Vector Graphic* (SVG) animation tool. That rumor turned out to be a bit premature. Although this first version of LiveMotion doesn't export SVG compositions, it's safe to say that a future version will. SVG export wasn't included in LiveMotion 1.0 for one basic reason—the SVG specification had yet to be finalized.

LiveMotion is not a one-trick pony. From the start, Adobe's marketing thrust has brought to light that SWF file export is just one of the program's export formats. LiveMotion isn't tied entirely to Flash. When the SVG format is finalized by the World Wide Web Consortium (WC3), there's good reason to believe that LiveMotion will be poised to deliver support.

For more information on SVG, see: **www.w3.org/Graphics/SVG/**

Delivering the Difference

When you fire up LiveMotion to create a SWF file, keep in mind that great Flashed pages and ornaments do what can't be done—or done well—with HTML and JavaScript. If you can do what you need to do with a simple animated GIF, perhaps that's what you should use. Let's take a look at some of the reasons you'll want to use the Flash format:

Adobe Illustrator Does SVG

Illustrator 9, which shipped slightly after LiveMotion, *does* support the SVG standard. In addition, Illustrator 9 exports in the SWF format.

- *Advanced animation*—Looking to build a Saturday morning television-caliber cartoon? Need to create a compelling product demo? LiveMotion puts you in the director's chair.

- *Sound*—Want your rollovers to produce an audible click? Need to add a soundtrack or sound effects to your composition? LiveMotion lets you incorporate a range of sound files.

- *Interactivity*—Want to create an environment, rather than a simple animation? Need to go past simple rollovers? LiveMotion can deliver basic interactivity through the use of *behaviors* (which are covered in depth in the next chapter).

Common Animation Techniques

LiveMotion's Timeline-based approach allows you to create impressive animations with a minimum of hassle. The Flash file format is infinitely more flexible than the animated GIFs you may be accustomed to working with. With SWF, you can use smooth multi-frame transitions that mimic traditional animation, rather than Spartan GIF techniques that use a frame or two to *imply* motion.

Let's take a look at some typical Flash animation techniques. As you work through the following examples, notice how they work backward—setting the ending keyframe first. This is a common procedure. The instructions in this section demonstrate how to sequentially build an animation effect. Once you've built the effect, you can save it to the Style palette for reuse at a later time.

Scaling Techniques

The bouncing ball project in Chapter 6 provided a taste of scaling animation. As the ball bounced twice to the right, it shrunk—creating the illusion that the ball was moving away from the viewer. As the ball made the big bounce back to the left, it grew—making it appear as if it was moving toward the viewer. Not that many animations use bouncing balls, but plenty of them use similar scaling techniques to zoom text and objects into and out of the composition. Figure 7.1 shows a handful of frames from a typical scaled text animation.

Figure 7.1
This text scaling animation plays back in one second.

PROJECT Animating Scale

Here's the step-by-step for a simple animated scale:

1. Open the Timeline and set the Current Time Marker (CTM) to the ending frame of the scaled animation.

2. Select the object to scale, turn down its twisty in the Timeline, and then, turn down the Transform twisty.

3. Click on the stopwatch next to Scale to set the ending keyframe.

4. Set the final size of the object, if necessary, by scaling with the Selection tool (or with the Transform palette).

5. Set the CTM to the starting frame of the scaled animation.

6. Set the initial size of the Object palette by scaling with the Selection tool (or with the Transform palette). Figure 7.2 shows the Timeline with the starting and ending Scale keyframes.

> ### Another Way to Animate Text Scaling
>
> You can also animate the scale of Text objects by setting Text Size keyframes. You'll find the Text Size attribute under the Object Attributes twisty.

Figure 7.2
One keyframe makes you larger, one keyframe makes you smaller.

Opacity Techniques

LiveMotion provides control over two different types of opacity—Object Opacity and Object Layer Opacity. *Object Opacity* affects the entire object, whereas *Object Layer Opacity* affects individual layers. You should use Object Opacity settings when working with single-layer, pure-vector objects destined for SWF export. (Object Layer Opacity fades will cause file size bloat.)

Opacity techniques are commonly used to fade objects in and out of a composition. Keep in mind that each individual frame of an opacity animation will add slightly to the overall size of the exported file. Opacity animation is frequently used in combination with position or scale animations (or both). These recipes can create convincing motion effects that fade into or out of view. Figure 7.3 shows an opacity animation added to the scaling animation.

Figure 7.3
This opacity animation is executed in the first 75 percent of the scale animation.

PROJECT Animating Opacity

Here's how to set a simple opacity fade:

1. Open the Timeline and set the CTM to the ending frame of the opacity fade (at approximately 08f on the Timeline).

2. Select the object to fade, turn down its twisty in the Timeline, and then, turn down the Transform twisty.

3. Click on the stopwatch next to Object Opacity to set the ending keyframe.

4. Set the final amount of Object Opacity with the Opacity palette. (This example uses 100%.)

5. Set the CTM to the starting frame of the opacity fade.

6. Set the initial amount of Object Opacity with the Opacity palette. (This example uses 30%.) Figure 7.4 shows the Timeline with Object Opacity keyframes in place. Notice the difference in timing between the ending Object Opacity and Scale keyframes.

Beware the Double Burst

Assigning the double burst opacity gradient to an object will cause it to export as a bitmap in the SWF file. All of the other opacity gradients (linear, burst, and radial) will export as vectors.

Figure 7.4
Try dragging the ending Opacity keyframe backward and forward on the Timeline to achieve different results.

Rotation Techniques

Put the spin on it. The Transform palette allows you to create object rotation animations in one degree increments. Once you set the first Rotation keyframe, you're able to set the amount of rotation in a number of ways:

- *Use numeric entry*—Enter the number of degrees directly into the Transform palette.

- *Spin the Rotation widget*—Spin the Transform palette's Rotation widget. The number field automatically keeps track of the total number of degrees of rotation.

- *Manipulate the object*—Click and drag on the object's top-right corner handle with the Selection tool, or any of the corner handles with the Transform tool. As you rotate the object, the Transform palette's rotation field displays the total amount of rotation.

Animating Rotation

Here's a quick rundown on how to animate object rotation:

1. Open the Timeline and set the CTM to the ending frame of the rotation.

2. Select the object to rotate, turn down its twisty in the Timeline, and then, turn down the Transform twisty.

3. Click on the stopwatch next to Rotation to set the ending Rotation keyframe. By default, this sets the degree of rotation to 0.

4. Set the CTM to the starting frame of the rotation.

5. Use the Transform palette to set the amount of rotation (15 degrees). Positive numbers cause the object to rotate to the right; negative numbers cause the object to rotate to the left. (If the starting degree is higher than the ending degree, the object will rotate in a clockwise manner; if the starting degree is lower than the ending degree, the object will rotate in a counter-clockwise manner.) Figure 7.5 shows the rotation animation as added to the scale and opacity animation.

Figure 7.5

With just 15 degrees of rotation, you'll impart a subtle spin.

Tweak Those Keyframes

Preview the animation to get a feel for the playback speed. If it feels a bit slow and clunky, you can easily speed things up. LiveMotion allows you to move keyframes—even multiple keyframes—by clicking and dragging. To move multiple keyframes, just drag a marquee around the keyframes you want to move, and then, drag them to a different spot on the Timeline. Figure 7.6 shows an accelerated Timeline.

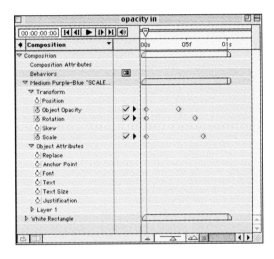

Figure 7.6

Move the ending keyframes up in the Timeline to speed up the motion.

Skew Techniques

Lean into it! Animating an object's horizontal or vertical skew can lend the impression of motion and speed. Want to get a quick idea of what I'm babbling about? Two animated skew styles are loaded with LiveMotion—Anim Leanslidefromleft and Anim Leanslidefromright—that do exactly as their names imply. In the following little project, you'll apply these styles to a pair of text blocks.

Moving an Object's Center of Rotation

LiveMotion provides two ways to move an object's center of rotation. Start by selecting the object with the Selection tool, and then, press Cmd/Ctrl. The cursor will change to a four-headed arrow, with a hollow square at the center. The two methods of moving the center of rotation are:

- *Move the object*—Click and drag on the object to drag the object around on its rotation point.

- *Move the rotation point*—Click and drag on the rotation point to drag the rotation point on the object.

The default rotation point varies, according to object type:

- *Geometric object*—Located at the center of the object.

- *Path object*—Located at the starting control point of the path.

- *Text object*—Based upon text alignment (left align is located at the left-most point of the text baseline, center align is located at the centerpoint of the text baseline, right align is located at the right-most point of the text baseline).

PROJECT **Using the Leanslide Styles**

The Leanslide styles serve as a neat example of what's possible when you combine an animated skew along a motion path. The two text blocks will start from opposite sides of the composition and smash into each other when they meet at the centerpoint. Here's how to do it:

1. *Open a new LiveMotion window.* Choose File|New.

2. *Set the composition dimensions.* In the Composition Settings dialog box, set the Width to 800 and the Height to 200. Select Entire Composition from the Export menu and click on OK.

3. *Add the text.* You'll add two separate text blocks. Start by selecting the Text tool, and then, click in the left side of the composition. Type "CRASH" in the Text dialog box, specify 36 point Helvetica Bold (or your typeface of choice), and click on OK. With the Text tool still selected, click in the right side of the composition, type "TEST" in the Text dialog box, and click on OK.

4. *Align and position the text.* Position the text blocks so that they're next to each other. Select both text blocks with Cmd/Ctrl+A, and then, choose Object|Align|Bottom. With both text blocks selected, drag them to the center of the composition. (Hint: Turn the rulers on with Cmd/Ctrl+R.)

   Save the file as "Crash Test" (Cmd/Ctrl+S) before you go any farther. You'll be able to reuse the basic elements in subsequent style tests. Set the Styles palette to Name View before proceeding to the next step (otherwise, it may be difficult to find the styles you need).

5. *Apply the Leanslide styles.* Once you've applied the styles, "CRASH" slides in from the left, whereas "TEST" slides in from the right. Shift-click on "TEST" to deselect it. With "CRASH" still selected, choose Anim Leanslidefromleft in the Styles palette and click on Apply Style. Select "TEST", and then, choose Anim Leanslidefromright in the Styles palette and click on Apply Style.

6. *Preview the animation.* Select Preview Mode from the lower right corner of the toolbox (or press Q) and click in the composition window to see your animation in action. Notice how the words lean back as they're sliding in, and then, lean forward as they make impact. Figure 7.7 demonstrates a handful of frames from the animation. To get a closer look, try scrubbing through the Timeline with the CTM. Press Q to switch back to Edit Mode.

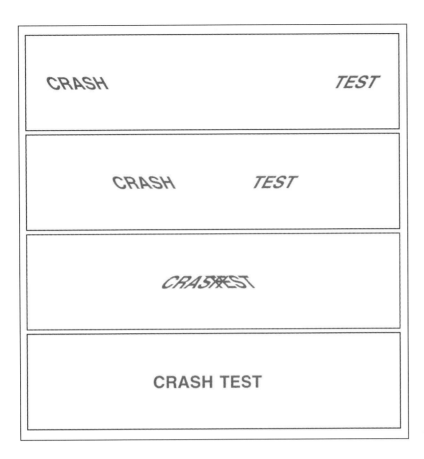

Figure 7.7
Here's how the animation appears. The Timeline shows where the action is.

If you'd like, save the file as "Crash Test Leanslide" (Shift+Cmd/Ctrl+S). Then, try altering the skew percentages and keyframes. You might want to have the words squish together upon impact or momentarily flash a different color or tint.

Advanced Animation Techniques

Now that you've seen some of the basic animation techniques, let's take a look at some slightly more advanced techniques that use individual character animation and object masking.

Broken Text Techniques

The Break Apart Text command lets you independently animate individual characters. The command comes in handy when flying in individual characters or with typewriter-like effects. With the characters broken apart, it's easy to create a staggered effect by shifting each object's arrival time in the Timeline. Once a motion path—or better yet, a full-blown animated style—is applied, you can achieve some marvelous effects. This next project demonstrates how it works.

PROJECT Creating Individually Animated Characters

You'll start this project by setting and breaking apart the text, before spacing the text arrival time. Once you've completed these steps, be sure to preview the animation—you'll have created a slick typewriter text effect. Here's how to do it:

1. *Open a new LiveMotion window.* Choose File|New.

2. *Set the composition dimensions.* In the Composition Settings dialog box, set the following:

   • Width: 600

   • Height: 300

   • Export: Entire Composition

   • Frame Rate: 12

   Click on OK.

3. *Set the composition time.* Open the Timeline (Cmd/Ctrl+T) and drag the composition end time to 02s.

4. *Add the text.* Select the Text tool, and then, click in the center of the composition. Type "SCRUMPTIOUS!" in the Text dialog box, specify a fun typeface in 48 point, and click on OK. (I used 54 point Cooper Black in this example.)

5. *Break the text apart.* Press V to switch to the Selection tool. Then, with "SCRUMPTIOUS!" still selected, choose Object|Break Apart Text. This will break the word into single characters (individual objects). Figure 7.8 shows the broken apart text in the composition window, along with the individual characters as shown in the Timeline.

6. *Space out the character timelines.* Click and drag the individual character timelines so that a one-frame stagger exists between each object, as shown in Figure 7.9.

7. *Preview the animation.* Click on the Play button to preview the animation. The type should pop into the composition in a typewriter-like manner. You might also want to try scrubbing through the animation by dragging the CTM back and forth in the Timeline.

8. *Save the file.* Save the file as "Scrumptious" before proceeding. (Undoing an animated style assignment to a bunch of characters can be sticky— it's best to have a file on the hard drive for backup.)

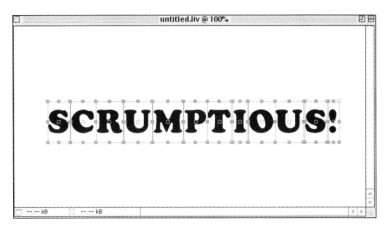

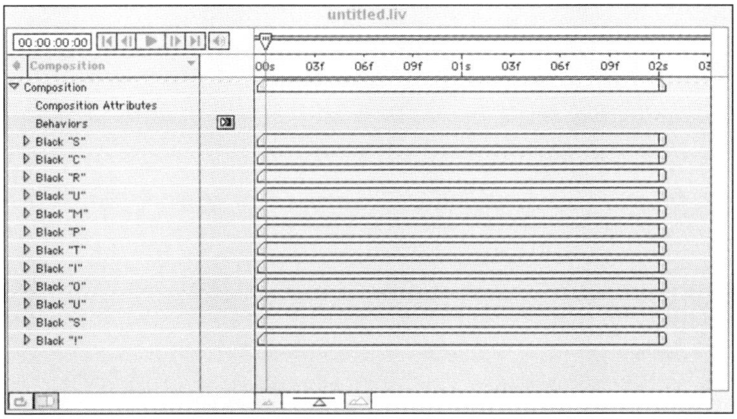

Before You Stagger

You may also want to apply the animated style *before* staggering the individual characters in the Timeline.

Figure 7.8
Notice how the text appears in the Timeline when first broken apart.

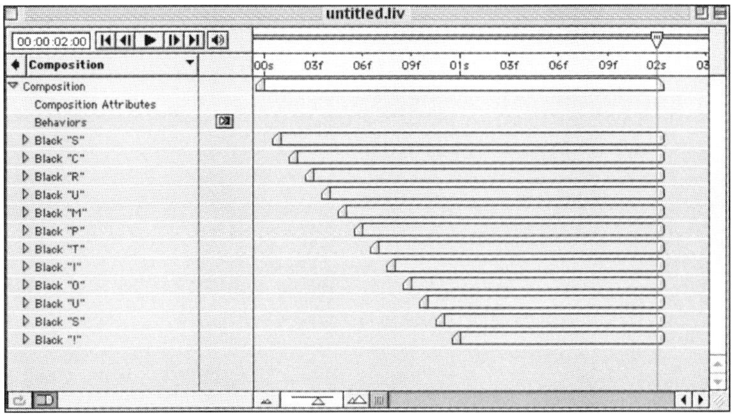

Figure 7.9
The staggered timelines create a cool effect all on their own. Watch what happens when you apply an animation style.

9. *Assign an animated style.* Drag the CTM to the end of the animation (02s). Select all of the individual characters with Cmd/Ctrl+A, and then, select an animated style from the Styles palette. Try either "anim arc fade left" or "anim arc fade right"—both of these animated styles should run well in a two-second timeline. (Other animated styles may require longer timelines to run properly.) Figure 7.10 demonstrates the "anim arc fade left."

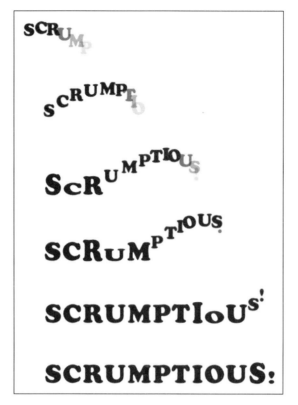

Figure 7.10
Combine a fun typeface and a playful motion path for a cartoon-like effect.

Preview the animation once the style has been applied to the individual characters. You'll see that a whole bunch of things are going on with this style—providing a fun mix of motion, scaling, and opacity animation.

Mask Techniques

Animated masks are a staple of interactive design. You'll use masks when creating animated effects, such as moving spotlights and scrolling text boxes. Once again, LiveMotion takes a straightforward approach.

PROJECT Creating Masked Spotlight Animation

This project creates a simple text mask:

1. *Open a new LiveMotion window.* Choose File|New.

2. *Set the composition dimensions.* In the Composition Settings dialog box, set the following:

   - Width: 400

   - Height: 200

   - Export: Entire Composition

   - Frame Rate: 12

Click on OK. Then, drag the composition window open in order to see a bit of the gray area that surrounds the active composition area.

3. *Set the composition time.* Open the Timeline (Cmd/Ctrl+T) and drag the composition end time to 03s.

4. *Add the text.* Select the Text tool, and then, click in the center of the composition. Type "SPOTLIGHT!" in the Text dialog box, specify 60 point Helvetica Bold (or a similar typeface), and click on OK. Select a medium gray from the Color palette.

5. *Create the spotlight.* Select the Ellipse tool. Draw a 50-pixel wide circle and select a pale yellow from the Color palette, and then, drag the circle so that it's sitting on top of "SPOTLIGHT!" The object should appear in the Timeline as "Pale Yellow Ellipse". Click in an empty area of the composition to deselect all objects.

6. *Change the background color.* Select the Document Background Color swatch on the toolbox, and then, select black from the Color palette. The composition should appear as at the top of Figure 7.11.

7. *Bring the text to the front.* Press V to switch to the Selection tool, and then, select "SPOTLIGHT!" and press Shift+Cmd/Ctrl+] (or choose Object|Arrange|Bring to Front). The composition should appear as at the center of Figure 7.11.

8. *Move the spotlight to its ending position.* Select the Pale Yellow Ellipse and drag it to the right of "SPOTLIGHT! (as shown at the bottom of Figure 7.11).

9. *Create the position animation.* Set the CTM to 03s. Select the Pale Yellow Ellipse in the Timeline, and then, turn down its twisty in the Timeline, and turn down the Transform twisty. Click on the stopwatch next to Position to set the ending Position keyframe. Set the CTM to the starting frame of the animation, and then, click and drag the Pale Yellow Ellipse to the left side of "SPOTLIGHT!" (hold down the Shift key *after* you start moving the ellipse to constrain movement). The composition should appear as at the left of Figure 7.12.

10. *Create the mask group.* Shift-click "SPOTLIGHT!" so that it is selected along with the Pale Yellow Ellipse. Press Cmd/Ctrl+G to group the two objects, and then, choose Object|Top Object Is Mask. Don't freak out when the text and ellipse disappear, as shown at the right of Figure 7.12.

Figure 7.11
The mask object must always be
at the top of the z-order stack.

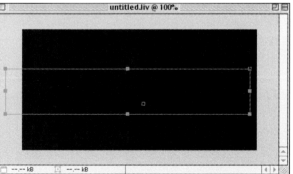

Figure 7.12
Hey! Where did they go?

Check out the animation with the Preview tool. The Pale Yellow Ellipse should slowly pan across the text, as shown in Figure 7.13.

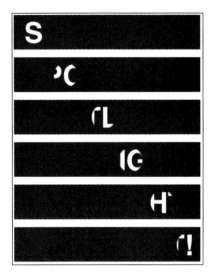

Figure 7.13
There they are!

Keyframe Modifiers

In the previous chapter, you got a taste of what's possible with motion paths in the bouncing ball and swimming fish projects. In this section, you'll learn about the commands that take your motion path animations to the next level. LiveMotion provides five modifiers that fine-tune your motion paths. The modifiers are:

- *Linear*—Provides an angular (rather than curved) transition

- *Auto Bezier*—Delivers a curved transition (keyframes have this attribute by default)

- *Hold Keyframes*—Prevents tweening (or interpolation) between keyframes (The attribute changes only at the next keyframe—not before.)

- *Ease In*—Provides a smooth transition into a keyframe

- *Ease Out*—Provides a smooth transition out of a keyframe. (A keyframe can be assigned both Ease In and Ease Out attributes.)

Controlling Sound

Sounds are integrated into LiveMotion compositions in one of two ways—they're either attached to an object state (most often, a rollover) or placed at the current time, as indicated by the Timeline. Although LiveMotion imports AIF, SND, and WAV format sounds, the program only exports MP3 format sounds within SWF files. This requires the use of the Flash 4 plug-in at the browser, because earlier versions of the plug-in don't support the MP3 format.

Importing Sound

You can place sounds into a LiveMotion composition in a number of ways:

- *Sound palette*—Select a sound, and then, click on the Apply button (or drag and drop the sound from the palette into the composition). If an object is selected, the sound will be applied to the object's active state. If an object is not selected, the sound will be placed into the composition at the current time.

- *Drag and drop*—Direct from the desktop (or Sound palette), just click and drag the sound file into the composition. If you drag and drop onto an object, the sound will be applied to the object's active state; if an object is not selected, the sound will be placed into the composition at the current time.

- *File|Place*—(Cmd/Ctrl+I) Use the dialog box interface to find and place the sound file. If an object is selected at the time you use the Place command, the sound will be applied to the object's active state; if an object is not selected, the sound will be placed into the composition at the current time.

The Sound palette, like other LiveMotion palettes, provides a Swatches view, a Preview view, and a Name view. Figure 7.14 shows the three views.

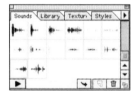 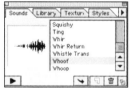 

Figure 7.14
The Preview view—shown at center—is the slickest way to scroll through the Sound palette.

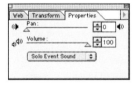

Figure 7.15
You'll find Pan and Volume controls on the Properties palette.

Pan and Volume

LiveMotion provides two basic controls over sound—Pan and Volume. You can animate these controls over time through the use of keyframes. You set Pan and Volume via the Properties palette, and set keyframes on the Timeline, under the sound's Object Attributes twisty. Figure 7.15 shows the Properties palette with a sound selected.

Here's a quick description of the sound controls:

- *Pan*—Adjusts the sound between the left and right stereo speakers. This allows for some nifty effects. A locomotive, for example, could thunder from one side of the computer to the other. (Listen to Jimi Hendrix's *Axis Bold As Love* for a more complete aural illustration.)

- *Volume*—Independently adjusts the playback level of each sound. Animating the Volume level allows for fade in and fade out.

Sound Tips

There are some sound anomalies in the initial shipping version of LiveMotion 1. With luck, these will be addressed in a bug fix. Until then:

- *Stick with 16-bit sounds*—Other bit rates may produce less than satisfactory results.

- *Looping must be done manually*—To loop a sound, drag out its right handle in the Timeline to the desired duration. (Each dark gray line in the sound's Timeline denotes an iteration.) This avoids the popping problems that can happen with Time Independent Group looped sounds.

- *No streaming*—LiveMotion 1 does not stream sound. This can make sound synching on long sounds a frustrating experience. Use smaller sounds instead.

Event Sound or Solo Event Sound?

The Properties palette allows you to set sounds as either Event Sounds or Solo Event Sounds. There's a subtle difference between the two—*Solo Event Sounds* do not repeat upon themselves, thus preventing the occurrence of overlapping sound. An *Event Sound* can play simultaneously upon itself (more than once at a time). (Two different Solo Event Sounds can play at the same time, however.) Don't confuse these two terms with sound looping—that's a whole separate issue.

Check the CD-ROM

Looking for more music and sound loops? Be sure to check the *Adobe LiveMotion f/x and Design CD-ROM.*

Flash Export Settings

At the risk of being redundant, let's reiterate some LiveMotion SWF export facts. Only simple, single-layer vector objects export as vectors. LiveMotion exports everything else as bitmap objects, which tend to be larger than vector objects. The larger the object, the longer the download.

Who can live on vector objects alone? Bitmaps will always be part of the game. Savvy designers accept that bitmaps take longer to download and use their design expertise, along with the tools that LiveMotion provides, to shave download times to the highest practical degree.

Image Compression with File Format Export Settings

When the SWF format is selected in the Export palette, you can choose among three different bitmap export formats—JPEG, PNG-Indexed, and PNG-Truecolor. LiveMotion provides the means to specify the overall bitmap format and settings for a composition, as well as object-specific formats and settings.

Here's a common situation. Let's say that your composition consists largely of flat color, along with a handful of photographs, such as the design shown in Figure 7.16. In this case, you would probably choose the Indexed format for the document export and the JPEG format for the photographic objects. This would provide the highest level of image control and compression for this specific type of composition.

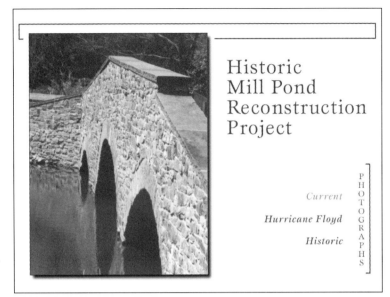

Figure 7.16
This composition would be best exported as indexed color, with the JPEG option specified for the photograph, on a per-object basis.

Each of the bitmap export formats provides control over specific settings:

- *JPEG*—Quality (0-100) and Opacity Resolution (0-8). Lower settings provide less quality and higher levels of compression.

- *Indexed*—Colors (2-256), Palette (Perceptual, Selective, Web Adaptive, Web, Mac OS, and Windows), Transparency, and Dithering.

- *Truecolor*—Quality (1-8) and Opacity Resolution (0-8). As with the JPEG format, lower settings provide less quality and higher levels of compression.

Frame Rates

You can set the Export dialog box to export SWF files at either the Document Rate—as set in the Composition Settings dialog box—or at a specific frame rate (8, 10, 12, 15, 18, 20, 24, 25, 30, 33, or 40 frames per second). Generally speaking, you'll want to export at the Document Rate. You may want to use a specific rate in special circumstances. Higher settings may provide smoother animations, but they will increase the file size. It's simple logic—the higher the frame rate, the more frames, the larger the export.

Sound Export Settings

Although LiveMotion can only export sound in the MP3 format, you have a good bit of flexibility as to the specifics in which you can export the sounds. You can export them at the Auto Data Rate or at 16, 20, 24, 32, 48, 56, 64, 80, 112, 128, or 160Kbps. You can keep file size to a minimum by converting stereo sound to mono sound—simply select the Stereo/Mono button.

As with other export settings, you can create documents with per-object sound export settings. This allows you to compress certain sounds at higher levels to achieve the smallest possible export.

Working with the Export Report

Want to get the skinny on file size and download flow *before* you export and upload your SWF composition? LiveMotion's handy Export Report lets you see exactly what's in your exported SWF and where it might bog on download. This allows you to construct your composition so that it downloads and plays smoothly, without noticeable delays.

When you select File|Preview In|Your Browser Of Choice (with the SWF export option chosen in the Export palette), LiveMotion will create a test export of your composition and open up the exported file in your browser. At the bottom of the exported test page, you'll see a text link ("Export Report"). Click on the link and you'll see that the Export Report provides information on Total Download Times, Download Streaming, and Resources for the SWF file. The Overview is a simple HTML page that shows the exported File Size (in kilobytes), Duration (in frames), and Frame Rate (in frames per second). Figure 7.17 shows a typical Export Report.

Download Streaming

The Download Streaming section provides a frame by frame report on the animation showing frame size (in bytes) and the status of preloaded frames, which are broken down by modem connection speeds (14.4, 28.8, and 56Kbps). When an element appears in the animation for the first time, the time code for that frame is hyperlinked to that time and element in the Resources section. The red zones signify heavy download areas.

Resources

The Resources section provides a comprehensive rundown on each and every element in the exported file, including sounds, sprites, bitmaps, and shapes. The listing delivers information on:

- *Sounds*—Format, Size, Settings, References, and Names
- *Sprites*—Size, References, and Names
- *Bitmaps*—Format, Size, Settings, References, and Names
- *Shapes*—Size, References, and Names

File Smashing and Staging

As you work on your composition, it's a good idea to test the export repeatedly. Careful manipulation of the object export settings will yield impressive file size savings. And just as importantly, smart staging will allow your file to play back smoothly. The idea is to build your compositions so that something (valuable) is happening while the content-to-follow flows down the pipe.

> ### What's a Sprite?
> We're not talking about lemon-lime soda! *Flash 4 Web Animation f/x and Design* defines a Flash sprite as "a self-contained movie within a movie." You might think of sprites as little characters, with minds of their own. (Okay, so maybe that's a bit much.) In LiveMotion terms, Time Independent Groups and rollovers are exported as sprites.

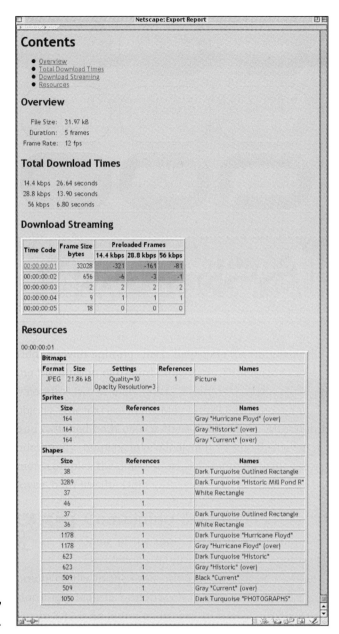

Figure 7.17
The Mill Pond Export Report.

The proper use of LiveMotion's Wait For Download behavior is essential for smooth running presentations. You don't want an animation to bog as the download streams to the browser. That's why it's important to stage the animation so that the crucial elements are present at the browser *before* they're called. Although the next chapter introduces the topic of behaviors as a whole, you'll see a good number of examples of the Wait For Download behavior in Chapter 9.

Flash vector purists love to note that LiveMotion will turn an object into a bitmap in the wink of an eye. Bitmaps aren't necessarily a bad thing, however. You can achieve impressive file size savings through meticulous attention to detail and careful manipulation of the per-object compression settings. The time you spend here will be paid back in gold at download time.

Moving On

Creating Flash files has never been so easy. In this chapter, you learned about some of the basics of the SWF Flash file format, and how you can use LiveMotion to create compelling animation, complete with MP3 soundtracks. The next chapter goes full force into the subject of LiveMotion behaviors, as it explains how these handy controls can turn your LiveMotion movies into interactive environments.

LiveMotion Studio

*Some things are best said with pictures. Color pictures,
that is. This LiveMotion Studio is chock full of tips,
CD-ROM content samples, and above all, inspiration.
I'll start with tips that illustrate a half dozen of my favorite
LiveMotion techniques. Then, I'll showcase a bunch of
the awesome elements that you'll find on the Adobe
LiveMotion f/x and Design companion CD-ROM.*

Desert Chrome (Masked Text)

Try this slick way to create totally vector chrome text for SWF export. This effect uses an object mask to contain the reflection of the desert horizon. Follow this rundown on how to create the effect:

1 Create the text.

2 Draw two or three gradient rectangles so that they are slightly taller and wider than the text. Select a color scheme that mimics a desert horizon line.

3 Bring the text to the front (Object| Arrange|Bring To Front); then drag the text on top of the rectangles.

4 Group the text with the rectangles; then select Object|Top Object Is Mask.

5 Create a new piece of text with the exact same settings as the original. Set the outline to 20, change the color to black, and align it with the masked text.

6 Duplicate the outlined text, change the color to light gray, and change the outline to 10.

7 Create one more version of the text, send it to back, and position it as a drop shadow. Set the Object Layer Opacity to a 90-degree Linear Gradient (10% to 90%).

When the artwork is complete, you can turn it into a Time Independent Group and subtly animate the movement (or colors) of the reflection. This technique animates the surface in vectors—which is far less bandwidth-intensive than animating a bitmap texture.

Sliding Mask Technique

Mask animation allows for a wide range of intriguing effects. In this example, I'll show you how to quickly build an animation mask to reveal text in a typewriter-like fashion:

Background

Text

Revealing rectangle

Mask

❶ Create four objects in the following order:

- A (background) rectangle. It should be large enough to contain all the elements.
- The text to be revealed.
- The (revealing) rectangle. It should be large enough to cover the text.
- The rounded corner rectangle (mask). It should be slightly smaller than the revealing rectangle.

❷ Because the z-order is extremely important, make sure the objects stack up as shown.

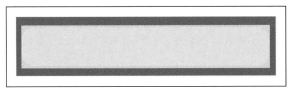

❸ Select Object|Align|Centers. The objects should appear as shown.

❹ With all the objects selected, group them (Cmd/Ctrl+G), and select Object|Top Object Is Mask. You should now see only a rounded corner rectangle with the color of the revealing rectangle. Select the revealing rectangle in the Timeline and assign the same color as the background rectangle.

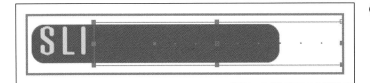

❺ Now, you'll use the Timeline to create a position keyframe animation to reveal the text. If you simply set a beginning and ending position keyframe, the revealing rectangle slides smoothly to reveal the text. This effect doesn't look much like a typewriter in action.

To create a typewriter-like effect, set a position keyframe to reveal each individual character. Select all the position keyframes, and then select Timeline|Hold Keyframe to ensure a character-by-character display.

Setting Text to a Circular Path

Looking for a way to set text to a circular path? This slick little tip uses Object|Break Apart Text and repositioned center points to do the deed:

❶ Create the text string (using center alignment), and draw an outlined circle as large as the rotation path. (See **Ⓐ**.)

❷ Drag out horizontal and vertical guidelines to intersect the circle's center point.

❸ Position the text so that its baseline touches the circle and select Object|Break Apart Text.

❹ With all the single characters selected, position the cursor over one of the character center points. Hold down Cmd/Ctrl, and then click and drag the center point down to the horizontal guideline. (This action drags all the character center points.) (See **Ⓑ**.)

❺ Select Object|Align|Horizontal Centers to stack all the characters on top of each other.

❻ With the characters centered on the vertical guideline, hold down Cmd/Ctrl and then click and drag the center point over to the vertical guideline. (See **Ⓒ**.)

❼ Deselect the characters; then select the first character via the Timeline. Click and drag the top right bounding box handle to rotate the character on the repositioned center point. Repeat this procedure for each character, positioning each character around the circle. (See **Ⓓ**.)

❽ Delete the circle when everything is aligned and looking good. Set the rotation animation properties for the text and turn the whole enchilada into a Time Independent Group, if necessary.

Setting Tight SWF Rollover Targets

Closely spaced and irregularly shaped rollover objects can present a special challenge. Overlapping bounding boxes make individual rollovers difficult to select. (The internal LiveMotion preview works just fine—the problem crops up when you're exporting the SWF file.) To avoid this situation, you need to create rectangular objects to create valid hot zones within the rollovers. These rectangular objects—which trigger the actual rollover buttons—can be invisible rectangle objects *or* text. To create them, follow these steps:

❶ Create rollover states for the irregular objects. Rename the **over** states to "true over". This way, you disable the rollovers from rolling over by themselves.

❷ Create the rectangular trigger objects and position them on top of the irregular objects, taking care so that the trigger objects do not overlap each other.

❸ Create **over** states for each of the trigger objects.

❹ Set up the targeting by using one of two methods:

- *Option 1*—Add a Change State behavior to the **over** state of each trigger object, targeting the "true over" state of its corresponding irregular object. Then, add a Change State behavior to the **normal** state of each trigger object, targeting the **normal** state of its corresponding irregular object.

- *Option 2*—Set a remote rollover for the **over** state of each trigger object, targeting the "true over" state of its corresponding irregular object. Then, add a remote rollover for the **normal** state of each trigger object, targeting the **normal** state of its corresponding irregular object.

❺ Set the trigger object's Object Opacity level to 0, as necessary.

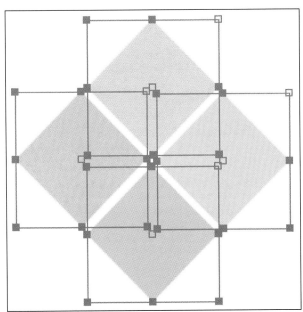

Overlapping rollovers

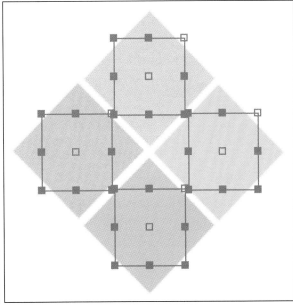

Tight (yet invisible) targets

Scrolling Text

You can create a scrolling text effect relatively easily with LiveMotion. To do so:

1 Set up a masked Time Independent Group (TIG) that contains your text. Then, create a position animation that slides the text from bottom to top. The masked group must have a Stop behavior in its first frame.

2 The forward and backward arrow buttons are (looping TIG) rollovers with Go To Relative Time behaviors in their **down** states; these behaviors target the masked TIG.

3 The forward button uses two Go To Relative Time forward frame behaviors. The backward button uses two Go To Relative Time backward frame behaviors. Each behavior moves forward or backward by only a single frame. These behaviors are placed at the beginning and end of the object lifetime.

When you press an arrow button, it sends a repeated stream of forward or backward frame instructions to the masked TIG.

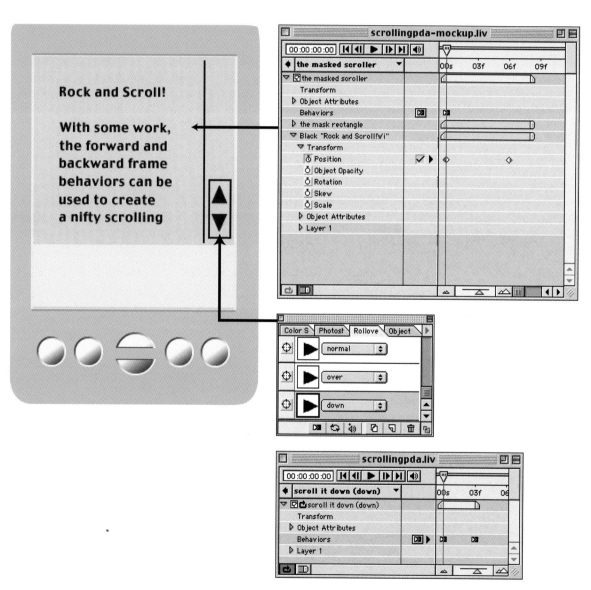

Applying Plug-in Filters to Vector Objects

Okay, so this heading is a bit misleading. You *can't* apply plug-in filters directly to vector objects. You must first convert the vector object(s) into a bitmap. Fear not; this process is easier than it sounds. Just follow these steps to find out how:

1 Select the object(s).

2 Copy (Cmd/Ctrl+C) or cut (Cmd/Ctrl+X) the object(s) to the clipboard.

3 Deselect the object(s), if necessary. (You might want to save the original.)

4 Select Edit|Paste Special|Paste Image and bingo! You can now apply plug-in filters to the new bitmap image object.

5 Delete the original vector object(s)—if it's still present in the file—or move it to a separate file for safe-keeping.

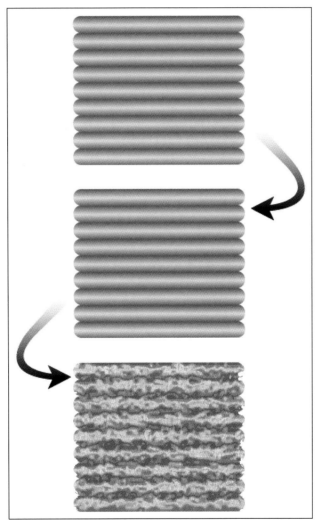

This example was created with a series of burst-filled rounded rectangles. The top image shows the individual vector objects, and the center image shows the bitmap image object created with Edit|Paste Special|Page Image. The Water Paper and Ocean Ripple plug-in filters were applied to the bottom image.

Dan's Styles

Because these crazy styles rely heavily on bitmap textures, they're best suited for JavaScript rollovers. You can find them, along with loads of others, on the *Adobe LiveMotion f/x and Design* CD-ROM. (If you decide to use them for SWF export, be sure to optimize the bitmap exports with LiveMotion's per-object compression feature.)

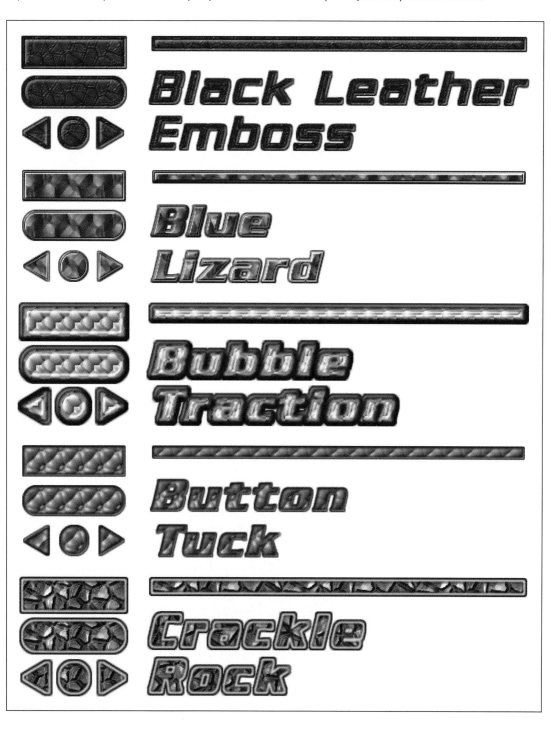

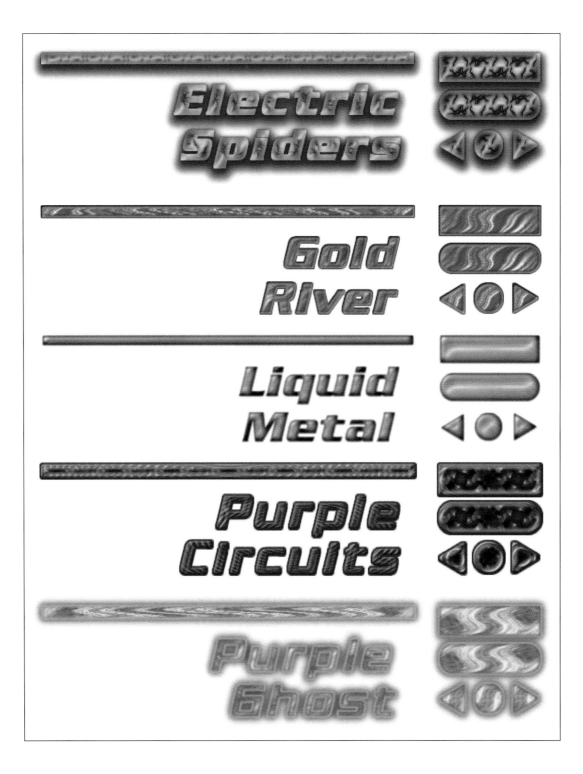

Dan's SWF Template Depot

Here, you can see a sampling of my wacky SWF-able templates. Above all, I aimed for speed, using vectors wherever possible (and slamming down the bitmap compression settings as necessary). As the old hot rodder's adage says, "If it don't go fast, chrome it!" All of the following designs make use of LiveMotion's auto symbol function to optimize downloads.

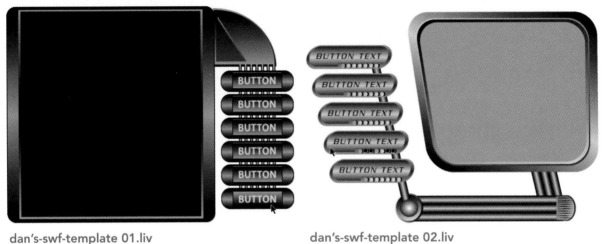

dan's-swf-template 01.liv

dan's-swf-template 02.liv

dan's-swf-template 03.liv

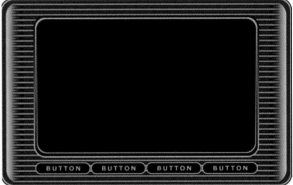

dan's-swf-template 04.liv

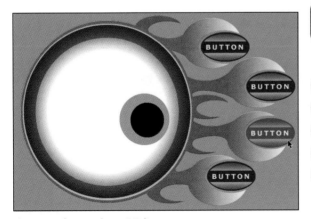

dan's-swf-template 05.liv

dan's-swf-template 06.liv

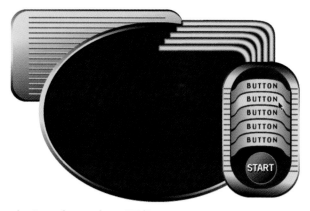

dan's-swf-template 07.liv

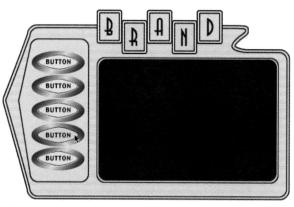

dan's-swf-template 08.liv

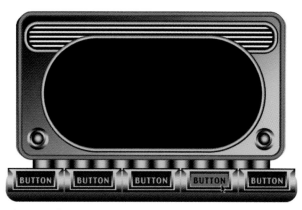

dan's-swf-template 09.liv

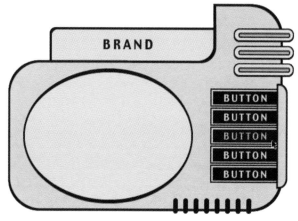

dan's-swf-template 10.liv

A Pair of Preloaders

This wacky pair of preloaders comes from the Preloader Depot in Chapter 9. Both the Purple Pager and the Island Radio preloaders are designed for lightning fast display.

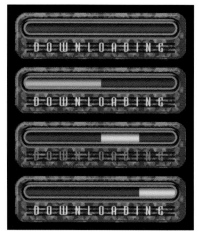

purplepreloader.tif

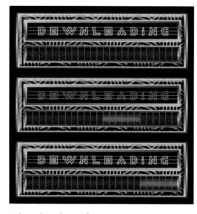

islandradio.tif

Charlie's Templates

Charlie Haywood, an artist who contributed to Adobe's content development efforts for LiveMotion, created these four intricate templates with rich textures and carefully crafted 3D effects. They're best exported in AutoLayout mode as sliced JPEG compositions. You can find Charlie's templates on the *Adobe LiveMotion f/x and Design* CD-ROM.

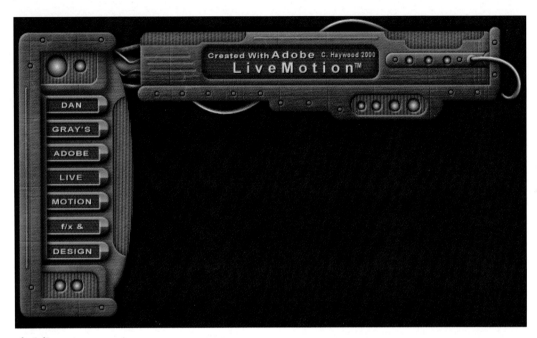

ch-1.liv

ch-2.liv

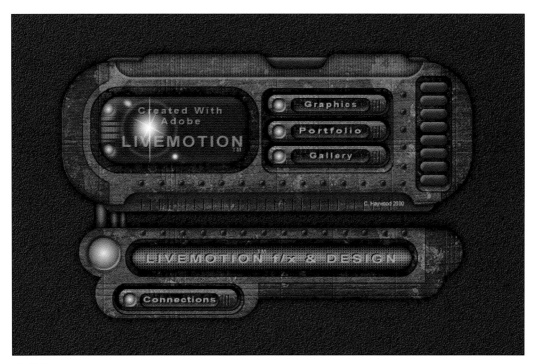

ch-3.liv

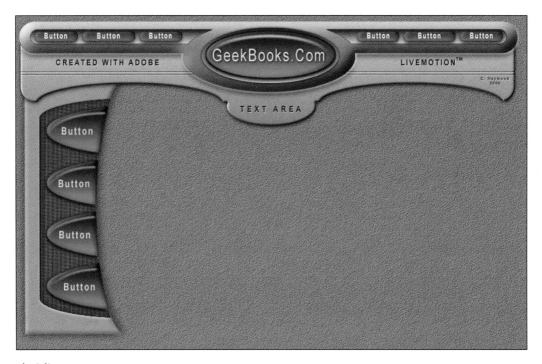

ch-4.liv

Charlie's HighLight and DeepBevel Buttons

Charlie Haywood's highlight buttons use a sliver object with a linear opacity gradient to achieve a candy-like appearance. His deep bevel buttons use a horizontally striped texture in one of the layers to achieve a crisp lighting edge. Look for the HighLightButton.liv and DeepBevelButton.liv files, on this book's companion CD-ROM.

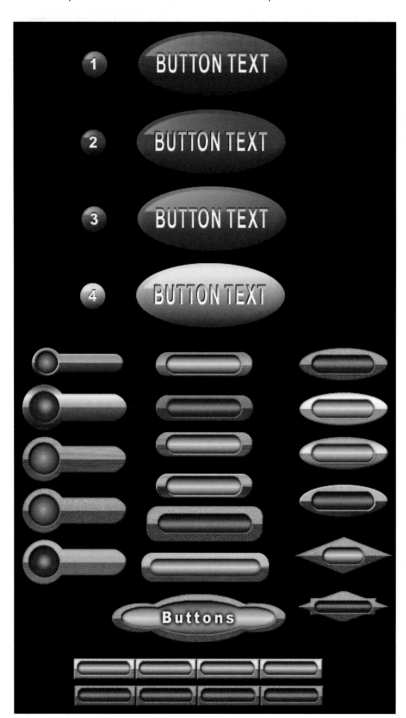

Charlie's Interface Components and SuperButtons

Here, you can see a bunch of Charlie Haywood's slick interface components and super buttons. Once again, he makes excellent use of textures, imparting subtle highlights and a realistic feel. See the files, Components.liv and SuperButtons.liv, on this book's companion CD-ROM.

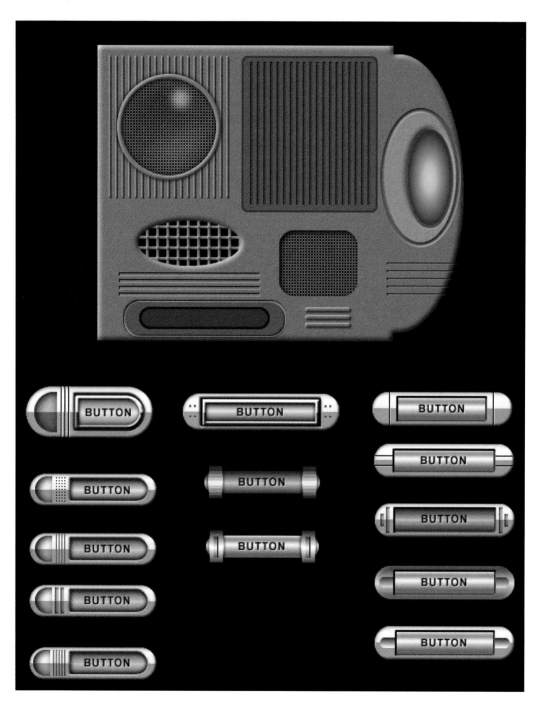

Charlie's Text Stylings

Charlie Haywood's text stylings show an intuitive sense of color and light.

BigGoldLetters.liv

The big, gold letters design features a gem-like center texture—created with the twirl distortion surrounded by a tasteful gold bezel. (Open the file on the CD-ROM to see how Charlie created this cool effect.)

BlueMetalic.liv

The blue metallic design uses a burst gradient layer on top of a brushed metal texture layer to achieve its subtle highlight.

Glass.liv

The glass design uses a twirl distortion on a background fill in one of the layers to great effect.

Chapter 8

Behaviors

LiveMotion delivers scripting functionality through its use of behaviors. In this chapter, you'll learn about behaviors and how each one operates. The chapter also covers a number of techniques for combining behaviors to build powerful interactivity.

Oh, Behave!

Did rollovers whet your appetite, or were you left hungry for more? Pull up a chair. This chapter covers some of LiveMotion's heaviest power tools: behaviors. Behaviors let you turn the most basic Web page into a truly interactive gem that keeps your visitors coming back for more. Fortunately, that power is wrapped up in a nice tidy package that requires no hand coding on your part. If you know code, you'll find your skills very useful as you swiftly combine behaviors into complex, yet elegant, interface elements. If you're a code-phobic designer, you, too, can add behaviors and look like a pro. For each type of LiveMotion jockey, behaviors provide a quick route to pages that jump from the screen.

Because I already discussed basic rollovers in Chapter 4, it's time to "move up to the next level" (as my son likes to say). Let's start with the basics.

What Is a Behavior?

A *behavior* is a specific way of triggering an event to occur. When all is said and done, a LiveMotion project will end up as an HTML page that may or may not refer to some assets also created by LiveMotion (such as GIF or Flash files). Even a basic Flash file will run happily along its intended Timeline until it hits the end and stops. Behaviors take charge of the proceedings by triggering actions to happen at a certain point, or by giving the end user the ability to determine what happens and when. Behaviors can be as simple as a loop command at the end of a Timeline, and as complex as a set of triggers that creates pull-down menus for interfaces. In either case, working with a behavior is a straightforward process.

LiveMotion 1 offers eleven behaviors:

- Stop

- Play

- Change State

- Go To Relative Time

- Go To Label

- Go To URL

- Run JavaScript

- Load Movie

- Unload Movie

- Wait For Download

- Stop All Sounds

When you export a project in the file format(s) of your choosing, LiveMotion translates the behaviors into the code that makes them work in a Web page. If you generate straight HTML with supporting image files, LiveMotion generates HTML and JavaScript. If you export to Flash, LiveMotion generates ActionScript (the language Flash files use for scripting). Again, LiveMotion takes care of the dirty work for you.

The Change State and Go To URL behaviors work with exported HTML compositions, as well as with SWF movies. The other behaviors are only functional for SWF exports.

Attaching Behaviors

Before you get into the weeds with the specific behaviors, let's talk about where to put them. You can trigger a behavior in two ways. First, the project can play along its Timeline, hit a frame in that Timeline, and then do something different. That's known as a *timeline behavior*. The second way to trigger a behavior is to associate it with an object on the page that will act as a button. That's known as an *object behavior*. You can use both types of behaviors in the same project. Any Timeline (including independent timelines) or any object can have multiple behaviors associated with it.

Timeline Behaviors

Timeline behaviors are triggered directly on the Timeline, and can be attached to the overall composition Timeline or to any independent timelines that exist in the project. To attach a behavior, move the Current Time Marker (CTM) to the desired frame and click on the Edit Behaviors button. The Edit Behaviors dialog box appears, as shown in Figure 8.1, allowing you to set the desired behavior and define its options. Once a timeline behavior is set, a behavior icon appears (along with its label) on the Timeline, as shown in Figure 8.2.

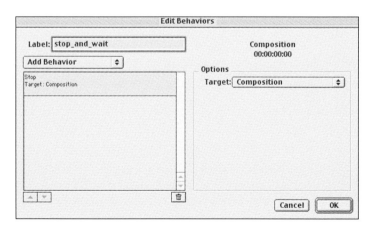

Figure 8.1
The Edit Behaviors dialog box. Take note of the targeting.

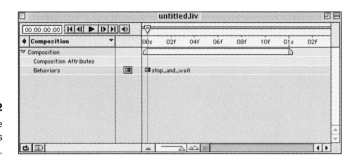

Figure 8.2
The Stop behavior sitting at the start of the Timeline (labeled as "stop_and_wait").

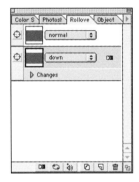

Figure 8.3
See that tiny doodad in the down state? It indicates that a behavior has been assigned to the state.

Normal State Behaviors

If you associate a behavior with an object's **normal** state, the behavior will trigger as soon as the object appears in the composition Timeline. If you associate a behavior with a custom state for an object, the behavior will trigger when (or if) the object is set to that state.

Object Behaviors

You add object behaviors via the Rollovers palette. Create a new state for the object and then click the Edit Behaviors button at the bottom of the palette. Again, the Edit Behaviors dialog box appears, asking for the behavior you want and giving you access to the options for the specific behavior you choose. Notice the slight difference in the dialog box—it has no place to label the behavior. We'll see why that is in a moment. Once an object behavior has been assigned to an object state, a behavior symbol appears on the state in the Rollovers palette, as shown in Figure 8.3. (To edit the state, click on the Edit Behaviors button.)

Which One When?

Sometimes, you can achieve the same effect by either adding a behavior to an object's Timeline or by adding to a rollover state for the object. Which is best? It all depends on the situation at hand. Because LiveMotion interprets your desired result into actual code, whatever methods you use to accomplish your goals are fine by LiveMotion—as long as the behavior works when you preview it. (Always preview the results in each browser; using LiveMotion's internal preview isn't enough.) However, let's answer the question in general terms. In most cases, if you want a behavior to trigger at a certain point in time, use a timeline behavior. If you want to associate the behavior with a specific object in the composition, use an object behavior.

Choosing Behaviors

When you attach a behavior to a Timeline or an object, you'll be greeted by the Edit Behaviors dialog box. Before getting into the nitty-gritty, let's add two simple behaviors to a project to get a feel for the way they work.

 Start and Stop

Follow these steps to add a Start and Stop behavior:

1. Start with a new composition (File|New).

2. In the Composition Settings dialog box, set the following:

    *   Width: 300 pixels

    *   Height: 200 pixels

    *   Frame Rate: 12

    *   Export: Entire Composition

    *   Select Make HTML

    Click on OK.

3. Open the Timeline window (Ctrl/Cmd+T), and drag the composition time to 01s (one second). Make sure that the CTM remains at 00s.

4. Click once on the Edit Behaviors button.

5. In the dialog box that appears, select Stop from the pop-up menu on the left.

6. In the Label field, type "stop_and_wait". Click on OK. Your Timeline should appear as in Figure 8.2.

7. To continue, add a 100-by-50-pixel, blue (R0, G0, B255) rectangle. Place it somewhere in the middle of the composition.

8. Use the Rollovers palette to create another state for the rectangle; it automatically creates this new state as an **over** state. Switch it to the **down** state by selecting **down** from the pop-up menu in the Rollovers palette.

9. Next, click on the Edit Behaviors button at the bottom of the Rollovers palette.

10. From the Edit Behaviors dialog box, select Play from the pop-up menu on the left of the palette. On the right side of the palette, select Composition from the Target pop-up menu. Click on OK.

11. Drag the right end of the rectangle's Timeline all the way to the left. Your Timeline will look like the one in Figure 8.4.

If you preview the project, you'll be greeted with a blue rectangle that just sits there. This is because the Timeline was stopped dead in its tracks with the Stop behavior. The button behavior plays the Timeline when the button is pushed. Because the button only exists for the first frame of the composition, it quickly blinks out of existence. You are on your way to interface design.

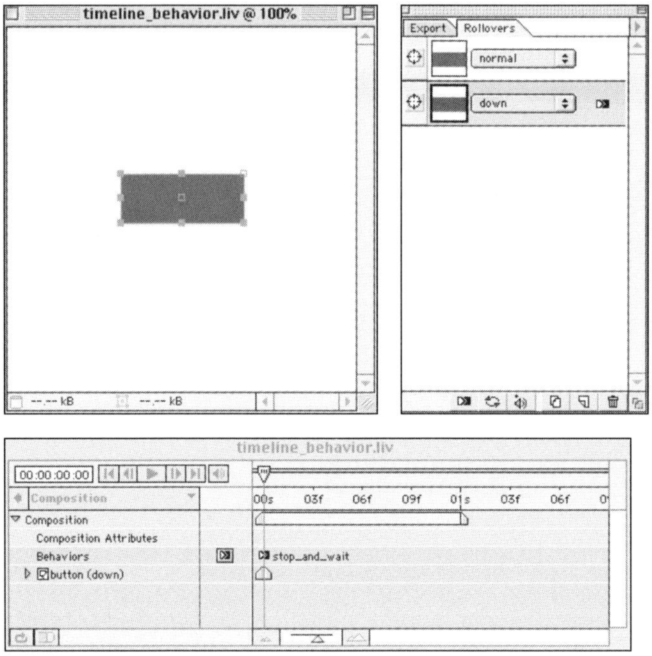

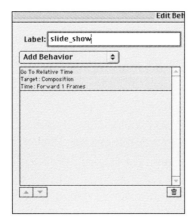

Figure 8.4
The finished composition—all dressed up with behaviors.

The Details

Let's take another look at the Edit Behaviors dialog box. This is where you'll add behaviors and set their options.

On the Left

On the left side of the dialog box, you choose, name, delete, and order your behaviors. The Label text field lets you assign a specific name to any behavior placed on the Timeline (or create labeled points on the Timeline). You should use descriptive names for your behaviors; generally, the name should indicate why you created the behavior where you did. Figure 8.5 displays the left side of the Edit Behaviors dialog box.

Figure 8.5
The left side of the Edit Behaviors dialog box.

Next, choose the particular behavior you want by selecting it from the pop-up menu. You can add as many behaviors as you like. (I've seen as many as 40. I can't imagine ever needing to add that many behaviors to something, but it's nice to know you can.)

The order of the behaviors is important to consider. If you have more than one behavior, the one listed at the top of the list will play first. As you work with behaviors, you might decide that the composition would work better if the behaviors played in a different order. To change the order of a particular behavior, select it in the list, and click on one of the arrow buttons at the bottom left of the dialog box. The behavior will change order. (If the behavior is at the top, the up button won't be available. The down arrow does the same when the behavior is at the bottom.)

On the Right

On the right side of the Edit Behaviors dialog box, you'll set the options for the behavior you have selected on the left. The options vary by behavior, and we'll cover them in detail in the next section.

Above the options area of the dialog box, you'll see a time indicator if you are creating a timeline behavior. This lets you know the precise frame you are applying the behavior to. At the bottom right of the Mac version, you'll see the ever-present Cancel and OK buttons, as shown in Figure 8.6. (The Cancel and OK buttons are at the top right of the Windows version.)

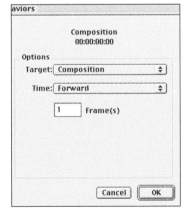

Where Are the Labels?

If you opened the dialog box by clicking on the Behaviors button on the Rollovers palette, you won't see the Label field. Only timeline behaviors have labels. We'll see why later.

Want to Discard a Behavior?

Select it, click on the Trash button at the bottom of the Edit Behaviors dialog box, and say goodbye. Note that this will only delete the behavior from the Edit Behaviors dialog box; the label will remain in the Timeline. To remove a label—or a label complete with behaviors—from the Timeline, select the label and press Delete.

Figure 8.6
The right side of the Edit Behaviors dialog box.

It Goes Up to 11

To understand details of behaviors, it's necessary to discuss each of the 11 behaviors in its own little world. The function and options provided by each behavior determine how it can be used. To help add some context, I'll mention a way each behavior can be applied. After that, you'll learn some ways to put behaviors together in a composition to add real interactivity. Figure 8.7 shows the 11 choices on the Add Behavior drop-down menu.

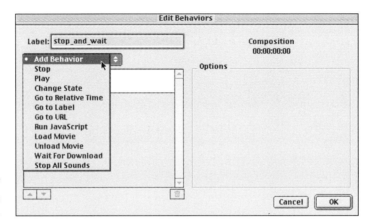

Figure 8.7
You must select behaviors from
the Add Behavior menu.

Stop

The Stop behavior is one of the two simplest behaviors (along with Play). When triggered, the Stop behavior halts either the composition Timeline or a Time Independent Group within a composition. The Stop behavior always acts on a Timeline; it can be attached to either a Timeline or an object.

Only one option is available for the Stop behavior: Target. It is the Target Timeline that you want to halt. The Target pop-up menu offers you any Timeline that exists in the project by the name of the object that owns it. For example, if I have created an independent time object and named its group Flame, then I have at least two Timelines from which to choose: Flame, and Composition. If I stop Flame somehow, but let the composition continue, the Flame halts and the rest of the composition continues to play.

Play

> **Always On**
>
> Timelines always default to Play. That's why you don't need to tell them to play if you simply want them to play as soon as they appear in the composition. However, when you set the CTM to a specific point in the Timeline (see Go To Label), it will not automatically play from that point. You must tell it to begin playing.

The Play behavior undoes the work of the Stop behavior. When the Play behavior is triggered, it starts something playing again. As with the Stop behavior, the Play behavior always acts on a Timeline, and may be triggered from the Timeline itself or through association with an object. Like the Stop behavior, the Play behavior is targeted to a particular Timeline. All Timelines available in the project will appear in the pop-up menu.

A basic way to add interactivity to a composition is to set a Stop behavior at the first frame of the composition, then add a Play behavior to a button. When the composition starts, it waits at the first frame until the visitor clicks the button, then the composition starts up. This is exactly what took place in this chapter's first project.

PROJECT Creating a Play Button

Let's use the Stop and Play behaviors to create a composition. The animation of the project will not start until the user clicks on a button to tell it to. First, let's create an animation of some sort (you can substitute Steps 1 through 5 with an animation of your own if you like):

1. Create a new LiveMotion document (File|New). Set the document size to 300 by 300 pixels, the Frame Rate to 12, the Export option to Entire Composition, and select Make HTML.

2. Create a rounded corner rectangle near the center of the composition. Make it 150 pixels wide by 40 pixels tall.

3. Bring the Timeline window to the forefront (Cmd/Ctrl+T). Drag out the composition Timeline to 01s. The Timeline for the rounded corner rectangle should also open to 01s.

4. Make sure the rounded corner rectangle is selected, and set keyframes at 00s for Transform|Rotation and Transform|Scale (see Chapter 6 for a refresher on setting keyframes).

5. Move the CTM to 01s, use the Transform palette to rotate the rounded corner rectangle to 360 degrees, and scale it down to make it smaller.

    Now you have created a basic animation. If you preview it, a rather unspectacular thing happens. The rounded corner rectangle spins 360 degrees and shrinks over the period of a second. Let's add the behaviors to make it a bit more interesting.

6. Move the CTM to 00s.

7. Click on the Edit Behaviors button on the Timeline. In the Edit Behaviors dialog box, give the behavior a label of "wait", set the behavior to Stop with the Add Behavior drop-down menu, and set the Target option to Composition. Click on OK.

    When you preview this using the Preview tool, nothing will happen. The composition's Timeline was stopped before it moved past Frame 00. Next, we'll add a Play Behavior to the rounded corner rectangle. This will make it a Play button for the composition.

8. Select the rounded corner rectangle with the Selection tool.

9. In the Rollovers palette, add a new state by clicking on the New Rollover State button at the bottom of the palette (see Chapter 4 for a refresher on rollovers). Set the state to **down** from the State drop-down menu.

10. Click on the Edit Behaviors button on the bottom of the Rollovers palette. Select the Play Behavior from the Add Behavior drop-down menu. Set the Target option to Composition (the rounded-corner rectangle itself will be selected by default), and click on OK.

Now, when you preview the composition, it will still just sit there. That is, it will sit there until you click on your rounded corner, play button. When you do that, the button will spin through 360 degrees and stop. Congratulations! You are well on your way to working with behaviors. Save this file as playbutton.liv—you'll use it later.

Change State

The Change State behavior interacts with a specific object. For Change State to be useful, the target object must first have multiple rollover states. When triggered, the behavior will switch the state of an object.

The two options for this behavior are the Target and the State to which the targeted object will be set. Any states the object has will appear in the State drop-down menu. This is an interesting behavior, because the result can also be achieved using the Rollovers palette. In fact, if you apply this behavior to a button and target a second object (which just creates a remote rollover), LiveMotion just makes it look like you used the method described in Chapter 4 for creating remote rollovers. Change State always targets an object, but can be attached to either an object or a Timeline.

Why do this? You can get the same effect by keyframing an object to change from the Timeline or by using the Rollovers palette to have objects change the state of other objects. Using behaviors in this manner happens for two reasons. The first is that it is a timesaving device. Perhaps you have an object that must change its appearance in the space of a single frame. This makes it appear to "pop" from one state to another. To get this on the Timeline, you might need to use three keyframes: one at the start of the animation, one at the frame just before the frame that will have the various changes applied to it, and the frame that has all of the various changes applied to it. Figure 8.8 shows this Timeline for a rectangle that will change from green to red.

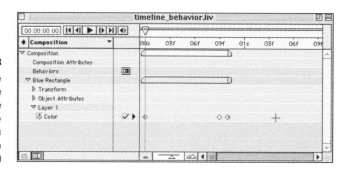

Figure 8.8

It takes three. Three keyframes are needed to make the color change from green to red in a single frame. The first two keyframes are for green; the third is for red. (You might also accomplish this with a Hold Keyframe command.)

The second reason is to use the Timeline to trigger a state change, and have it trigger any behaviors associated with that state. For example, say you have an ellipse that has a Custom State called *red* that turns the ellipse red. You want the ellipse to change to the **red** state after 2 seconds. You also want the project to stop a spinning, blue diamond whenever the ellipse hits the **red** state. Place a Change State behavior on the Timeline at 2 seconds, target the ellipse, and tell it to send the ellipse to the **red** state. Next, create an object behavior for the **red** state that stops the Timeline for the diamond you want to stop. Now at 2 seconds, the ellipse turns red and the Timeline for the other stops. In fact, anytime you change the state of the ellipse to the **red** state, that Timeline for the other object will stop (see Figure 8.9).

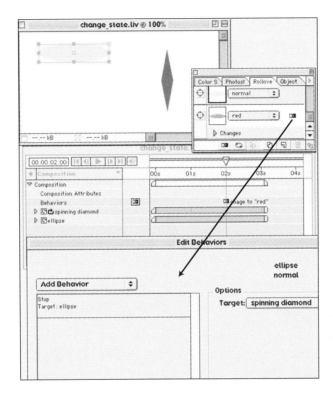

Figure 8.9
The Change State behavior, sitting on the Timeline, tells the ellipse to turn red. The ellipse, in turn, tells the spinning diamond to stop.

Go To Relative Time

The Go To Relative Time behavior allows you to step through a Timeline frame by frame. It does this by sending the composition to a frame that is either before or after the current frame. For example, if the composition was sitting at frame 10, you could back it up or move it forward a frame at a time with this behavior.

This behavior has three options: the Target, the Time, and the Number of Frames. The Target is the Timeline that you want to move around in. The Time is essentially the direction you want to go—forward or backward. The Number of Frames determines the number of frames you want to jump.

PROJECT "Now for Our Place Sequence Slide Show"

One good example of a way to use the Go To Relative Time behavior is to make a slide show. Here's how:

1. Create a file in Photoshop that has at least five layers, each layer having a different image. Save it where you can easily find it. If you don't

want to create your own, use the go_to_rel_time.psd file on the Adobe LiveMotion f/x and Design companion CD-ROM (look inside the Chapter 8 folder).

2. Create a new LiveMotion document. Make sure that the LiveMotion composition size is larger that the Photoshop file, in order to have room for the buttons that will control the slide show. The Photoshop file is 300 pixels wide by 300 pixels tall. The LiveMotion project should be 300 pixels wide by 400 pixels tall.

3. Place the multilayered Photoshop image into the new composition by selecting File|Place and locating the file you created (or place the go_to_rel_time.psd file from the CD-ROM).

4. Select Object|Convert Layers Into|Sequence and you will have an object on the Timeline. Its name will match the name of the first layer in the Photoshop file (that's the layer on the bottom of Photoshop's Layers palette).

5. Place the CTM at the first frame, and add a Stop behavior. This ensures that the composition doesn't barge right along through the frames as soon as the file loads (the first project in the chapter will guide you through adding a Stop).

6. Create a button somewhere at the bottom of the composition.

7. Use the Rollovers palette to create a **down** state.

8. To the **down** state, add the Go To Relative Time behavior. Set the Target option to Composition, set the time to Forward, and set the Number of Frames to "1".

   You now have a Forward button. Preview it to see if it works. Click on the button and the picture in frame 1 should change to the second layer in the sequence. Now, to back up, you'll need to add a Back button.

9. Copy and paste the Forward button. This also copies the rollover state for **down** and the behavior tied to it.

10. Select the **down** state of the new button, and click on the Edit Behaviors button on the Rollovers palette.

11. Change the Time option from Forward to Backward.

You now have a slide show. Select File|Preview In|your browser of choice to try it out. Click on the Forward button to step through the frames of the Photoshop file. When you get to the end, you can click on the Back button you made to step back through the slides.

Blank Frame

Note that LiveMotion creates a blank frame in the first frame position (00s) of the exported SWF file. Hit that back button one too many times and the movie will seem to vanish. To avoid the white-out effect, try placing the photo sequence and the forward/backward buttons into a Time Independent Group. (Don't forget to add a Stop behavior at the beginning of the Time Independent Group's Timeline.)

Label

Did you notice that behaviors on the Timeline have a slightly different dialog box than behaviors for objects? The timeline behaviors have a Label field above the Behaviors pop-up. This allows you to refer to a certain frame in a Timeline. To create a label, insert a behavior at a point on the Timeline, but don't add any actual behaviors in the Edit Behaviors dialog box. Just be sure to add a label that describes the reason for having a label there. Figure 8.10 provides an example.

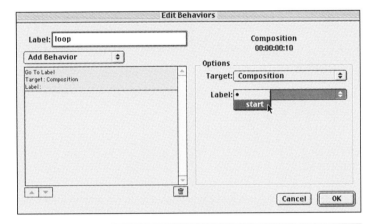

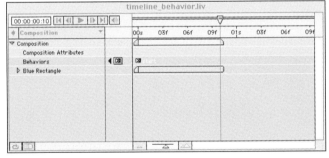

Figure 8.10
After you drop a label onto the Timeline, you can refer to it in other behaviors. In this case, you'll send the composition to the start label.

This label will now be a place where you can send the Current Time. When you do, the Timeline will stop doing what it was doing and move to that new point on the Timeline. To get it to play from that new point, you'll need to add a Play behavior to the mix (either in the label or as a part of the Go To Label behavior used to get you to the label). That way you know the composition will do what you want it to.

Go To Label

The Go To Label behavior lets you point an animation to a specific label on the Timeline. Whenever the Go To Label behavior is triggered, it will send the animation to the frame at the label you choose and either sit there or continue playing—depending on what was happening when you sent the animation to the label.

The two options for Go To Label are Target and Label. The Target is the intended Timeline you want to affect, and Label is a pop-up of all labels available on that Timeline.

PROJECT Make a Reset Button

Let's use the Label/Go To Label combination to create a Reset button for a composition. If you kept it, open the playbutton.liv file you created in the "Creating a Play Button" project (if you didn't keep it, go back to that project and redo it).

1. Move the CTM to the last frame of the composition.

2. Click on the Timeline's Edit Behaviors button. Label the behavior "Reset," choose Go To Label from the Add Behavior drop-down menu, set the Target option to Composition, and select the wait label. Click on OK.

   This will automatically reset the composition when it gets to the end. It will seem like nothing happened, but you will be able to play the animation again by clicking on the button. (LiveMotion's internal preview may not function properly. Instead, you'll want to preview this in a browser with File|Preview In|Your Browser Of Choice.)

   Let's change the file so that a Reset button appears at the end of the animation.

3. Delete the timeline Go To Label "reset" behavior. Select it with the cursor and press the Delete key.

4. Move the CTM to the end of the animation.

5. Create a small rectangle at the bottom of the animation centered below the button.

6. In the Rollovers palette, create a new Rollover state for the new rectangle and set it to **down**.

7. Click on the Rollovers palette Edit Behaviors button. Choose Go To Label from the Add Behavior drop-down menu, set the Target option to Composition, and select the wait label.

Preview this project in a browser. Click on the rounded corner button. It will rotate and shrink. At the end of the rotation, the rectangle will appear. Click on the rectangle button, and the project will reset itself to the beginning.

Go To URL

The Go To URL behavior provides rudimentary control over elements outside of the SWF file. It operates basically like any <**HREF**> in an HTML file would act (in fact it operates exactly that way if you output the file to HTML instead of SWF). When triggered, the behavior loads the contents of the file at a particular URL into the browser window or frame within the browser.

Pick a Frame—Any Frame

The Frame setting you choose tells LiveMotion where to load the object at the URL. If you have a site with frames, you can have the file you are loading go into a specific frame in the window. The four built-in Frame options are: "_parent", "_self", "_top", and "_blank". Choosing "_blank" will load the URL into a new browser window. You can also target a custom frame by typing the frame name into the Frame text field.

The options are URL and Frame. The URL is the address for the composition to go to. It can be either a relative or an absolute URL, depending on your needs. However, remember that if you are using a link to a page outside of your site, you need the "http://" part of the address. If you don't add that, browsers will complain that they cannot find the server or page. The second option, Frame, is the frame you want to target. Parent, Top, Self, and Blank are the four options from the drop-down menu, and they match the HTML definitions for targeting frames. You can also type the name of a frame into the text field, so you can target frames to which you have given custom names.

One way to use this behavior is to create a button with a link. Say you want to link to your favorite clam shack on the Web (let's say that it's at http://www.clamshackheaven.com). To add the link, create a button with a **down** state. Add the Go To URL behavior, enter "http://www.clamshackheaven.com" into the URL field, and set the Frame Target to self. When the user clicks on the button, it will take him or her off to the clam shack Web site.

For those paying attention, you might be asking what the difference is between adding a link this way, and adding it via the Web palette. The answer to that question is, "No difference." Either way, you will get an appropriate HTML or SWF file with a button that takes the end user to a clam shack on the Web.

A second way to use this behavior is to add Go To URL behaviors along the Timeline. Set them to fill a different frame in a frameset than the one occupied by the SWF file. As the animation plays along, it will trigger these behaviors to load the other frame with different information. To extend the clam shack example, if you were listing the 12 most elegant clam shacks, you might want to have each one's Web site appear in another frame of the composition as it is listed in the animation.

PROJECT Putting the Go To URL to Work

Have you ever wanted to create a document that uses a SWF navigational system to call HTML content? This short project shows how LiveMotion content can be combined with straight, everyday HTML (like the stuff that, say, GoLive makes). Look inside the Chapter 8 folder on the *Adobe LiveMotion f/x and Design* CD-ROM, and locate the folder named go_to_URL. Inside, you should find an HTML file named "go_to_URL.html." Use a browser to view the file.

What's in a Name?

Bear in mind: These names are arbitrary. I could have used "king kong," and "sharleena." I didn't, because I wanted to give each frame a name that made sense to its purpose in the site. I didn't, but I could have.

This file includes a SWF file in a frame alongside some HTML files. The frameset that holds them together has two frames: SWF and HTML.

When you click on the yellow button (as you are instructed to do), watch the information in the right-hand frame (html) change as the movie unfolds in the left-hand frame (.swf). Each time the right-hand frame changes, a Go To URL behavior was triggered. Let's reconstruct it a little:

1. Locate the go_to_URL folder on the CD, and copy it to the hard drive in your computer.

2. In the go_to_URL folder, locate the Projects subfolder. In this subfolder, locate and open the file called go_to_URL.liv.

3. If it isn't visible, open the Timeline window by selecting Timeline|Show Timeline Window (or pressing Cmd/Alt+T).

4. Locate the behavior at 5s with the label "go to URL 1" and open it. Note that it has http://www.geekbooks.com as the URL. You'll change it to hook it up to one of the provided HTML files by redoing the URL.

5. In the URL text field, type "slide_one.html", and enter "html" in the Frame field.

6. Next, locate the behavior on the Timeline at 10s and open it.

7. In the URL text field, replace http://www.geekbooks.com with "slide_two.html" and enter "html" in the frame field.

8. Last, locate the behavior at 15s and open it. Replace the http://www.geekbooks.com URL with "slide_three.html", and enter "html" in the Frame field.

9. Make sure the Export palette is set to SWF, set the Composition settings (Edit|Composition Settings) to Entire Composition with Make HTML deselected, and then export the file into the Projects folder (the same folder you found the .liv extension file in).

When you load the HTML file called "go_to_URL.html" in the projects folder (it's just a copy of the one you loaded earlier to preview the work), it should work the same way the preview did. By the way, I like grape jelly.

Run JavaScript

The Run JavaScript behavior allows you to call JavaScript functions from your exported SWF files. This allows for a realm of possibilities. (The only option for the behavior is the JavaScript code itself.) If you know how to code it, drop it in and go. This behavior extends the scripting capabilities of LiveMotion by allowing you to connect to code outside of the project at hand. You'll need to define the functions within the HTML code of the file that contains the SWF file, and then call those functions in the behavior.

 **Alert!**

Try this self-contained example:

1. Create a new composition. Make it any size you like, set the Export option to Entire Composition, leave the Frame Rate at the default, and select Make HTML.

2. Use the Rounded Rectangle tool to create a button in the middle of the composition.

3. Select the button, and create a new state in the Rollovers palette. Set the state to **down**.

4. Click on the Edit Behaviors button on the Rollovers palette. In the Edit Behaviors dialog box, select Run JavaScript from the Add Behavior drop-down menu.

5. In the option field, type the following text:

```
alert('Quit pushing me!');
```

6. Close the dialog box and preview the project. When you click on your button, it should provide the results as shown in Figure 8.11.

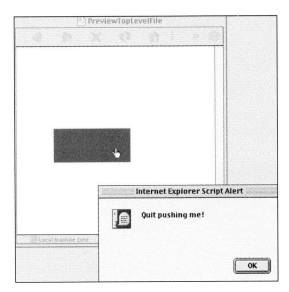

Figure 8.11
If you did it right, your computer will have a bone to pick.

Load Movie

You may have created other SWF files that you want to use as small movies within the project; however, you can't add a SWF file to a LiveMotion project directly. That's where the Load Movie behavior comes into play. Trigger this behavior to add the SWF movie you choose—via a URL—to the currently playing project. The loaded file will sit in the upper-left corner of the current composition.

The options for the behavior are URL, Replace or Append, and Layer:

- *URL*—The location of the SWF file you are targeting with the Load command. As with any of the URL options in LiveMotion, the address can be absolute or relative.

- *Replace or Append*—Determines what happens to any movie that might already have been loaded. If a movie is already loaded when this behavior is triggered, Replace unloads the previous movie and loads the new movie in its place. Append adds the SWF file to the overall composition without removing any movies that might be playing. This effectively piles movies on top of each other in a stacking order determined by the Layer option.

- *Layer*—Allows you to assign a movie to load in a particular place in the stack. If you had four movies loaded into layers 1, 3, 5, and 7, you could load a fifth movie into the middle of the pile by setting its Layer option to 4.

PROJECT Propeller Head

This project requires three files from the *Adobe LiveMotion f/x and Design* companion CD-ROM: load_movie_1.swf, load_movie_2.swf, and load_movie_3.swf. (They can be found in the load_movie folder, inside the Chapter 8 folder.) To get started:

1. Move the load_movie folder from the CD-ROM onto your computer's hard drive. This will be the folder where you'll save your files. It's important not to move the files from the CD into any subfolders (if you created any) within the load_movie folder (otherwise, the URL you'll use will be different than the one you'll be instructed to use).

2. Create a new composition (File|New). Set the Width to 300 pixels, the Height to 400 pixels, the Frame Rate to 12 (although it's really up to you), the Export option to Entire Composition, and select Make HTML.

   Now that you have set yourself up, you'll create a project to use them.

3. Create a small rectangle at the bottom of the composition. This will become the first of three buttons to which you'll attach the behavior.

4. Create a **down** state for the button with the Rollovers palette.

5. Click on the Edit Behaviors button at the bottom of the Rollovers palette. In the Edit Behaviors dialog box, choose Load Movie from the Add Behavior drop-down menu. In the URL option text field, add the following text:

```
Load_movie_1.swf
```

6. Select the Append option, and set the Layer option to 1.

7. Copy the button (Edit|Copy) and paste it (Edit|Paste). Paste it again (Edit|Paste). This produces three buttons on top of each other. Use the Selection tool to arrange them so that the three buttons are at the bottom of the composition.

8. Because you copied the buttons after you completed the first one, all you will need to do is change the options for the second and third buttons. Select the second button and click on its **down** state in the Rollovers palette.

9. Click on the Edit Behaviors button to get to the Edit Behaviors dialog box. Change the URL to load_movie_2.swf and the Layer to 2.

10. Select the third button you made, click on its **down** state, and change the URL to load_movie_3.swf and the Layer to 3.

11. Export the project into the folder you copied onto your computer. To see the project, you'll need to open the HTML file that LiveMotion created for you. (If you choose File|Preview In, the URL won't find the file. This is because LiveMotion builds the temporary files in a directory other than the one in which you have placed the movies.)

12. Click on the three buttons to preview the action.

Dizzy? Next we'll add buttons to stop this. Save the file you created for the next project, and name it "load_movie.liv".

Unload Movie

The Unload Movie behavior simply unloads a movie that has been loaded. The only option is the layer of the movie you wish to unload. (You can't unload a movie by name; instead, you must unload it by layer.)

 Please Stop!

This project adds three buttons, each tagged with a specific Unload Movie behavior, to vanquish the movies in the "Propeller Head" project.

1. Open the file you created in the "Propeller Head" project (if you didn't do the last project, do it now).

2. Drag to select all three of the buttons you created, copy them (Edit|Copy), and paste them (Edit|Paste) so that they are positioned below the original three.

3. Because you copied the buttons after you completed the first set, all you will need to do is change the behavior attached to them. Select a second button and click on its **down** state.

4. Click on the Edit Behaviors button to open the Edit Behaviors dialog box. Delete the Load Movie behavior and add an Unload Movie behavior. For the first button, set the Layer option to 1.

5. Repeat this for the other two buttons, setting the Layer options to 2 and 3, respectively.

6. Save this file as unload_movie, and export it into the same folder into which you exported the previous file into. When you play the movie, the first three buttons will load the propeller movies as before, whereas the second set of buttons will unload the movies.

Wait For Download

Sometimes, when you create larger projects, you often want to give the page visitor something to look at until the main part of the project loads in. These are often referred to as *preloader* scripts. Typically, you'll set up a small, looping animation that repeats until the rest has loaded. However, if you have a complex project with many areas that require a few seconds to download, you can add breaks with small repeaters anywhere along the Timeline.

The options for Wait For Download are Loop To, and Until <insert label> Has Loaded. These require a little bit of explanation. The Loop To option sends the animation back to a label you set somewhere on the Timeline. Until <insert label> Has Loaded is a label at the end of the piece of the animation you are waiting for. Each time the animation hits the Wait For Download behavior, it checks whether the composition components have loaded between the Wait For Download spot on the Timeline and the Until <insert label> Has Loaded. If not, it returns to the Loop To label you set. The best way to use this is to create a very small, efficient animation as the preloader that repeats quickly. Figure 8.12 diagrams the flow of the Wait For Download behavior.

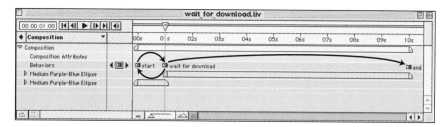

Figure 8.12
Preloaders help to ease the pain of hefty downloads.

Using a Preloader

Open the wait_for_download file from this book's companion CD-ROM. This is an animation file that we'll use as a Wait For Download example. The animation has been created, so we'll just add the Wait For Download behavior to the mix. Once you get the hang of this file, you can use it as a template for your projects. All you need to do is to swap in your own animation, and move some of the labels around a bit. Let's dig in:

1. Open the Timeline window and locate the element named "preloader animation." This element will repeat until the rest of the project has loaded.

2. First, add a behavior on the Timeline at 00s. Label it "start", but add no actual behaviors. This will become the Loop To label for the Wait For Download behavior.

3. Move to the end of the last element on the Timeline, frame 10s and set another Label behavior. Set the Label to end.

4. Locate the last frame of the element named "preloader animation." It will be frame 01s. Add a behavior to this frame of the Timeline, and set the Add Behavior drop-down choice to Wait For Download. Set the Loop To option to start, and set the Until option to end.

This one is difficult to preview, simply because it is hard to create a movie that is too complex to load quickly with a local copy. However, consider your audience. If they are likely to be using anything but a broadband connection, test your projects by putting them up on a test Web site. If they take anything more than a few seconds to download, create a Wait For Download piece for the project to give people something to build a little anticipation before the whole thing is loaded and ready.

The Mother Lode of Preloaders

Can't get enough preloaders? Fear not...you're well covered. Chapter 9 dives back into the topic of preloading in the Preloader Depot, and the *Adobe LiveMotion f/x and Design* companion CD-ROM contains a slew of ready-to-go widgets. (And don't forget to check out the groovy preloader image previews in this book's color LiveMotion Studio.)

Stop All Sounds

The Stop All Sounds behavior has a solitary purpose in life. Whenever this behavior is triggered, all sounds cease. (It is so easy that it has no options.) One common way to use the Stop All Sounds behavior is to provide a Sound Off (or Boss) button.

Combining Multiple Behaviors

Behaviors by themselves are quite useful tools. When you start to combine them, however, you unlock real power that is easy to control. The next section provides a set of examples that show how you can use behaviors to create relatively interactive interfaces.

PROJECT Repeating Button

In this project, you'll create a button that, when pressed and held down, triggers a behavior and repeats it. To create this effect, you'll build a button that has a **down** state with a separate Timeline that loops. At the beginning of that Timeline, you'll place a behavior that gets triggered each time the Timeline loops. When you let up, the button reverts to the **normal** state and the triggering stops. The concept demonstrated in this example shows how it's possible to create Timelines for each state of an object. Furthermore, those differing Timelines can trigger different behaviors.

Before getting started, let's open the starter file from the CD-ROM's Chapter 8 folder. Locate the files repeating_button.liv and non-repeating_button.swf. Copy the LIV file onto your computer's hard drive, and open it in LiveMotion. This file has a purple ellipse with an independent Timeline that is triggered by the red, rectangular button below it. If you click on the button, it sends the ellipse's Timeline one frame forward, causing it to rotate by 45 degrees. However, if you hold the mouse button down, nothing more happens. You must release the mouse button and click again to get it to rotate another 45 degrees. Test this by opening the SWF file in a browser.

Now, let's fix the button, so that it repeats the rotation of the ellipse when you keep the mouse button pressed down:

1. Open repeating_button.liv.

2. Examine the ellipse (purple ellipse) in the Timeline window and the red button (red button). Each has an independent Timeline.

3. Select the red button with the Selection tool and look at the three states it has in the Rollovers palette.

   The **down** state of the button triggers the Go To Relative Time behavior targeted to the purple ellipse. When you click on the button, it sends the ellipse one frame forward, which rotates it through 45 degrees. You'll change this state of the button to make the button repeat.

4. Press the Edit Behaviors button at the bottom of the Rollovers palette. In the Edit Behaviors dialog box, select the Go To Relative Time behavior, and delete it by clicking on the Delete Behavior button at the bottom of the palette. (Don't worry, we'll add it back to the state shortly.) Click on OK.

5. With the **down** state of the red button still selected, note that the name of the button has changed slightly in the Timeline with the addition of the word "down" (in parenthesis).

6. Double-click on the button's name in the Timeline to drill down and access the Timeline for the button.

7. Increase the length for the Timeline to one frame by dragging one "click" to the right.

8. Set the CTM to the start of the Timeline.

9. Click on the Edit Behaviors button for the Timeline to get at the Edit Behaviors dialog box.

10. From the Add Behavior drop-down menu, select Go To Relative Time. Target the purple ellipse, set the Time to Forward, and the number of frames to 1.

11. As a last step, set the red button to loop by selecting Timeline|Loop.

When you export this to a SWF file, you will have a repeating button.

PROJECT Jumping in the Timeline

Jumping in the Timeline is one of the more basic and functional uses of behaviors. This behavior changes scenes within a composition by moving to specific places on the Timeline. At each one, a different, looping animation occurs. Try this out by opening the jumping_in_timeline.html file (from this book's companion CD-ROM) in a browser. Click on the red, yellow, or blue button to see a different animation.

Copy the folder jump_in_timeline from the CD-ROM to your computer's hard drive. You'll add the behaviors required to make the blue button work in the project:

1. Open the file jump_in_timeline_start.liv. Move the CTM to frame 3.

2. This is the start of the object called "ellipse and ball." Click on the Edit Behaviors button to get to the Edit Behaviors dialog box.

3. Name the label "ball start". From the Add Behavior drop-down menu, choose Play and target the composition.

4. Move the CTM to 1 second, frame 3. Click on the Edit Behaviors button to get to the Edit Behaviors dialog box. Enter "loop ball" as the label. Add the Go To Label behavior, target the composition, and choose the ball start label.

   Now that the labels and the behaviors are set for the ball, you need to hook up the button so that it will play the ball animation by sending the composition to that point in the Timeline.

5. Select the blue button and create two new states with the Rollovers palette. The first new state is the **over** state (which you'll ignore), and the second new state will be the **down** state. To match the other buttons, you can color the **down** state to a light blue. Set the RGB values for the **down** state to R0, G255, B255.

6. Add a behavior to the state by clicking on the Edit Behaviors button on the Rollovers palette. In the Edit Behaviors dialog box, choose Go To Label, target the composition, and select the ball start label.

7. Save the file and preview it in a browser.

Now, when you click on the blue button, the ball will move.

A Word on ActionScript

Although LiveMotion 1 does not offer all of the high-end possibilities afforded by ActionScript in Macromedia Flash 4, it does provide a great deal of interactivity required by most designers. As your needs and experience increase, you may want to investigate Flash...or wait until LiveMotion 2.

Moving On

The best way to get a real grip on behaviors is to start using them. Experiment with different methods to get to the same result; also, check the exported result to see what the file size might be and how quickly the project plays after it loads. When you create an interesting project with behaviors, consider saving it as a component you will use in future projects. Because LiveMotion allows you to place other LiveMotion projects into a composition, you can quickly add elements to your project. You'll learn more about how this works in the next chapter, as it tackles the subject of building kinder, gentler, and smarter SWF files.

Chapter 9

Flash, Splash, and Burn

*Avoid the pitfalls of bad Flash. Create SWF pages and
sites that load quickly, and above all, do their job.*

The Message (Not the Medium) Is the Message

When it's used in the right manner, the SWF format can be a wonderful thing. When it's used in the wrong manner, it's one of the fastest ways to lose a visitor. You want flash and splash, without that nasty crash and burn feeling. This chapter will help you steer clear of many common Flash accidents. Among other things, you'll:

- Learn from the mistakes of others and gain maximum exposure for your site content.

- Build manageable SWF files to deliver your message without a hitch.

- Design with the search engines in mind to get your Flashed site the visitor traffic it deserves.

- Preload like a pro with the Preloader Depot, where you'll find a sample of 10 of the ready-to-use preloaders included on the *Adobe LiveMotion f/x and Design* companion CD-ROM.

Learn from Their Mistakes

Flash designers can go wrong at so many points, but none more frequently than on the introductory, or *splash page* of a Web site. You can go astray in lots of ways. Let's take a look at some of the most obvious.

Knock Knock...Anybody Home (Page)?

Here's an experiment worth trying. Find a computer that has a Web browser without the Flash plug-in installed (alternatively, you can simply move the plug-ins out of your browser). Surf for a few hours to see how this browser without plug-ins reacts when it hits a Flashed site. When you land on the site's front door, how does the site greet you?

The absolutely worst thing you can do on the front page of a Web site is to merely include a SWF file *without* also including at least one HTML link. When a browser lands on a page that's been designed (and I use the word in the loosest terms possible) in that manner, the only thing that the visitor might see is a big fat broken plug-in icon, as shown in Figure 9.1. (Take note of the URL in the browser's status bar.)

The heinous nature of this design crime is so obvious, yet novice Flash designers repeat it time after time. And still, it can be avoided with a simple HTML link into the site. If you want your home page to feature a big SWF, don't forget to also include that all-important HTML link, as demonstrated by Figure 9.2.

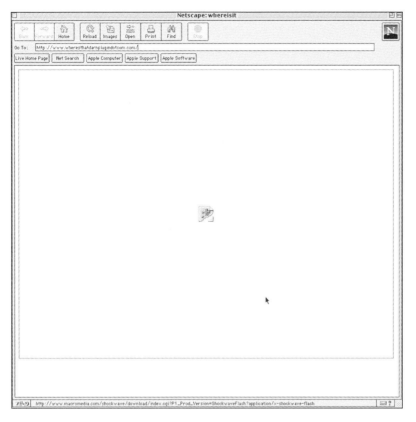

Figure 9.1
Q: How do they get into the site?
A: They can't.

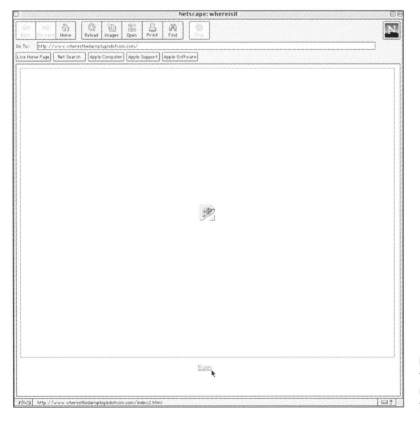

Figure 9.2
The plug-in is still not installed; nonetheless, your visitors will have the means to enter your site.

Sniffing the Plug-In

It's not a bad idea to sniff the browser to determine whether the Flash plug-in (or ActiveX control) is installed at the browser, *before* you send the SWF file. Thankfully, a good number of ready-made JavaScript routines are designed expressly for this purpose.

You can find an excellent Flash detection system at:

www.moock.org/webdesign/flash/index.html

The support section of Macromedia's Web site offers some sage advice on Flash detection, as well:

www.macromedia.com/support/flash

Older browsers (in this case Netscape Navigator 3 for Macintosh), might only show the broken plug-in icon. Newer browsers may display a dialog box (or automatically call up a new browser window) to facilitate download of the plug-in.

Is This a Tunnel to Nowhere?

You've seen this site before. The front page is a one-way Flash trip into the site, without the choice to opt out. Like it or not, visitors hit your home page and have to endure the infomercial. Truth be told, they might not endure; they might just click away someplace else. (I'm reminded of the time I suckered my wife into the Star Trek Experience at the Las Vegas Hilton. She thought the museum was cool, but when she figured out—too late, I must add—that it was merely a prequel to the virtual reality ride, she wanted to bail in the worst way. When the door to the shuttlecraft slammed shut, it was all over.)

The Flash medium allows for interactivity. Don't make your visitors sit through what might (at best) be considered a commercial. What do you need to avoid the tunnel to nowhere? Just include a simple Skip Intro button, like the one shown in Figure 9.3. Give them the means to bail—better they bail *into* your site, than bail *elsewhere*.

How About a Choice?

What if your visitors would rather view an HTML site, instead of a SWF site? LiveMotion makes it easy for you to repurpose your layouts as sliced JavaScript/HTML pages. Take advantage of this ability and provide both SWF and HTML versions, as necessary. Let folks choose what route they want to take, right on the front page, as in Figure 9.4. But don't make too much of a big deal over it—you merely want to inform your audience, not run an advertisement for Macromedia.

Is That an Elephant Coming Down the Pipe?

Looking for a fast way to infuriate your audience on anything less than a broadband connection? Stuff a huge SWF file down their gullets without warning. Be polite and let your visitors know how large the file is *before* it starts

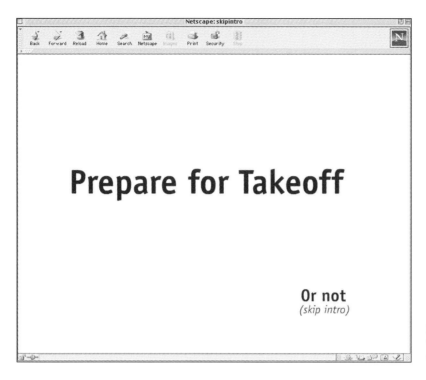

Figure 9.3
With a Skip Intro button, your visitors can get right to the site.

Figure 9.4
Give your visitors a choice.

lumbering down the pipe. Anything more than a few hundred K or so deserves a tip-off, as shown in Figure 9.5. Although you might have the good fortune of being on a broadband connection, your visitors may not. Be kind and consider the shortcomings of their Internet connection.

Figure 9.5
Let your site visitors know what's
coming their way.

Do I Have to Listen to That Annoying Music?

Okay, so your visitors' opinion of annoying is a good bit different from your own. Who's to say who's the arbiter of taste? Don't add background music to your SWF movie unless you also include the means to mute the tunes. A simple button, like the examples shown in Figure 9.6, tagged with the Stop All Sounds behavior, will do the trick.

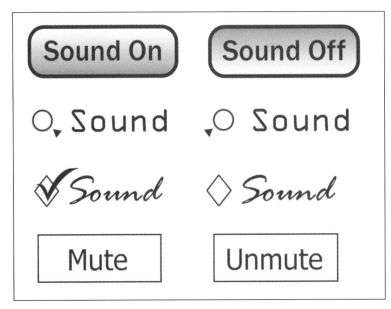

Figure 9.6
Turn that down!

Building Manageable Files

In this section, you'll learn about staging downloads, and how to deal with bitmaps. I'll also clue you in on LiveMotion's smart SWF export engine and how it can cut down on file size with nary a fuss.

Stage Downloads

You needn't cram your elephant all down the pipe at once. If your Flash movie weighs in at a hefty rate, consider using some techniques to manage the download routine. As shown in Chapter 8, LiveMotion's Load Movie behavior comes in handy when building more complex interfaces. With Load Movie, you can bring down the resources *when* they are needed, rather than *whether* they're needed.

Suppose your visitor lands at a page that asks, "Lady or the Tiger?" It's not necessary to bring down *both* the Lady and the Tiger. You only need to bring down the option (movie) they choose. Clicking on the Lady's door should trigger a Load Movie behavior for the Lady; likewise, clicking on the Tiger's door should trigger a Load Movie behavior for the Tiger. Figure 9.7 shows the Edit Behaviors dialog box for the Lady button's **down** state. When the Lady button is clicked, the ladymovie.swf file is loaded into layer 1, while layer 2 (which may contain the tigermovie.swf file) is unloaded.

With careful implementation of the Load Movie behavior, you can allow your visitors to customize their experience. You might set up a button to download the soundtrack, for example, offering visitors the choice of whether they want to wait for that techno drone. Although LiveMotion doesn't provide conditional logic, you can achieve basic branching using Load Movie.

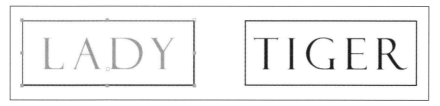

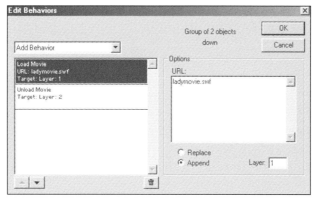

Figure 9.7

Only give them what they ask for, never more.

Deal with Bitmaps (or Not)

Without a steady hand on the wheel, LiveMotion will turn many objects into bitmaps upon SWF export. It's all up to the operator. With the Active Export Preview, LiveMotion will *always* tell you when it's going to bitmap something. Always keep in mind that those bitmaps can be highly compressed through judicious use of the per-object settings in the Export palette.

Nonetheless, there are plenty of times when you don't want your objects to export as bitmaps; don't let these occasions come as a surprise. Here's a set of conditions that will cause an object to be exported as a bitmap, along with some workarounds that you may want to try:

- *Using multiple layers*—Create multiple objects or use per-object compression.

- *Making changes to the Adjust, 3D, or Distort palettes*—Deal with the bitmaps by using per-object compression. Mimic 3D effects with the pure vector 3D technique described below.

- *Making changes to Layer Width or Softness*—Create multiple iterations of the object, place the duplicates behind the original, and tweak the duplicates' dimensions and Object Opacity settings.

- *Combining text with another object*—Break the text into paths in Illustrator before combining it with another object.

- *Applying a gradient to an outlined object*—Create a doughnut object, as demonstrated in Chapter 1, instead of using the Outline option.

- *Applying the Double Burst gradient*—Create two identical objects, both using (single) Burst gradients. Rotate the second object's gradient 90 degrees from the first and fiddle around with the front-most object's Object Opacity settings.

- *Cropping an object*—Try using the Combine Minus Front function, rather than the Crop tool.

Some of these conditions may seem fairly limiting. Although it's important to create the smallest practical export, don't feel that you have to rely exclusively on vector artwork. With judicious use, the per-object export compression settings can achieve impressive results. Don't compromise your vision. Instead, keep the artist and technician in balance.

When you use the per-object compression settings, it's important to select the right format for the selected object. Use the JPEG or TrueColor settings for continuous tone objects, including photographs and textured artwork. Use the Indexed color settings for flat color artwork, such as logos, basic cartoons, and the like.

Pure Vector 3D Effects

In certain cases, you can mimic the look of some bitmap effects through the careful construction of vector objects. A beveled button effect, for example, can be created with two or three objects stacked on top of each other. Fiddling with gradient values can impart the effect of highlight and shadows. You can see the vector bevel/gradient technique demonstrated in the LiveMotion section of **geekbooks.com**.

Use Smart Symbols

LiveMotion's SWF export engine has real smarts. It sorts through the output of your file, looking for situations when the same exact object is used more than once. When identical objects are found, LiveMotion exports the object as a shape only once—let's call it a *smart symbol*—and references the shape as needed. If you've designed your composition to take advantage of this time-saving feature, it can cut down the size of the exported file by a considerable amount. Using this technique, you can construct a bountiful field of flowers, a sky full of stars, or a drawer jammed with marbles using just a handful of objects. Or more likely, you'll build a page with a set of identical buttons.

The trick here is that the objects must be exactly identical. Any change between certain object properties—such as color or dimensions—will cause the objects to export as separate shapes. (Object rotation is fine, however.)

What Does Alias Have to Do with This?

Nothing. LiveMotion's Alias function is an editing feature. It's not tied to the smart symbol export feature. That is, identical objects don't have to be aliases (although they can be) to be automatically exported as smart symbols.

Export Magic

In this project, you'll create six buttons that export using just one single shape. You'll see the power of not only LiveMotion's automatic symbol generation, but also its superb bitmap optimization, as well. Let's begin with a new composition:

1. *Start with a fresh canvas.* Create a new composition (Cmd/Ctrl+N). In the Composition Settings dialog box, set the following:

   - Width: 580

   - Height: 350

   - Export: Entire Composition

   - Select Make HTML

   Click on OK.

2. *Create the navigational structure.* Select the Rounded Corner Rectangle tool and draw a rounded corner rectangle 150 pixels wide by 230 pixels high. Use the Properties palette to set the rounded corner Radius to 32. Select a deep cyan-blue from the Color palette (R0, G102, B153).

3. *Create the first button.* Here's how:

   - With the Rounded Corner Rectangle tool still selected, draw a rounded corner rectangle 130 pixels wide by 30 pixels high.

   - Select Linear from the Gradient palette and set the angle to –270.

   - Set the starting (left) gradient color to pale blue (R204, G240, B255), and set the ending (right) gradient color to medium gray-blue (R51, G51, B102).

4. *Duplicate and position the buttons.* Follow these steps:

- Press V to switch to the Selection tool.

- With the rounded corner button selected, press Cmd/Ctrl+D five times to create a total of six buttons.

- Select the topmost button and drag it downward, approximately 160 pixels (or reposition it with the Transform palette).

- Drag a marquee around all of the buttons and select Object| Distribute|Vertical to space them out, then, select Object|Align|Left to align the buttons.

- Position the buttons on top of the deep cyan-blue navigational structure.

5. *Preview the exported file.* Make sure that SWF is selected in the Export palette, and then, select File|Preview In|your browser of choice. The file will be displayed in the browser. Click on the Export Report link to view the exported file statistics. You'll see that the composition is quite lean (mine measured in at just 444 bytes, as shown in Figure 9.8). Scroll

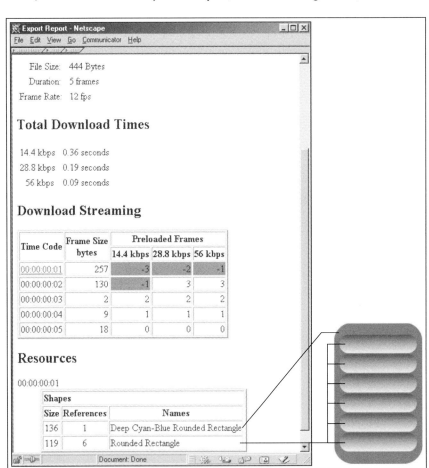

Figure 9.8

These buttons will download in the blink of an eye.

down to the Resources section of the report and notice that the Rounded Rectangle (button shape) was exported just once, but referenced six times.

6. *Give the buttons some (3D) depth.* Now that you've seen how small you can make the file with pure vectors, you'll add a 3D effect to the buttons to see how large the file will grow to be (as bitmaps). With all of the buttons selected, assign a bevel with the 3D palette, using the default settings for depth, softness, and lighting. Don't touch the export settings (keep the JPEG default) and preview the exported file again. (My example weighed in at a respectable 2K, with the single 3D button accounting for 1.64K.)

7. *Hammer down the export settings.* Now, go to work and see how tight you can squeeze the button bitmap. With a TrueColor export, I was able to lean on the settings (Color Resolution of 5, Opacity Resolution of 3) to get the entire composition to 1.11K, as shown in Figure 9.9. In this case, going with a pure vector button, rather than a highly optimized bitmap saved less than 600 bytes. With export control over bitmaps like this, you needn't always pass them over for the vectors.

Of course, you'll probably add bitmapped **over** and **down** states to the button, but even so, you can still squeeze a remarkable amount of detail into just a few kilobytes. (The button text is best kept as a vector, to separate it from the bitmapped button.)

Get Ranked or Get Lost

How do most folks find the Web sites they frequent for the very first time? Statistics point to the search engines, which means great danger for pages that rely exclusively on Flash to deliver their content. A page must be properly constructed in order for it to rise to the top of the search engine listings. Quite simply, Flash-only pages will not be properly indexed by the search engine spiders. Most robots do not currently have the ability to crawl through Flash files. They won't pick up information contained in the files and they won't follow the links contained therein.

I've touched on search engine topics in a number of my books, including *Looking Good on the Web* and *The Complete Guide to Associate and Affiliate Programs on the Net*—it's a subject that bears repeating. I write about search engines for one basic reason: If you haven't designed your site so that it can be easily (and well) indexed, the site will not get the traffic it deserves. It's like planting the most beautiful garden in the world, but no one stops by to see it, because they don't know it's there.

An Active Export Preview File Size Caveat

The Active Export Preview file size figure does not take automatic symbol optimization into account. Turn on Active Export Preview and take note of the (sometimes dramatic) difference between the total file size reported there and in the Export Report.

Figure 9.9
The bitmapped button weighs in at just 771 bytes—it's only downloaded once.

Nonetheless, human-driven (rather than bot-driven), indexes, such as Yahoo and the Open Directory Project, should index and summarize your Flashed site. It's the bots that you need to worry most about. Humans will click into a SWF movie, a spider will not.

Lay the Spider Bait

You must be extremely vigilant in order for your Flashed pages to be effectively crawled and ranked. At a minimum, here's a bit of the spider bait you'll need on each of the HTML container pages:

- *Page title*—Should be clear and concise, while containing the page's most pertinent keywords. Don't go overboard with a lengthy title.

- *Body text*—Include at least a sentence worth of real text, containing the most important keywords. Nail the page topic on the head.

- *<META> keyword and description tags*—Although not used by all of the search engines, clean <META> tags are always a good idea. Don't bother with spurious keywords; they should be relevant to the page (as reflected by the HTML body text).

A great page title and descriptive body text are absolutely essential. You can run the body text underneath the main SWF. If you are concerned about the HTML text clashing visually with the SWF movie, add a bit of space between the movie and the HTML text.

Internal Search Engines

Some search engines can index Flash content, but as of this writing, they're limited to *internal* search engines. Atomz.com, is one shining example. With Atomz, you can index your Flash content and offer searching for SWF within your site.

Preloader Depot

Looking for preloader ideas? The "Preloader Depot" offers a flock of nifty (and yes, even tacky) preloader widgets that you can drop into your LiveMotion compositions. You'll find all of these examples and many more on the *Adobe LiveMotion f/x and Design* companion CD-ROM. Here's a rundown on some of the preloaders included on the CD.

Three Arrows Down

The Three Arrows Down preloader is clean and basic. The bright green arrows loop in a chase light fashion, with the color fading in through the use of an Object Opacity animation. The area within the outlined rounded corner rectangle is left open for you to place your own text. This preloader consists entirely of vector objects and is easy to modify. Figure 9.10 shows the Three Arrows Down preloader in action.

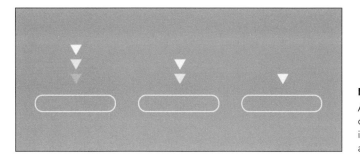

Storm Watch

The Storm Watch preloader spins a dozen white circles on a black background to deliver the feeling of a swirling storm on a radar screen. The circles are divided into three incrementally scaled groups that spin around a shared center point. As with the Three Arrows Down preloader, Storm Watch uses Object Opacity animation. Figure 9.11 provides a glimpse of the Storm Watch preloader.

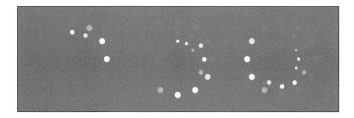

Figure 9.11
Batten down the hatches.

Red Dot Dance

The Red Dot Dance preloader is a fun little animation that consists solely of red circles that pulse in and out, spinning merrily around a center point. Pure vectors export to a highly optimized SWF file (a shade over 4K). Figure 9.12 shows the Red Dot Dance in mid step.

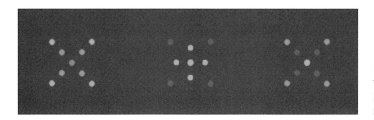

Figure 9.12
This little ditty would look at home on the centerfield scoreboard.

Ratchet Scope

The Ratchet Scope preloader is an uncommon design. With magenta outlined circles and medium purple scope marks, this preloader is intended for sci-fi interfaces. The circles pulse in and out, whereas the scope marks rotate, creating an interesting targeting effect. You can add a bit of descriptive text at the center. Figure 9.13 provides a preview of the Rachet Scope design.

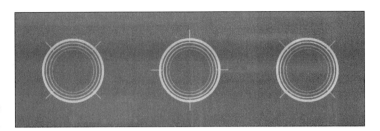

Figure 9.13
Lock into those coordinates.

Digital Square Dance

The Digital Square Dance preloader has nothing to do with traditional square dancing; it's merely made up of dancing digital squares. Eight outlined cyan squares frolic to and fro, bouncing about as if they're held down by rubber bands. Figure 9.14 provides three views of the dancing squares. This whimsical little animation (the exported SWF is less than 4K) is one of my favorites.

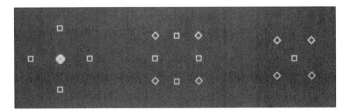

Figure 9.14
Toss your digital partner, do-si-do!

Purple Pager

The Purple Pager preloader contains two looping animations. The word "DOWNLOADING" flashes from purple to pale pink, and the cyan indicator bar flashes from left to right. The pager surface uses a highly compressed bitmap texture. (The exported SWF is just 5K.) As you can see in Figure 9.15, it's not exactly a subtle combination.

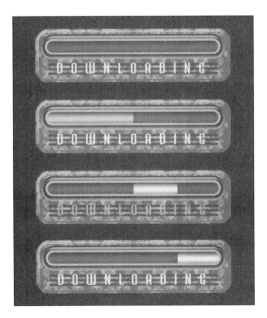

Figure 9.15
Take a look in the color LiveMotion Studio to see this one in glorious screaming color.

Island Radio

The Island Radio preloader is full of action. Like the Purple Pager preloader, the word "DOWNLOADING" flashes—although in this case it's between deep red and pale pink. The red LED indicator bar pulses both left and right. Vector gradients create the chrome bezels, and the grayscale texture comes from the original Adobe LiveMotion CD-ROM. See Figure 9.16.

Figure 9.16
The Island Radio preloader weighs in at only 5K.

Simple Text Track

The Simple Text Track preloader does as its name implies. LiveMotion makes text tracking animation a cinch—just set a Text Tracking keyframe (under Object Attributes), change the CTM, and make an alteration to the text tracking value. Figure 9.17 demonstrates a simple text tracking animation, in conjunction with opacity and a scaling rectangle.

Figure 9.17
Bingo! Instant text tracking animation.

Burst Gradient Wipe

The Burst Gradient Wipe preloader uses a text mask in a rather unique manner. A burst gradient slides through the text, moving from top to bottom. The text is invisible at the start, then, it slowly fades into and out of view. Figure 9.18 shows the effect in action.

Figure 9.18

A smooth loop fades the burst gradient text in and out of view.

10-9-8-7-6-5-4-3-2-1

While you wouldn't want to loop a numeric countdown, this technique can be a very useful piece of the performance; it helps you gain time. Count down from 10 and you'll gain 10 seconds' worth of download time. This can help ease the download up front, as well as within sections of the movie. You'll find a number of numeric countdown animations in the LiveMotion section of **geekbooks.com**.

Moving On

The Flash format isn't a raison d'être, it's merely a means to an end. You must accept that if you want your sites—and more importantly, your clients—to succeed. Don't let the Flash bells and whistles get in the way of the meat and potatoes. The site content is what matters, above all. In the next chapter, you'll learn how to build complete Flash interfaces with LiveMotion. Effective, compelling sites just don't happen. They're inspired and engineered.

Chapter 10

SWF Navigation

Want more than a simple intro, banner, or ornament?
This chapter tackles the topic of building a complete
Flash interface with LiveMotion.

Taking It to the Next Level

Once you've had a taste of real interactivity through the SWF format, you may never want to go back to the mundane world of HTML and JavaScript rollovers. Success doesn't happen at the click of a button, however. To prevail, your work must be fresh, compelling, and well engineered. Great SWF delivers more than just a commercial, and more than just a bunch of flying text and gyrating logos syncopated to a thumping beat.

In the previous chapter, I stressed the importance of building smart SWF—shaving file sizes and staging downloads. This chapter takes things to the next level, as it dives into the subject of Flash interfaces and animated styles.

All SWF or SWF and HTML?

How are you going to build your site? Do you want to take the leap and create the whole enchilada as SWF files? Or do you want to mix SWF and HTML content? In the previous chapter, I tried to drive home the importance of opening up your site content to the search engines. If you have that angle covered, you can indulge in a deep SWF interface. If not, you'll likely want to mix SWF and HTML.

One popular method of doing so is to use a SWF movie as the navigational element—linking to additional HTML pages (which also contain the same SWF navigation file). The HTML pages should also provide basic navigation through HTML links to appease the search engine spiders and plug-inless browsers, alike. Another method is to place the SWF navigation in a separate frame from the HTML content. This can work nicely—but once again, you must be assured that the site content is accessible from the search engines. (Framed sites are notorious for under performing in search engine results.)

Let's take a look at some SWF navigational approaches.

Drop-Down Menus

The drop-down menus used in the Macintosh and Windows operating systems have spawned many a Web navigation scheme. In this section, I'll demonstrate the creation of a basic drop-down menu scheme with LiveMotion, as shown in Figure 10.1. The following project shows how to create SWF drop-down menus in a fairly straightforward manner. You can apply this method to more complex designs as you become more comfortable with the procedure.

Here's an overview:

1. Create each individual drop-down menu. Add links and rollovers, as necessary. Make each drop-down menu a Time Independent Group. Name each menu accordingly.

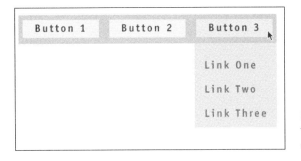

Figure 10.1
The end result—a basic drop-down menu.

2. Position the drop-down menus in their "dropped down" position.

3. Draw a rectangle to cover the entire drop-down area.

4. Select the drop-down menus along with the covering rectangle and group.

5. Select Top Object Is Mask to turn the covering rectangle into a mask.

6. Name the menu drop-down group via the Timeline.

7. Create a custom rollover state for each of the menu drop downs. (The **normal** state contains all of the menus in a rolled up mode.)

8. Create rollovers and target each of the drop-down menu custom rollover states.

PROJECT Drop (Down) and Give Me Twenty

Ready to build a nifty navigational scheme? This project uses three basic rollover buttons and drop-down menus:

1. *Create a new composition (Cmd/Ctrl+N).* In the Composition Settings dialog box, set the following:

   - Width: 600

   - Height: 400

   - Export: Entire Composition

   - Select Make HTML

   Click on OK.

2. *Create the first drop-down menu.* Follow these steps:

   - Select the Rectangle tool and draw a rectangle 140 pixels wide by 140 pixels high. Assign it a light blue color.

   - Select the Text tool and add the menu text as separate text blocks (in 18-point type)—called Link One, Link Two, and Link Three. Assign a dark blue color to the text.

- Use the Web palette to assign links to each of the text blocks (linkone.html, linktwo.html, and linkthree.html, respectively).

- Position the text as shown in Figure 10.2.

Figure 10.2

The drop-down menu, shown with the third link targeted via the Web palette.

In the next step, you'll duplicate the first drop-down menu. If this were a live project, you'd then alter the text and links. (Those steps have been omitted for simplicity's sake.)

3. *Group and duplicate the drop-down menu.* Follow these steps:

    - Select the light blue rectangle and text, and then, select Timeline| Make Time Independent Group (Shift+Cmd/Ctrl+G).

    - Press Cmd/Ctrl+D twice to duplicate the drop-down menu group (to create a total of three).

    - Position the three drop-down menus as shown in Figure 10.3. (Leave 10 pixels between the menus.)

4. *Name each drop-down menu.* Open the Timeline (Cmd/Ctrl+T), select each drop-down group (they'll all be named "Group of 4 objects" with a little Time Independent icon), press Enter, and rename each as "dropdown1", "dropdown2", and "dropdown3".

5. *Create the mask.* Follow these steps:

    - Select the Rectangle tool and draw a rectangle 440 pixels wide by 140 pixels high; it should exactly cover the drop-down menus.

    - Select all of the menus, along with the rectangle. You can position the rectangle with the Transform palette or (temporarily) set the Object Opacity level to 30% in order to see through the mask, as demonstrated by Figure 10.3.

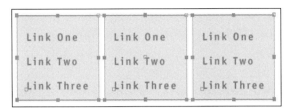

- With all three menus and the 440-by-140 rectangle selected, press Cmd/Ctrl+G to group, and then, select Object|Top Object is Mask. (You can change the Object Opacity of the masking rectangle back to 100% by first selecting it in the Timeline.)

Before you go any further, select the "Masked Group of 4 objects" in the Timeline. Press Enter and rename the group as "the drop down group", and click on OK. (This will make it easy to find later on.)

6. *Create the custom rollover states.* With the masked drop-down menu group selected, click on the New Rollover State button (on the Rollovers palette) three times to create a total of four rollover states. Use the Rollovers palette to:

   - Select the **out** state, then, select Custom State from the **out** state's drop-down menu. Assign "dropped 1" in the Custom State dialog box, and click on OK.

   - Select the **down** state, then, select Custom State from the **down** state's drop-down menu. Assign "dropped 2" in the Custom State dialog box, and click on OK.

   - Select the **over** state, then, select Custom State from the **over** state's drop-down menu. Assign "dropped 3" in the Custom State dialog box, and click on OK.

7. *Position the elements in each custom rollover state.* Here's where the magic starts to appear (as the menus disappear). These steps are highly repetitive, so make sure that you're selecting the correct items in each step:

   - Select the **normal** state in the Rollovers palette. Double-click on "the drop down group" to drill down in the Timeline, and then, select dropdown1, dropdown2, and dropdown3 (hold down the Shift key to add the second and third selection). Press Cmd/Ctrl+T to switch focus back to the Composition window. Hold down the Shift key and press the Cursor Up key 15 times. (This moves the three menus up 150 pixels, in 10 pixel increments.) Notice how the mask group expands as the menus disappear and slide upward.

- Deselect the drop-down menu group, then, reselect it. Select the **dropped 1** state in the Rollovers palette. Select **dropdown1** in the Timeline. Hold down the Shift key and press the Cursor Down key 15 times.

- Deselect the drop-down menu group, then, reselect it. Select the **dropped 2** state in the Rollovers palette. Select **dropdown2** in the Timeline. Hold down the Shift key and press the Cursor Down key 15 times.

- Deselect the drop-down menu group, then, reselect it. Select the **dropped 3** state in the Rollovers palette. Select **dropdown3** in the Timeline. Hold down the Shift key and press the Cursor Down key 15 times.

The drop-down menus should now be functional (although not yet targeted). Deselect the drop-down menu group, and reselect it one more time. Preview each of the four states with the Rollovers palette. Make any adjustments as necessary. The next step is to build the horizontal button bar from which the drop-down menus will fall.

8. *Create the button bar.* Select the Rectangle tool and draw a rectangle, 440 pixels wide by 48 pixels high to create a button bar. Assign it a slightly darker blue color than the drop-down menus. Draw three rectangles, 130 pixels wide by 30 pixels high, and assign an aqua color to create the buttons. Position them as shown in Figure 10.4.

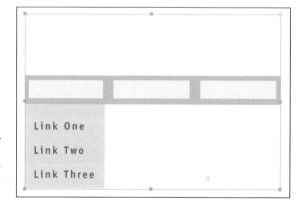

Figure 10.4

Select the drop-down menu group's dropped 1 state to gauge the height of the drop-down menu.

9. *Add text and rollover states.* Add and position three text blocks (Button 1, Button 2, and Button 3) on top of the respective aqua buttons. Then, select all three aqua buttons and click on New Rollover State to add **over** states to each of the three buttons. Assign a light purple color to the **over** states.

10. *Target the custom drop-down menu states.* At last, now you tell the rollovers to drop down the menus. Once again, this shows a bit of repetition:

     • Target the first state. Select the **over** state of the first button and click on the Behaviors button (on the Rollovers palette). Select Change State from the Add Behavior menu in the Edit Behaviors dialog box. Select "the drop down group" from the Target menu and "dropped 1" from the State menu, as shown in Figure 10.5, and click on OK.

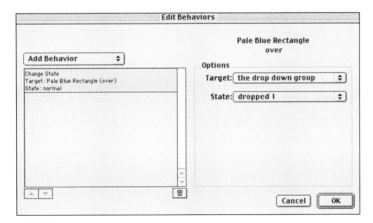

Figure 10.5
It's important to name your objects, groups, and states descriptively. Otherwise, they can be frustrating to find and target.

     • Target the second state. Select the **over** state of the second button and click on the Behaviors button (on the Rollovers palette). Select Change State from the Add Behavior menu in the Edit Behaviors dialog box. Select "the drop down group" from the Target menu and "dropped 2" from the State menu, and click on OK.

     • Target the third state. Select the **over** state of the third button and click on the Behaviors button (on the Rollovers palette). Select Change State from the Add Behavior menu in the Edit Behaviors dialog box. Select "the drop down group" from the Target menu and "dropped 3" from the State menu, and click on OK.

Save the file and take a look at your handiwork with LiveMotion's Preview tool. Then, try previewing in your browser of choice.

Want to spice things up? LiveMotion allows for a multitude of possibilities. Figure 10.6 shows how the drop-down menus can contain linked rollovers, rather than just simple links. (Of course, adding additional rollovers will increase the size of the exported SWF, so plan carefully.)

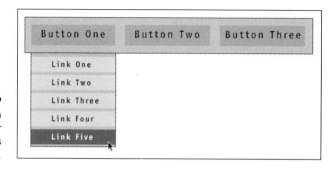

Figure 10.6

Drop-down menus with rollovers can mimic the familiar Macintosh and Windows interface components.

To add rollovers to a drop-down menu:

1. Create the menu object.

2. Create the rollovers and assign the links (either URLs or remote rollovers).

3. Position the rollovers, then, select the menu object (along with all of its rollovers) and create a Time Independent Group.

It's just as easy to create menus that fly out from a vertical navigation bar, as shown in Figure 10.7. When the button is rolled over, the fly-out menu appears; it is persistent until another button is rolled over. (The button's **normal** state doesn't hide the fly out. Instead, the fly-out menus are hidden by the **over** states of the other buttons.) You can animate the appearance of the menus. Because they are Time Independent Groups, they slide into view.

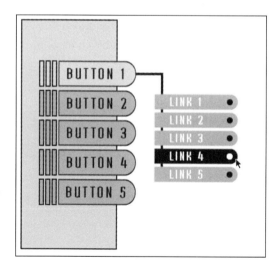

Figure 10.7

This example happens to use an object (the vertical rectangle), rather than a masked group, to hide the fly-out menus.

Here are some hints to create drop-down (or fly-out) menus that slide into view:

- *Put your things away.* The **over** state on one button should target the **normal** (hidden state) of all of the other fly-out menus, in addition to flying out the menu for that button.

- *Don't use more time (or whiz bang motion) than necessary*. Slide those puppies out, but don't make too much of the deal. It's easy to fall into gratuitous implementation mode—this bloats file size and feels heavy handed.

Slide Out Consoles

Would you like your visitors to have the option of sliding their buttons in and out of view? Slide out consoles are similar to drop-down (or fly-out) menus. They hide link selections until requested, and can be used to reduce screen clutter. The biggest difference between consoles and drop-down (or fly-out) menus is that the consoles provide the means to hide the exposed navigational buttons. The example shown in Figure 10.8 is a bit thingamajigish, but it's a fun demonstration, nonetheless. No doubt you'll come up with far more exciting variations.

Slide out console

Mask or Not

You can hide rolled up menus in a number of ways. Although the drop-down menu's Time Independent Group is often a masked group, you can also create a knock-out rectangle to cover the menus when they are rolled up—this lets you hide the menus without the use of a mask (the drop-down menus are placed *behind* the rectangle). Figure 10.7 provides one example. In some cases, you can make the knock-out rectangle the same color as the background. It's a cheap trick, but it works.

Figure 10.8
One click slides the nav buttons out, one click slides the buttons in.

PROJECT Building a Sliding Console

Let's take a look at how to create a basic sliding console:

1. *Create a new composition (Cmd/Ctrl+N)*. In the Composition Settings dialog box, enter the following:

   - Width: 720

   - Height: 500

   - Export: Entire Composition

   - Select Make HTML

   Click on OK.

2. *Create the lower console.* Select the Rounded Rectangle tool and draw a rounded rectangle 680 pixels wide by 46 pixels high; set its corner radius to 16 via the Properties palette and assign a medium gray color.

3. *Create the upper console.* Follow these steps:

   - Duplicate the lower console (rounded corner rectangle) object with Cmd/Ctrl+D.

   - Change the width of the new upper console object to 700 pixels and the height to 48 pixels via the Transform palette.

   - Change the color of the upper console object to a slightly lighter gray.

   - Position the objects as shown in Figure 10.9.

Figure 10.9
It doesn't look like much (yet).

4. *Add rollover buttons to the lower console.* Select the Rounded Rectangle tool and draw a rounded rectangle 100 pixels wide by 24 pixels high; set its corner radius to 16 via the Properties palette and assign a dark gray color. Position the button at the left side of the lower console, then:

   - Create the rollover. With the 100-by-24-pixel rounded corner rectangle (button) selected, click on New Rollover State on the Rollovers palette. Change the color of the over state to black.

   - Add text to the rollover button. Select the Text tool, click on the center of the button, and type "BUTTON 1" in the Type tool dialog box's text area. Set the text to 14 point Helvetica Bold (or something similar), with a centered horizontal alignment. Click on OK. Switch to the Selection tool (V), select white from the Color palette, and position the text on the button.

   - Group the text with the rollover button. Select the BUTTON 1 text, along with the underlying button. Group the two together with Cmd/Ctrl+G.

   - Duplicate the button. Press Cmd/Ctrl+D five times to create a total of six rollover buttons.

   - Position the buttons. Click and drag the top button to the right side of the lower console. Drag a marquee around all of the buttons (but not the lower console), and select Object|Distribute|Horizontal to distribute the buttons across the lower console, as shown in Figure 10.10.

Figure 10.10
The buttons in position.

- Alter the button text. Double-click on each button to summon the Text Tool dialog box. Change the names of buttons 2 through 6 to read "BUTTON 2" through "BUTTON 6", respectively.

5. *Group the buttons with the lower console.* Drag out a marquee to select all of the buttons, along with the lower console. Select Timeline|Make Time Independent Group. Select Object|Arrange|Send to Back.

6. *Group the lower console with the upper console.* Shift-click to select the upper console, along with the lower console. Select Timeline|Make Time Independent Group.

7. *Name the console group.* Press Cmd/Ctrl+T to open the Timeline. Select the "Group of 2 objects" (the console), then, press Enter to summon the Name dialog box. Enter "the slider" and press OK. Then, double-click on "the slider" in the Timeline—this will drill down into the group. Select "Group of 7 objects," press Enter, and rename as "lower console".

8. *Slide the lower console up and create a custom state.* Select the Subgroup Selection tool, and then, select the lower console in the Timeline. Press the Up cursor key repeatedly to hide the lower console behind the upper console. The next steps are a little tricky. It's easy to go astray when assigning the rollover:

   - Deselect the group. (This is crucial. You don't want to create the rollover with the wrong piece selected.)

   - Select the Selection tool, and then, select "the slider" in the Timeline. Click on New Rollover State on the Rollovers palette—this will create an **over** state. Select the **over** state, and then, select Custom State from the drop-down menu. Type "slider down" in the Custom State dialog box and click on OK. Select the lower console in the Timeline, and move it down with the Down cursor key (so that the buttons fully appear).

   - Deselect the group, and then reselect it again with the Selection tool. Preview the normal and slider down states with the Rollovers palette.

9. *Create the down and up arrow buttons.* Select the Polygon tool. Draw a 3-sided polygon (a triangle), approximately 20 pixels wide by 30 pixels

high. Select the Selection tool, assign a dark gray from the Color palette, and rotate the triangle by 90 degrees clockwise, so that it points down-ward, then:

- Press Cmd/Ctrl+D to duplicate the triangle. Click on Object| Transform|Flip Horizontal—this will flip around the duplicate triangle so that it points upward. Use the Up cursor key to move the upward pointing arrow above the lower pointing arrow.

- Select both triangles, and then, click on New Rollover State on the Rollovers palette. Change both of the **over** states to **down** states via the drop-down menu.

- Position the arrows on the right side of the upper console.

10. *Target the slide out.* Shift-click the up arrow button to deselect it. With the **down** state of the down arrow still selected, click on the Behaviors button (on the Rollovers palette). Select Change State from the Add Behavior menu in the Edit Behaviors dialog box. Select "the slider" from the Target menu and "slider down" from the State menu, and click on OK.

11. *Target the slider's **normal** state.* Click on the up arrow button to select it. Make sure that the **down** state is selected, and then, click on the Behaviors button. Select Change State from the Add Behavior menu in the Edit Behaviors dialog box. Select "the slider" from the Target menu and "normal" from the State menu, and click on OK.

Press Q to preview the sliding console and rollovers. Note that LiveMotion's internal preview *may* quit working after the first time you slide up the console. (Press Q twice to switch to Edit mode, and then back to Preview mode.) Preview in your browser of choice to ensure that everything functions as it should. Figure 10.11 shows the finished sliding console.

Figure 10.11

Click on the down arrow to slide the button console down. Click on the up arrow to hide the button console.

Layering Content with Load Movie

As you build a complex SWF site, you'll want to make the most of LiveMotion's Load Movie and Unload Movie behaviors (introduced in Chapter 8). When properly implemented, Load and Unload Movie let you quickly swap movies in and out of the presentation space. This helps to streamline downloads by downloading only the information as needed. Instead of a single 250K SWF, for example, you may be able to break the composition into half a dozen SWF files—allowing the container (navigational) SWF to download in the wink of an eye. As a rollover button is clicked, the individual SWF streams to the browser on demand. Figure 10.12 provides an example of the flow.

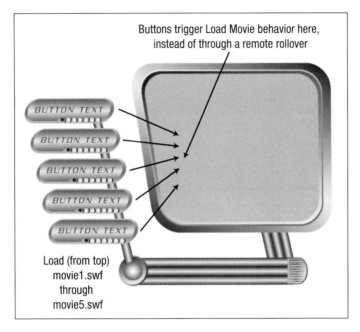

Buttons trigger Load Movie behavior here, instead of through a remote rollover

BUTTON TEXT
BUTTON TEXT
BUTTON TEXT
BUTTON TEXT
BUTTON TEXT

Load (from top)
movie1.swf
through
movie5.swf

Figure 10.12
With Load Movie, you can set up your files to download content as it is called.

While a plain old remote rollover works well with static rollovers, you should take advantage of Load Movie for more complex implementations. Think of a television set with a push-button console. As you push the buttons, different channels are loaded into the screen. The content appears (and is downloaded) as it is requested. (Imagine how it would be if your television set displayed a "downloading" screen—yeeech!)

Using this scenario has a number of additional benefits:

- Content creation can be split between members of a workgroup.

- It's easier to update individual LIV component files, rather than a gargantuan LIV file.

- LiveMotion should deliver better operating performance when editing smaller files.

The drop-down menu, fly-out menu, and sliding console examples shown in this chapter would work well with Load Movie behaviors assigned to the rollover buttons. As you build your sites in this manner, think about how the navigational structure will float over (or under) the page content.

Where Does It Fall?

The Load Movie behavior drops the movie at a coordinate of X: 0, Y: 0—the top-left corner of the SWF. In order to align the individual elements, you should build the separate movies with the exact same composition size. If your navigation is built in a 580-by-350-pixel space, so, too, should be the content. (Think of drawing on layers of acetate or tracing paper.)

Animated Styles

While the subject of styles was introduced back in Chapter 3, it's worth another look now. LiveMotion's capability to store and apply animated styles holds the potential for substantial time savings. As with graphic and rollover styles, animated styles allow you to create the style just once—and apply it with just a mouse click (or two). With a set style, you can apply the same exact motion effects to a number of elements within your movie. This can help to create a sense of continuity over multiple scenes of a presentation.

When creating animated styles for files that will be exported as SWF, it's wise to take extra care to forgo any attributes that cause bitmap output—unless you take the steps to optimize the resulting elements. To that end, I've created a whole bunch of SWF-friendly animated styles. These little critters play with safe attributes, such as opacity, scale, position, rotation, and skew, to great effect.

 ## Animated Style Depot

Here's a sampling of some of the many animated styles that you'll find on the *Adobe LiveMotion f/x and Design* companion CD-ROM. I've tried to name the styles as descriptively as possible—but of course, me being me, you'll find some wacky names there, too. It's a bit futile to portray these with static figures, so a text description will have to do (for now). Load up the CD-ROM and get a live look at the LIVs when you have the chance.

Here's a taste:

- *lmfx-drop-n-blink-3x.liv*—Falls from the top of the composition window, with an opacity fade-in as the object falls. When the object hits the vertical plane, it flashes and expands with scale and opacity tweaks.

- *lmfx-bounce-3x*—Zooms from back, with opacity and scale. Bounces three times when the object hits the vertical plane.

- *lmfx-breakingball.liv*—Imagine that you're the batter. This one flies from the back, growing larger and more opaque as it nears home plate. Also includes an opacity rollover effect.

- *lmfx-flyin-arc-top-left.liv*—Arcs in from the top-left side, starting out huge, with a low opacity level. The object rotates 45 degrees clockwise as the size decreases and the opacity level hits 100 percent.

- *lmfx-flyin-arc-top-right.liv*—Arcs in from the top right side, starting out huge, with a low opacity level. The object rotates 45 degrees counter-clockwise as the size decreases and the opacity level hits 100 percent.

Use the Library and Alias Features

LiveMotion's Library palette is a handy place to store everything from alpha channel image mattes, to dingbats, to frequently used navigation objects. Bitmap files, vector files, and complete LiveMotion files (including rollovers and animations) are all valid. If you build a complex element that will be used repetitively—especially when it's across a number of compositions—think about putting the element into the Library for safekeeping. The element will then always be just a click away.

Note that unlike Flash, it isn't necessary to store objects in the Library to gain the benefits of smart object optimization. (LiveMotion automatically applies its optimization scheme upon SWF export, rather than forcing the use of the Library palette.)

LiveMotion's Alias feature is provided purely as an editing convenience. When one object is an alias of another, all changes to one object will take place in the other object. This can be a convenient means to ensure optimized SWF export— identical objects will be exported only once in the SWF file. However, two identical objects do *not* have to be aliases to be optimized upon export. LiveMotion's export engine is smart enough to do the automatic symbolization on its own.

- *lmfx-rubberband.liv*—Slides in from the left with low opacity, on a vertical plane. The object pauses at the center of the screen, rears back, and takes off again (fading out as it slides to the right). A subtle skew adds to the feeling of motion.

- *lmfx-spin-in-boop.liv*—Completes four clockwise rotations as it fades in from back. When the object hits the wall, it splats and retracts with size and opacity. Also includes an opacity rollover.

- *lmfx-twirlingbuzzsaw-left.liv*—Think of a bouncing buzz saw blade, thrown from left to right. Uses an opacity fade in, along with a slight skew.

- *lmfx-zoomspin-in.liv*—Completes four clockwise rotations as it fades in from back with size and opacity tweaks. Think of the paper boy throwing you the morning news.

- *lmfx-zoomspin-out.liv*—Completes four counter-clockwise rotations as it fades away to back with size and opacity tweaks. Delivers that "down the drain" feeling.

Moving On

A great interface takes inspiration, careful planning, and thorough execution. To that end, this chapter's happy rant on the subject of building SWF interfaces with LiveMotion endeavors to put you on the road to success. The next chapter explains how LiveMotion works with other programs—importing resources and exporting Web layouts—with a focus on Adobe Photoshop and Illustrator.

Chapter 11

Working with Other Apps

LiveMotion was designed to work in tandem with Adobe's formidable suite of tools. This chapter provides hints on integrating with Adobe Photoshop and Illustrator; but it's only meant to be a beginning.

Exact Change Only

LiveMotion isn't an island, it's more like a bridge—allowing you to move content among the vector drawing, bitmap paint, and Web page layout worlds. But, this bridge has its tolls. You need to know where the costs lie. To that end, this chapter spells out some of the irregularities you'll find in the road, as it provides direction and alternative routes. The interaction between LiveMotion and other applications is a rapidly developing area. New things *always* come to light in the time it takes for a book to go from manuscript to your hands. This is a voyage that will be continued online at **geekbooks.com**.

Before going too far down the road, let's hit some of the key detours:

- *Illustrator 9 format: no go*—LiveMotion will not place Illustrator 9 formatted documents. Although you can drag and drop from application to application, you can't drag and drop a version 9 file from the desktop into LiveMotion, nor can you import it via the Place dialog box. If you are using Illustrator 9, you should save your files in the version 8 format (or earlier).

- *Work in RGB, not CMYK*—As you create your artwork in Illustrator and Photoshop, you should stick with RGB color mode, rather than CMYK. If you bring CMYK artwork into LiveMotion, you will experience the color shifts that are typical when moving between color modes (as with any application).

- *Text imported from Illustrator exports as SWF bitmaps*—Want to take advantage of Illustrator's character kerning and text on a path capabilities? Unfortunately, LiveMotion will turn imported Illustrator text objects into bitmaps upon SWF export. If you're working with flat colored text, use the Indexed Color export option to prevent file bloat. (Alternatively, you can convert the type to outlines in Illustrator—this object will export as vectors in SWF—but the weight of the text will likely swell upon conversion.)

- *No path*—Objects dragged and dropped from an Illustrator 9 composition window into a LiveMotion composition window cannot be edited with LiveMotion's Pen Selection tool. Save the object as a version 8 Illustrator file, and then, bring the file into LiveMotion (via the Place dialog box or by dragging and dropping from the desktop).

- *Simple paths*—Only simple black vector objects can be edited with LiveMotion's Pen Selection tool. The simple object must consist of a single path; if it contains more than one path, it can be altered via Edit Original.

Controlling Who Opens What

LiveMotion's Helpers folder (directory) contains four subfolders (subdirectories) where you can assign the Edit Original Helper applications. The installation process should automatically populate these folders (although it may not). You can make additions or changes to the Helpers at any time, simply by dragging an alias or shortcut for the helping application into the appropriate folder. Here's a list of the different helper types, along with some of their most common applications:

- *Graphic Editors*—Photoshop, Paint Shop Pro
- *HTML Editors*—GoLive, PageMill, FrontPage, Dreamweaver
- *Preview In*—Netscape Communicator, Microsoft Internet Explorer
- *Vector Editors*—Illustrator, Freehand, CorelDRAW

Edit Original

Once Illustrator or Photoshop artwork is placed into a LiveMotion composition, you can make changes to the artwork in the original application with the Edit|Edit Original command (Shift+Cmd/Ctrl+M). This capability is invaluable when altering artwork. When you select an imported object and summon the Edit Original command, LiveMotion launches the helper application and opens a file that is identical to the original. When you make changes in the application and close or quit the file, an alert dialog box appears, as shown in Figure 11.1. You must save the file in order for the changes to appear in LiveMotion.

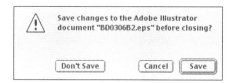

Figure 11.1
The revised file will be named with a cryptic alphanumeric.

Why is this feature so cool? Let's say that you've applied a bunch of special effect filters and adjustments to a photograph. Upon review, the client finds something in the photograph that must be removed, such as a logo or a departed employee. Instead of ditching all of your special effects work, you can use the Edit Original command to open up a copy of the photograph in Photoshop, make the changes (removing the logo or person), and simply close the file. When you return to LiveMotion, all of the effects and adjustments will be made to the altered original image.

The edited file is stored temporarily (until LiveMotion is closed) in a special folder:

- *Macintosh*—System Folder\Preferences\Adobe\LiveMotion\External Edits
- *Windows*—Windows\Application Data\Adobe\LiveMotion\External Edits

What If I Don't Have the Original App?

You can set up the Helper folders to use whatever applications you have at hand. If the image was originally edited in Adobe Photoshop, for example, you can get by with JASC Paint Shop Pro.

Placing Photoshop and Illustrator Files

Once you place layered Photoshop and Illustrator files into a LiveMotion composition, you can convert them with the Object|Convert Layers Into command. Then, you can animate them at will. This feature enables you to accomplish feats, such as drawing complex cartoon characters in Illustrator while handling the animation chores in LiveMotion.

Object|Convert Layers Into provides four options:

- *Objects*—Each layer is converted into a separate object.
- *Group of Objects*—Each layer is converted into a separate object; all of the resulting objects are grouped.
- *Sequence*—The layers are converted into a sequenced object.
- *Sequence With Background*—The layers are converted into a sequenced object that includes a background image, which is displayed consistently throughout the object's lifetime.

Commence Sequence

In addition to the Object|Convert Layers Into|Sequence and Object|Convert Layers Into|Sequence With Background commands, LiveMotion provides two additional ways to place a sequence of images—enabling a mini movie within a composition. The first method works with a series of files in any importable format (AI, EPS, TIFF, JPEG, PSD, and so on). The second allows for the placement of GIF89a animations. A sequence of images will appear as one object, regardless of the chosen placement method. When the sequence object is selected, the Properties palette displays a Time slider, as shown in Figure 11.2.

The image sequence concept is relatively simple, although it can be a bit difficult to grasp at first. When a sequence is placed into a LiveMotion composition, the Timeline is automatically set with starting and ending Object Time keyframes (under Object Attributes). The number of frames shown in the Time slider (and entry field) corresponds to the total number of frames in the sequence. These sequence frames can be freely tweaked—you can change the

---

Layer Conversion Tips

This pair of tips may come in handy when converting layered objects:

- *Those annoying bounding boxes*—When converting a layered Illustrator file into objects (or a group of objects), LiveMotion assigns an identically sized bounding box to each object, regardless of the object's size. This can make it difficult to select each object. The best solution is to make your object selections via the Timeline.
- *Throw out what you don't need*—Once you place a layered object and convert it to separate objects, delete any unnecessary layers to avoid any needless bloat in the exported SWF.

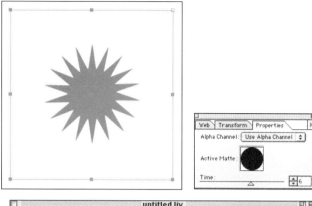

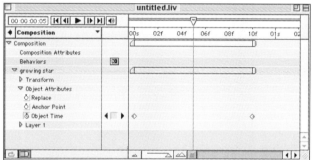

Figure 11.2
The Properties palette controls the image frame, whereas the Timeline's Object Time attribute displays the keyframes. The overall duration of the sequence is controlled by moving the ending keyframe.

order in which they are displayed, as well as the duration of exposure. The total Object Time can be quickly shortened or lengthened by simply moving the ending Object Time keyframe.

Placing a Sequence of Files

LiveMotion does not allow the placement of QuickTime, AVI, or other movie formats. If you want to simulate a movie, you must first generate a series of still files from your video editing application. Then, you'll need to use the File|Place Sequence command (Opt+Shift+Cmd+I on a Mac or Alt+Shift+Ctrl+I in Windows) to place the series of still files into your LiveMotion composition. (Keep in mind that these techniques can lead to hefty SWF exports, because they deal with lots of bitmaps.)

The files you place with Place Sequence must be named sequentially (say that three times fast): dog-1.psd, dog-2.psd, dog-3.psd, and so on. You need only specify one file with the dialog box, as shown in Figure 11.3. LiveMotion will import all of the sequentially named files present in the folder/directory.

You can also use the Place Sequence command to add three-dimensional animations into LiveMotion compositions. The still files are generated from a 3D application capable of rendering in Adobe Illustrator or EPS format, such as Adobe Dimensions or Swift3D.

Watch the Numbers!

The sequence numbers should be the only numbers in the file name—more than one set of numbers in the sequence name may cause the import to fail.

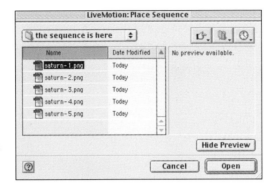

Figure 11.3

Just pick one. LiveMotion will gobble them all.

Placing GIF Animations

When you place GIF animations into LiveMotion, the program identifies the object as a sequence, as evidenced by the Properties palette's Time slider. However, the Object Time keyframes may not be properly set (preventing the sequence from playing). Once you place the file, you'll probably need to open up the Timeline and set the Object Time keyframes manually.

Working with the Web Page Editors

The most common way to get your LiveMotion composition into a Web page editor is to export the composition with the Make HTML option selected in the Composition Settings dialog box. Once the composition has been exported, open the exported HTML file in your Web page editor of choice. With all of the code in place—whether it's JavaScript or the SWF embedding commands—you can build the remainder of the page and make any tweaks, as necessary.

You'll probably want to keep the coding as intact as possible. Let's take a look at a sample of exported code for a typical SWF page (named "basic template"):

```
<HTML>

<HEAD>

    <TITLE>basic template</TITLE>
</HEAD>
<BODY BGCOLOR="#ffffff">
<OBJECT CLASSID="clsid:D27CDB6E-AE6D-11cf-96B8-444553540000"
 CODEBASE="http://active.macromedia.com/flash2/cabs/swflash.cab#
version=4,0,0,0"
ID="basic template" WIDTH="580" HEIGHT="300">
 <PARAM NAME=movie VALUE="basic template.swf">
 <PARAM NAME=quality VALUE=high>
 <PARAM NAME=bgcolor VALUE=#ffffff>
<EMBED SRC="basic template.swf" QUALITY=high BGCOLOR=#ffffff
WIDTH="580" HEIGHT="300" TYPE="application/x-shockwave-flash"
```

Converting ImageStyler Files to LiveMotion Files

A handful of issues affect the translation of ImageStyler files into LiveMotion styles. When you open an ImageStyler .ist extension file in LiveMotion, you'll likely encounter one of the following situations:

- *Rollovers*—Some rollovers may not make the transition between ImageStyler and LiveMotion. You may have to deconstruct intricate ImageStyler rollovers and reassemble them in LiveMotion.

- *Text*—LiveMotion treats text in a different manner than ImageStyler; LiveMotion places extra space at the top and bottom of the text bounding box. For this reason, text set in ImageStyler may be distorted when the file is opened in LiveMotion. Delete the text from the file and re-enter it in LiveMotion.

- *Combined objects*—Certain combined objects will not make the transition between ImageStyler and LiveMotion; there are alignment issues. It may be best to re-create the combinations from scratch in LiveMotion.

```
PLUGINSPAGE="http://www.macromedia.com/shockwave/download/
index.cgi?P1_Prod_Version=ShockwaveFlash"> </EMBED>
</OBJECT>

</BODY>

</HTML>
```

It's worth noting that LiveMotion uses both **<OBJECT>** and **<EMBED>** tags to handle the display of the SWF file in a range of browsers. (Thus, the repetition with regard to file names and dimensions.) The **CODEBASE** parameter tells Microsoft Internet Explorer where to find and download the Flash Player ActiveX control, should it be missing; this works in IE 4 and later. Likewise, the **PLUGINSPAGE** parameter tells Netscape Communicator where to find and download the Flash plug-in.

Some applications are more LiveMotion-friendly than others, with Adobe GoLive 5 being the most LiveMotion-friendly of all. (Unfortunately, GoLive 5 was still under development as this last chapter was submitted, so I could not provide in-depth coverage of LiveMotion/GoLive 5 integration in these pages.)

This book had to go to press before GoLive 5 was released. Rather than work with a pre-release version of the software, I made the decision to deliver the LiveMotion/GoLive integration information online. Point your browser at my Web site, **www.geekbooks.com**, to obtain the latest on using these two excellent applications together. You'll also find additional resources for LiveMotion and inter-program issues, as well as the LiveMotion FX [LMFX] mail list.

> **Building SWF into HTML Layouts**
>
> You can integrate SWF movies into your HTML layouts by placing the whole enchilada—from the **<OBJECT>** tag to the **</OBJECT>** tag—into a layout table cell. This provides basic control over layout for the widest range of browsers.

Moving On

LiveMotion provides a bridge between the conventional Adobe design tools and the Web design world. This chapter covered some of the intricacies of working with those applications, and brings to a close the tutorial section of the book. In the following appendixes, you'll get a taste of the original textures, vector objects, and bitmaps that come on the *Adobe LiveMotion f/x and Design* CD-ROM.

Appendix A

Image Mattes and Shapes

This appendix provides a visual index to the image mattes and shapes contained on the Adobe LiveMotion f/x and Design companion CD-ROM.

The image mattes and shapes you'll find on the *Adobe LiveMotion f/x and Design* companion CD-ROM are provided royalty-free. You're welcome to use these components in any of your designs. The only restriction is that you may not repackage or redistribute the files themselves.

Image Mattes

Oval-matte-01.eps   Oval-matte-02.eps   Oval-matte-03.eps   Oval-matte-04.eps

Oval-matte-05.eps   Oval-matte-06.eps   Oval-matte-07.eps   Oval-matte-08.eps

Oval-matte-09.eps   Oval-matte-10.eps   Oval-matte-11.eps   Oval-matte-12.eps

Rec-matte-01.eps   Rec-matte-02.eps   Rec-matte-03.eps   Rec-matte-04.eps

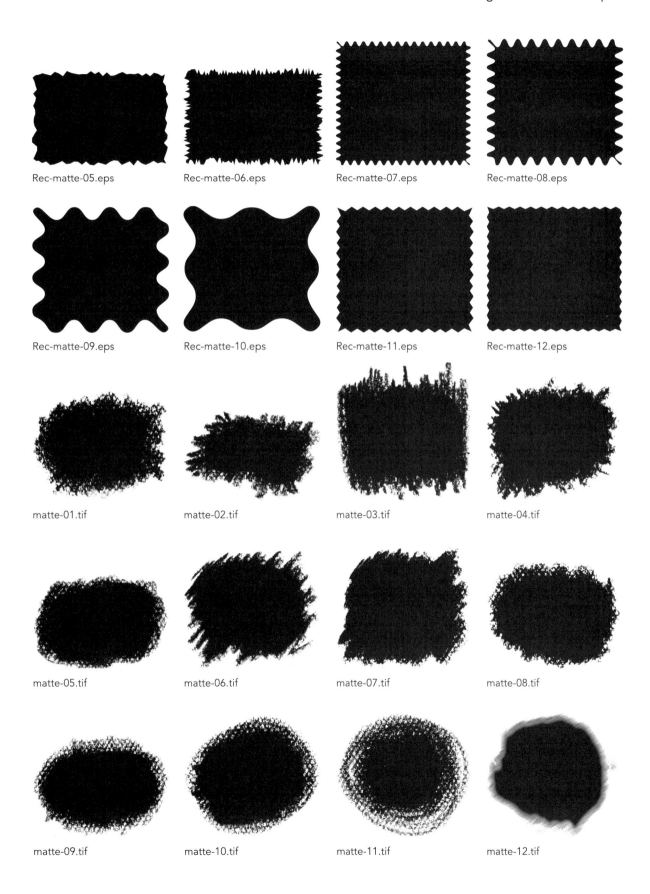

Rec-matte-05.eps

Rec-matte-06.eps

Rec-matte-07.eps

Rec-matte-08.eps

Rec-matte-09.eps

Rec-matte-10.eps

Rec-matte-11.eps

Rec-matte-12.eps

matte-01.tif

matte-02.tif

matte-03.tif

matte-04.tif

matte-05.tif

matte-06.tif

matte-07.tif

matte-08.tif

matte-09.tif

matte-10.tif

matte-11.tif

matte-12.tif

matte-13.tif

matte-14.tif

matte-15.tif

matte-16.tif

matte-17.tif

matte-18.tif

matte-19.tif

matte-20.tif

matte-21.tif

matte-22.tif

matte-23.tif

matte-24.tif

matte-25.tif

matte-26.tif

matte-27.tif

matte-28.tif

matte-29.tif

matte-30.tif

matte-31.tif

matte-32.tif

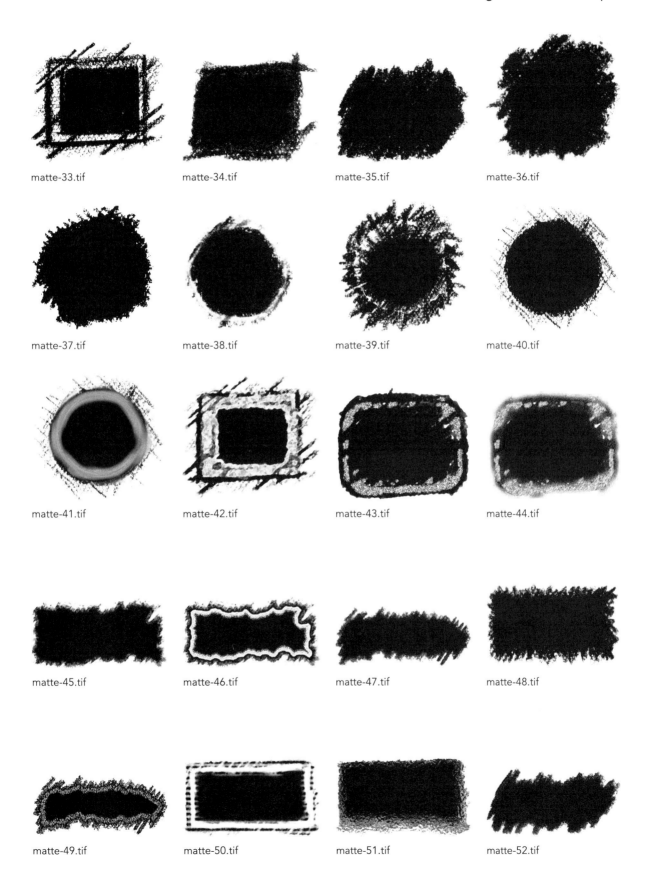

matte-33.tif

matte-34.tif

matte-35.tif

matte-36.tif

matte-37.tif

matte-38.tif

matte-39.tif

matte-40.tif

matte-41.tif

matte-42.tif

matte-43.tif

matte-44.tif

matte-45.tif

matte-46.tif

matte-47.tif

matte-48.tif

matte-49.tif

matte-50.tif

matte-51.tif

matte-52.tif

matte-53.tif

matte-54.tif

matte-55.tif

matte-56.tif

matte-57.tif

matte-58.tif

matte-59.tif

matte-60.tif

matte-61.tif

matte-62.tif

matte-63.tif

matte-64.tif

matte-65.tif

matte-66.tif

matte-67.tif

matte-68.tif

matte-69.tif

matte-70.tif

matte-71.tif

matte-72.tif

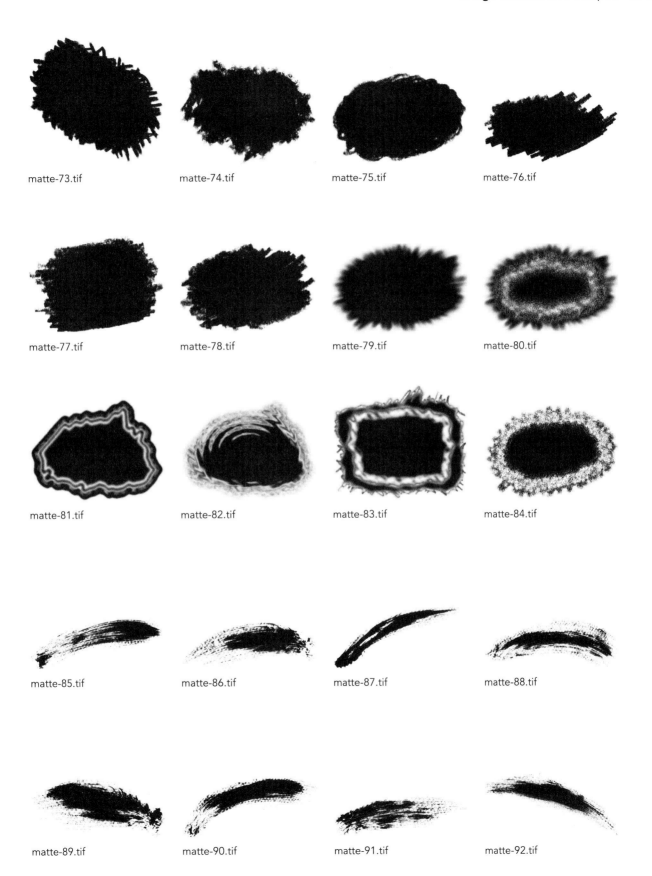

matte-73.tif

matte-74.tif

matte-75.tif

matte-76.tif

matte-77.tif

matte-78.tif

matte-79.tif

matte-80.tif

matte-81.tif

matte-82.tif

matte-83.tif

matte-84.tif

matte-85.tif

matte-86.tif

matte-87.tif

matte-88.tif

matte-89.tif

matte-90.tif

matte-91.tif

matte-92.tif

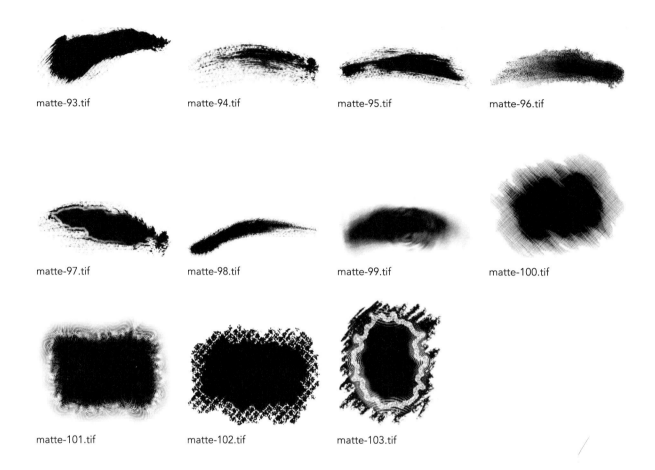

matte-93.tif   matte-94.tif   matte-95.tif   matte-96.tif

matte-97.tif   matte-98.tif   matte-99.tif   matte-100.tif

matte-101.tif   matte-102.tif   matte-103.tif

Shapes

Thang-01.eps

Thang-02.eps

Thang-03.eps

Thang-04.eps

Thang-05.eps

Thang-06.eps

Thang-07.eps

Thang-08.eps

Thang-09.eps

Thang-10.eps

Thang-11.eps

Thang-12.eps

Burst-01.eps

Burst-02.eps

Burst-03.eps

Burst-04.eps

Burst-05.eps

Burst-06.eps

Burst-07.eps

Burst-08.eps

Burst-09.eps

Burst-10.eps

Burst-11.eps

Burst-12.eps

Burst-13.eps

Burst-14.eps

Burst-15.eps

Burst-16.eps

Burst-17.eps

Burst-18.eps

Burst-19.eps

Burst-20.eps

Burst-21.eps

Burst-22.eps

Burst-23.eps

Burst-24.eps

Burst-25.eps

Burst-26.eps

Burst-27.eps

Burst-28.eps

Burst-29.eps

Burst-30.eps

Burst-31.eps

Burst-32.eps

Burst-33.eps

Burst-34.eps

Burst-35.eps

Burst-36.eps

Burst-37.eps

Burst-38.eps

Burst-39.eps

Burst-40.eps

Burst-41.eps

Burst-42.eps

Burst-43.eps

Burst-44.eps

Burst-45.eps

Burst-46.eps

Burst-47.eps

Burst-48.eps

Burst-49.eps

Burst-50.eps

Burst-51.eps

cigarband1.eps

cigarband2.eps

cigarband3.eps

cigarband4.eps

cigarband5.eps

cigarband6.eps

cigarband7.eps

cigarband8.eps

cigarband9.eps

doodle1.eps

doodle2.eps

doodle3.eps

doodle4.eps

doodle5.eps

doodle6.eps

doodle7.eps

doodle8.eps

firecracker01.eps

firecracker02.eps

firecracker03.eps

firecracker04.eps

firecracker05.eps

firecracker06.eps

firecracker07.eps

firecracker08.eps

firecracker09.eps

firecracker10.eps

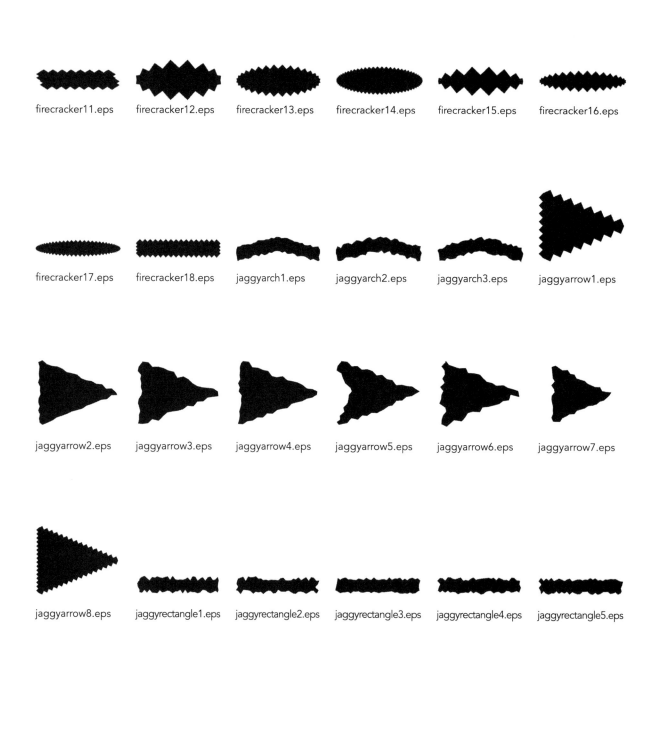

firecracker11.eps   firecracker12.eps   firecracker13.eps   firecracker14.eps   firecracker15.eps   firecracker16.eps

firecracker17.eps   firecracker18.eps   jaggyarch1.eps   jaggyarch2.eps   jaggyarch3.eps   jaggyarrow1.eps

jaggyarrow2.eps   jaggyarrow3.eps   jaggyarrow4.eps   jaggyarrow5.eps   jaggyarrow6.eps   jaggyarrow7.eps

jaggyarrow8.eps   jaggyrectangle1.eps   jaggyrectangle2.eps   jaggyrectangle3.eps   jaggyrectangle4.eps   jaggyrectangle5.eps

jaggyrectangle6.eps   jaggyrectangle7.eps   jaggyrectangle8.eps   jaggytab1.eps   jaggytab2.eps   jaggytab3.eps

seal1.eps   seal2.eps   seal3.eps

Appendix B

Seamless Textures

This appendix provides a visual index to just a sampling of the seamless textures contained on the Adobe LiveMotion f/x and Design companion CD-ROM.

The thousands of original PNG, GIF, and JPEG seamless textures you'll find on the *Adobe LiveMotion f/x and Design* companion CD-ROM are provided royalty-free. You're welcome to use these components in any of your designs. The only restriction is that you may not repackage or redistribute the files themselves. I've included this visual index to provide a peek inside the CD-ROM—the textures shown here represent some of my favorite selections.

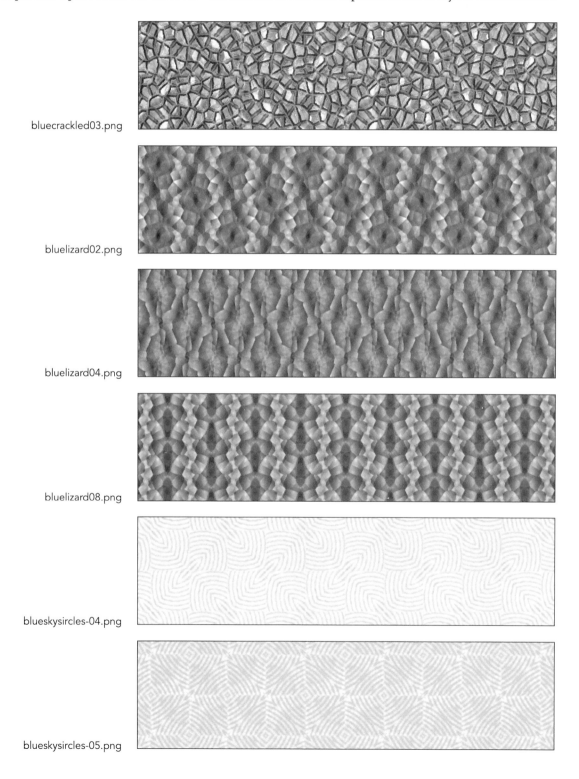

bluecrackled03.png

bluelizard02.png

bluelizard04.png

bluelizard08.png

blueskysircles-04.png

blueskysircles-05.png

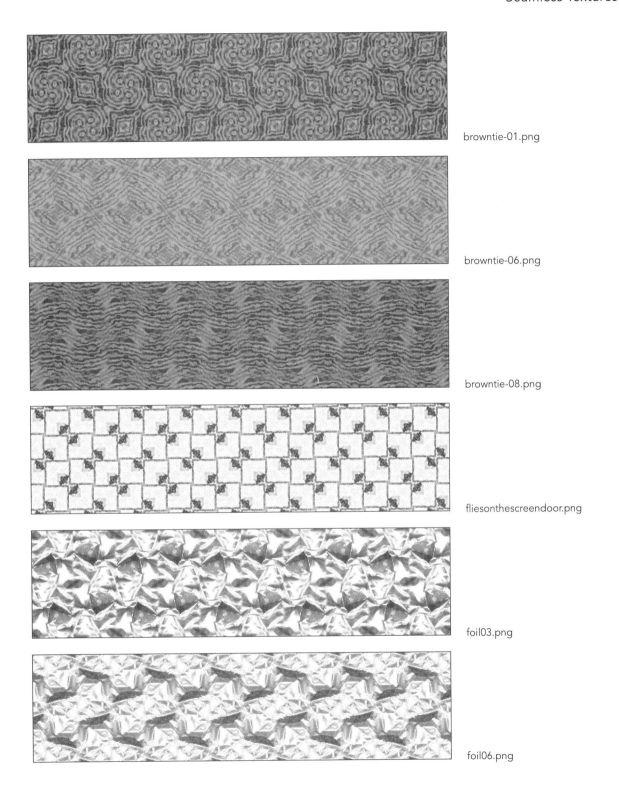

browntie-01.png

browntie-06.png

browntie-08.png

fliesonthescreendoor.png

foil03.png

foil06.png

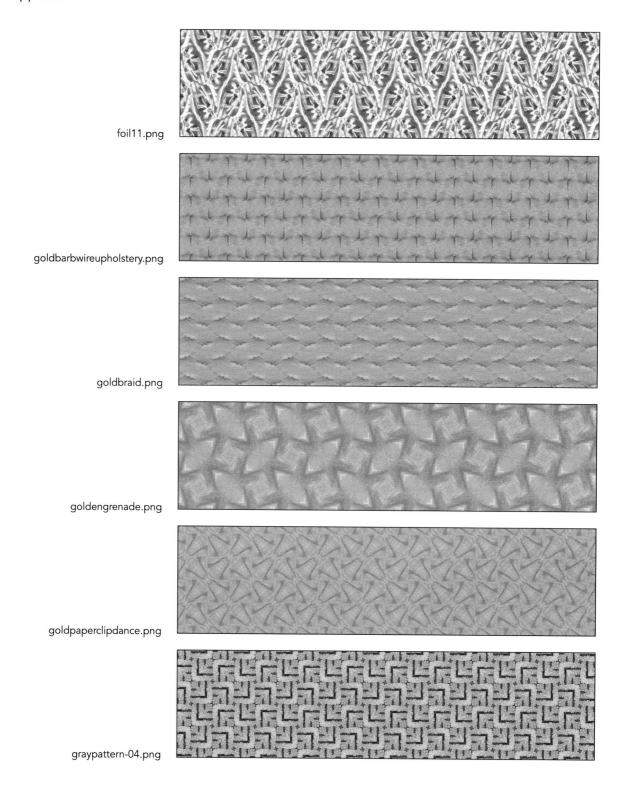

foil11.png

goldbarbwireupholstery.png

goldbraid.png

goldengrenade.png

goldpaperclipdance.png

graypattern-04.png

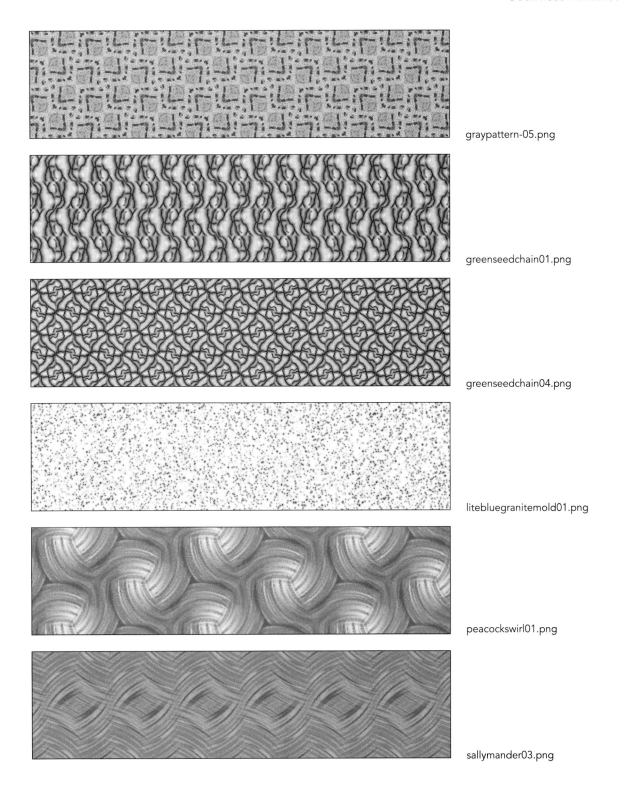

graypattern-05.png

greenseedchain01.png

greenseedchain04.png

litebluegranitemold01.png

peacockswirl01.png

sallymander03.png

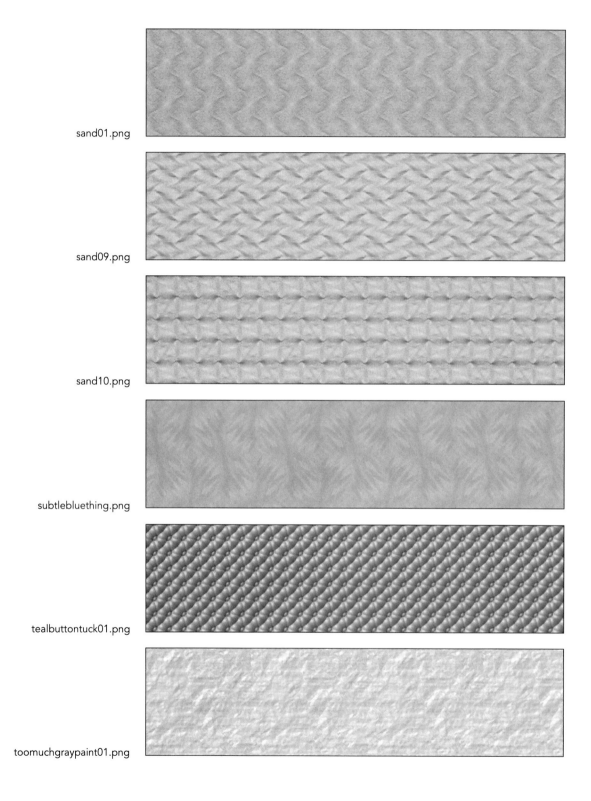

sand01.png

sand09.png

sand10.png

subtlebluething.png

tealbuttontuck01.png

toomuchgraypaint01.png

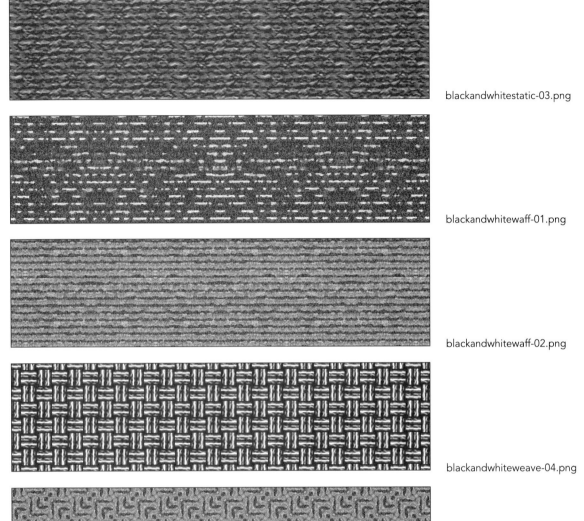

blackandwhitestatic-03.png

blackandwhitewaff-01.png

blackandwhitewaff-02.png

blackandwhiteweave-04.png

graypattern-01.png

graypattern-03.png

bloodnguts.jpg

retrocouch.jpg

slickwick.jpg

snakeskin.jpg

twirlingstarfishdance.png

vincent.jpg

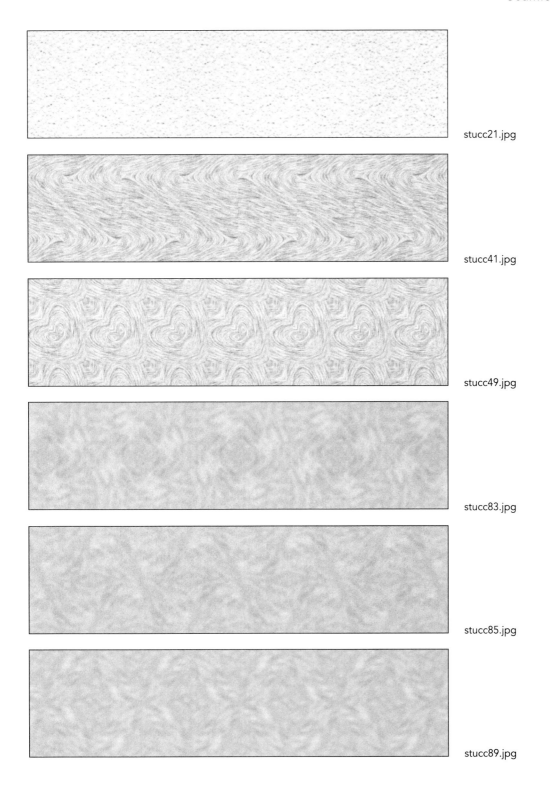

stucc21.jpg

stucc41.jpg

stucc49.jpg

stucc83.jpg

stucc85.jpg

stucc89.jpg

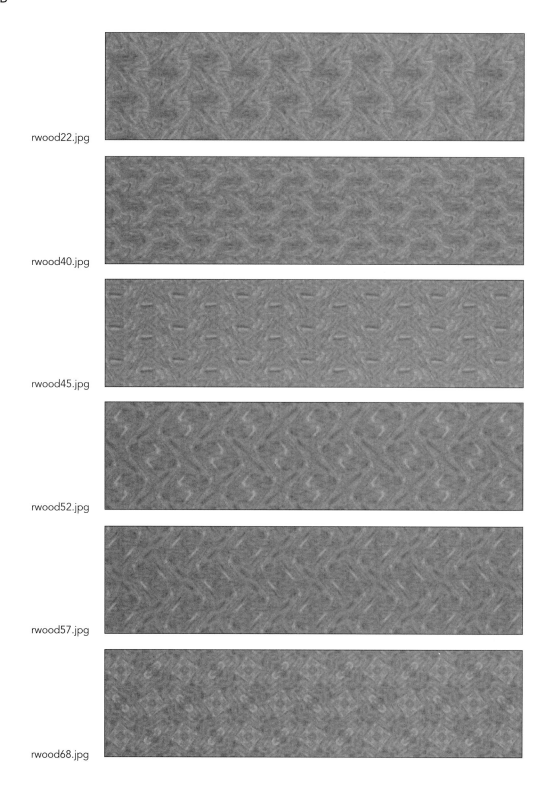

rwood22.jpg

rwood40.jpg

rwood45.jpg

rwood52.jpg

rwood57.jpg

rwood68.jpg

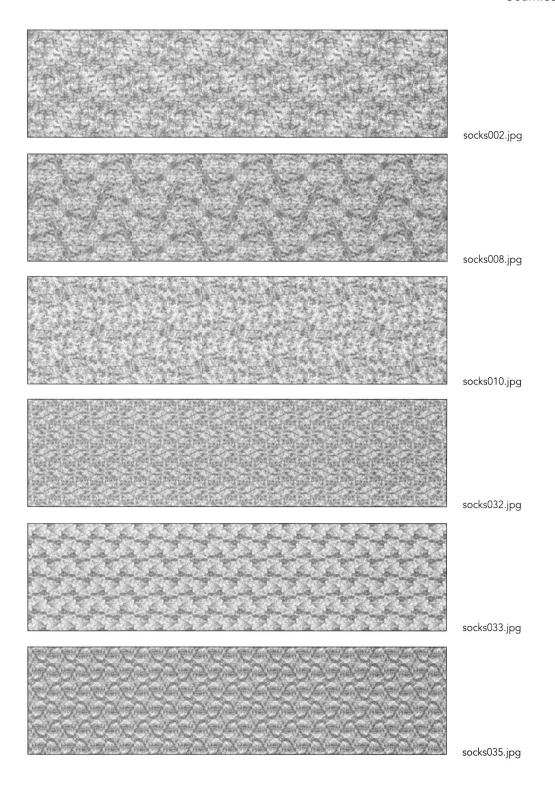

socks002.jpg

socks008.jpg

socks010.jpg

socks032.jpg

socks033.jpg

socks035.jpg

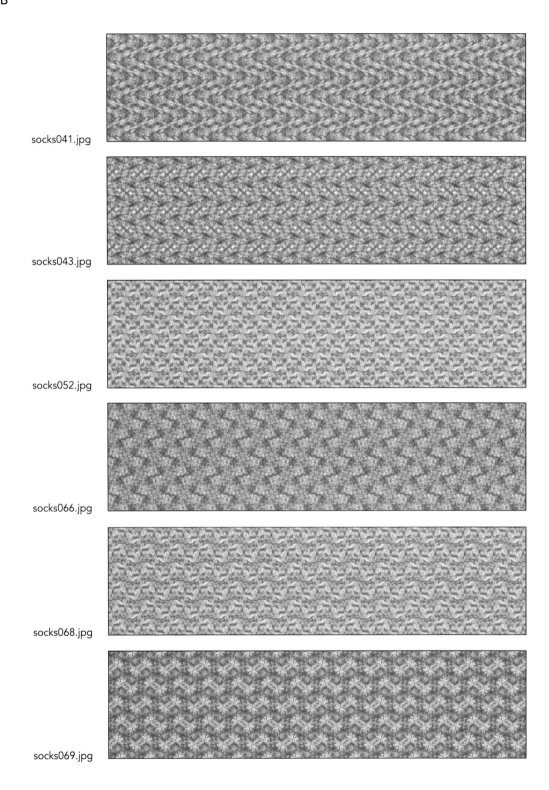

socks041.jpg

socks043.jpg

socks052.jpg

socks066.jpg

socks068.jpg

socks069.jpg

socks071.jpg

socks072.jpg

socks074.jpg

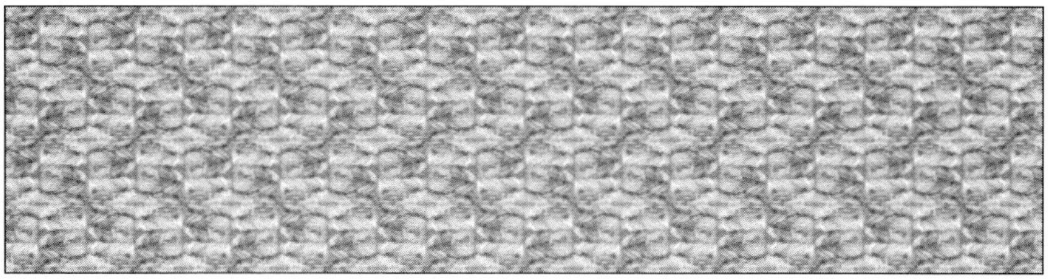

socks076.jpg

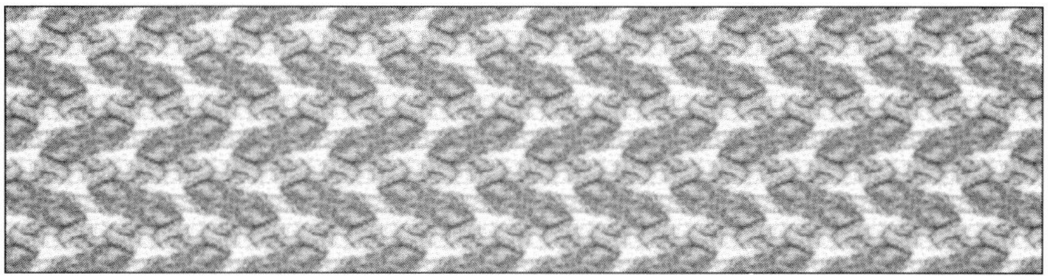

socks081.jpg

socks083.jpg

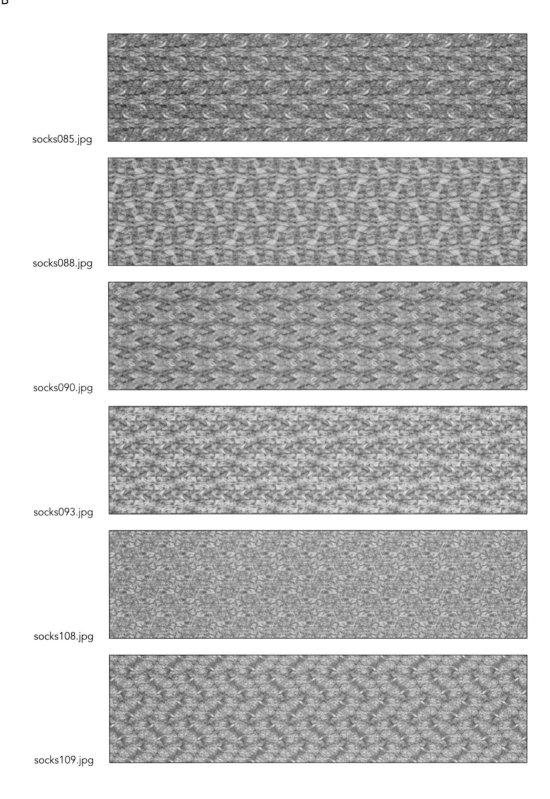

socks085.jpg

socks088.jpg

socks090.jpg

socks093.jpg

socks108.jpg

socks109.jpg

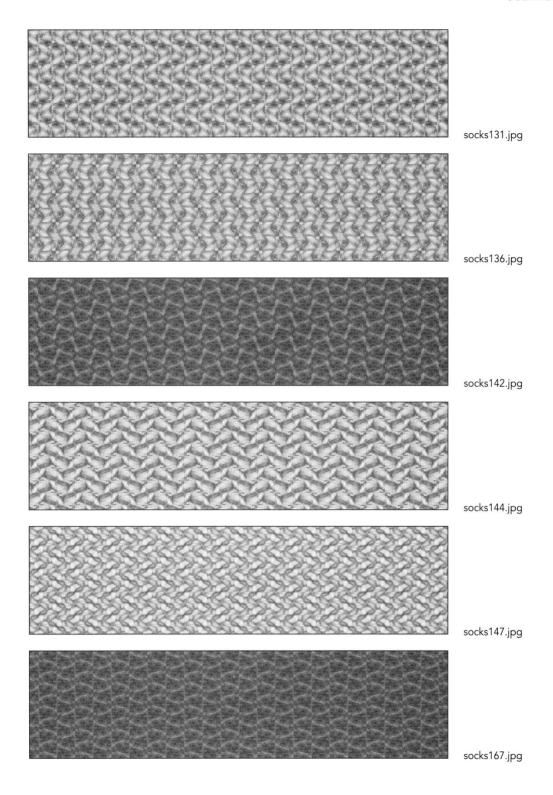

socks131.jpg

socks136.jpg

socks142.jpg

socks144.jpg

socks147.jpg

socks167.jpg

Index

C

D

If you like this book, you'll love these...

LOOKING GOOD ON THE WEB
Daniel Gray
ISBN: 1-57610-508-3 • $29.99 U.S. • $43.99 Canada
224 Pages

Speaking from the user's perspective, this book provides a comprehensive, non-technical introduction to Web design. You'll learn how to design and create friendly, easily navigable, award-winning Web sites that please clients and visitors alike.

PAINT SHOP PRO™ 6 VISUAL INSIGHT
Ramona Pruitt and Joshua Pruitt
ISBN: 1-57610-525-3 • $29.99 U.S. • $44.99 Canada
350 Pages

With concise instructions and screenshots on every page, *Paint Shop Pro™ 6 Visual Insight* teaches the most useful elements of the program to get you started. You'll get straight to work producing everyday effects, such as touching up photos, sprucing up colors, and creating eye-catching text effects.

CORELDRAW® 9 F/X AND DESIGN
Shane Hunt
ISBN: 1-57610-514-8 • $49.99 U.S. • $73.99 Canada
400 Pages with CD-ROM

Pick and choose the effects and techniques you want to emulate—from traditional to avant-garde, retro to techno, clean to chaos—all perfect for use in everyday design tasks. Load files off the companion CD-ROM—or use your own artwork—and walk through simple, step-by-step tutorials to get immediate results.

FLASH™ 4 WEB ANIMATION F/X AND DESIGN
Ken Milburn and John Croteau
ISBN: 1-57610-555-5 • $49.99 U.S. • $74.99 Canada
400 Pages with CD-ROM

Dedicated chapters and real-world projects highlight key features of Flash™ 4, including editable text, automated publishing, and forms capability. World-renowned Flash expert, John Croteau, provides added insight to teach you the most professional Flash effects being used today.

The Coriolis Group, LLC   Telephone: 1.800.410.0192 • www.coriolis.com
Coriolis books are also available at bookstores and computer stores nationwide.

Look for these books, coming soon...

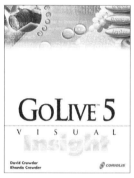

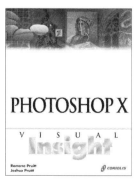

What's on the CD-ROM

The *Adobe LiveMotion f/x and Design* companion CD-ROM contains elements specifically selected to enhance the usefulness of this book, including:

- *Adobe LiveMotion 1*—A 30-day trial version of LiveMotion for Mac and PC. (The demo is fully functioning.)

- *Adobe Photoshop 5.5*—A trial version of the industry standard bitmap editing software for Mac and PC. (The trial version does not save, export, or print.)

- *Adobe Illustrator 9*—A try-out version of the vanguard vector-drawing software for Mac and PC. (The try-out version does not save, export, or print.)

- *SoundApp 2.7*—An awesome freeware sound conversion utility for Mac.

- *Sound Forge 4.5 and Acid Music 2*—Demo versions of Sonic Foundry's powerful sound editing and music composition programs for PC.

- *Music loops*—Twenty professional music loops from SoundShopper.com. Each music loop can be used free for one individual project in a commercial environment. To use them for multiple commercial projects, contact **info@soundshopper.com** for licensing details.

- *LiveMotion (.liv) files for the book's projects and examples*—Start with the concepts illustrated in these files, and build on them to create your own LiveMotion masterpieces.

- *LiveMotion compositions and resources*—More than 100 original styles, 5,000-plus textures, more than 250 shapes and image mattes, 15 preloaders, over 20 templates, and other goodies from the author and Charlie Haywood.

System Requirements

Software

- Macintosh users need operating system 8.5 or higher.

- Windows users need Windows 98, Windows NT (with Service Pack 4), or Windows 2000.

- Adobe LiveMotion is needed to complete the projects included in this book. (The 30-day trial version software provided on this CD-ROM can suffice.)

- A Web browser with the Flash plug-in is needed to view the output of LiveMotion compositions.

Hardware

- For Macintosh users, a Power PC processor is required.

- For Windows users, a Pentium II processor is required (as a minimum).

- 48MB of RAM is the minimum requirement. Adobe recommends 64MB of RAM. You'll be happier with far more.

- The LiveMotion application requires approximately 100MB of disk storage space. Be sure to leave plenty of extra room. (When importing sounds and photographs, the files can get quite large, quite fast.)